The content in this meal planning book is meant for educational purposes exclusively and not as medical advice. Although we aim to provide precise and current information, it is crucial to recognize that individual dietary needs may vary.

Welcome

to your guide to a reimagined approach to meal planning, where the foundation is rooted not just in feeding your family but nurturing your soul. In these pages, you'll embark on a journey that goes beyond the kitchen, learning what it means to nourish yourself and your family from the inside out.

As parents, we understand the daily juggle of balancing the demands of family, work, and self-care. The relentless cycle of meal planning can feel overwhelming, leaving us drained and uninspired. But what if meal planning could be more than just a chore? What if it could be a source of joy, connection, and renewal?

We invite you to explore an approach to meal planning that honours your mind, body, and spirit. Here, you'll discover that meal planning is not just about filling bellies but feeding souls – yours included.

In the pages that follow, you'll find practical tips, inspiring affirmations, and tools for personal growth to support you on this journey. You'll learn how to infuse your meal planning with mindfulness, gratitude, and a deep sense of purpose.

Together, let's redefine meal planning as an opportunity to nourish not just our bodies but our spirits – so that we may show up as our best selves, ready to cook with love and serve our families a slice of joy.

With warmth and nourishment,

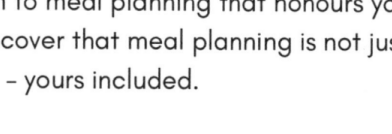

Diana Gottschalk-Miller

Introduction to the
4-MONTH MEAL PLANNER

We have opted for a 4-month meal planning structure to ensure that your meal plans stay fresh, adaptable, and manageable. This timeframe allows you to try out new recipes, incorporate seasonal ingredients, and adjust to any dietary changes with ease.

Life is ever-changing, and so are our dietary requirements. By creating a 4-month roster of go-to meals, you have the freedom to tweak your meal plans as your schedule, preferences, or nutritional objectives evolve.

Sustaining interest and dedication to meal planning can be tough over extended periods. By focusing on a 4-month plan, our goal is to keep you motivated and engaged, increasing the likelihood that you will stay committed and reap the benefits of the meal planning process.

In this book you will find loads of resources to help you navigate these 4 months with ease:

- **Utilize a Staples List to track monthly food rotation accurately**
- **Engage the Family with Family Favors while planning meals**
- **Employ Family Meal Rotation Lists to streamline weekly meal planning**
- **Address Toddler Nutritional needs to tackle picky eating phases**
- **Incorporate Theme Meal Ideas for creative meal planning and to avoid monotony**
- **Opt for Ways To Stretch Your Meals to reduce your food expenses**
- **Try Busy Days Meal Ideas for quick, nutritious meals on hectic days**
- **Explore 5 Minutes or Less Snack Ideas for busy days filled with family activities**
- **Use Alternative Ingredients to customize meals to meet your family's nutritional requirements without sacrificing taste**
- **Refer to the Glycemic Index List and Macro-nutrients Food List for balanced, satisfying meals for your family.**

And so much more!

1 KITCHEN HQ

- Kitchen Safety
- DIY Cleaning Products
- Closing the Kitchen Checklist
- Measurements Conversion
- Common Cooking Terms and Techniques
- Understanding Behind Baking

2 NOURISHING AFFIRMATIONS

- Confidence in the Kitchen
- Healthy Habits
- Picky Eaters
- Meal Planning Exhaustion
- Doing Dishes

3 ESSENTIAL RECIPES & BASICS

- Pancake Mix
- Pancake Syrup
- Granola/Granola Bars
- High Fiber Whole Wheat Bread
- Versatile Dough
- Seasoning Mixtures
- Ketchup
- Mayonnaise
- BBQ Sauce
- Honey Mustard
- Salad Dressings
- Pasta Sauce
- Pesto Sauce
- Alfredo Sauce
- Peanut Butter
- High Iron Dark Chocolate
- Nut Milk
- Smoothie Café
- Infused Water

4 MEAL PLANNING ESSENTIALS

 Section ONE

- Staples List (Dry Goods List)
- Staples List (Refrigeration List)
- Family Favors
- Family Meal Rotation Lists (3 pages)
- Toddler Nutritional Needs
- Theme Meal Ideas
- Ways To Stretch Your Meals
- Busy Days Meal Ideas
- 5 Minutes or Less Snack Ideas
- Alternative Ingredients (Gluten Free/Dairy-Free)
- Alternative Ingredients (Refined Sugar Free)
- Glycemic Index List
- Macro-nutrients Food List

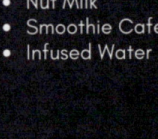 Section TWO

- Month Overview Guide
- Month Overviews
- Batch Planner Guide
- Batch Planners
- Meal Planning Reflection
- Inventory Checklist Guide
- Inventory Checkkists

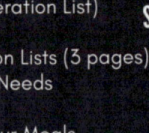 Section THREE

- Avoiding Store Tactics
- Produce Shopping Guide
- Produce In Season
- Storage Guide (Fruits)
- Storage Guide (Vegetables)
- Storage Guide (Proteins & Carbs)
- Shopping List
- Events & Parties Planners

Welcome

to your Kitchen Headquarters section! Here, you'll uncover a treasure trove of resources designed to elevate your culinary experience and make cooking an enjoyable adventure. From essential tips for a safe kitchen environment to practical DIY solutions for maintaining cleanliness, every aspect of your kitchen routine is addressed.

- **Kitchen Safety**
- **DIY Cleaning Products**
- **Measurements Conversion**
- **Common Cooking Terms and Techniques**

Kitchen SAFETY

Kitchen safety is crucial for cooking efficiently and securely. By establishing a safe environment, you can elevate your cooking experience and safeguard everyone in the kitchen.

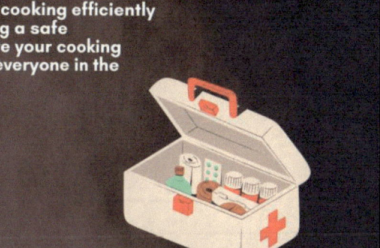

To prevent cross-contamination, use separate chopping boards for meat and fruits/vegetables.

Remember to sanitize chopping boards after each use with hot, soapy water or baking soda solution. Replace worn boards to prevent bacteria buildup.

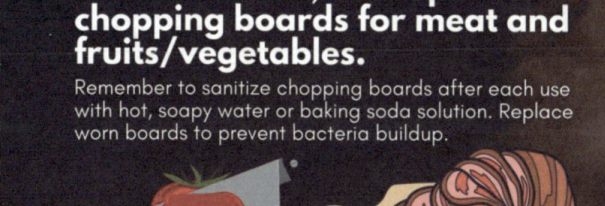

Proper Way to Chop

To chop veggies like a pro, arm yourself with a razor-sharp knife, a confident grip, a claw-like hand to secure the produce, and smoothly rock the knife back and forth while the tip stays put on the cutting board.

"Using water to put out a cooking fire is never recommended."

When faced with a cooking fire, refrain from using flour or water as they can escalate the situation. Opt for a kitchen fire extinguisher, metal lid (using a glass lid could result in shattering the glass) or covering flames with baking soda to safely put out the flames.

The main way to treat a kitchen burn...

- Submerge the burn in cool water, refraining from using ice-cold water.
- Apply a thin coat of antibiotic ointment or petroleum jelly to the burn.
- Cover the burn with a non-adherent bandage, ensuring regular replacement.
- Refrain from popping any blisters to minimize the likelihood of infection.
- Shield the burn from sun exposure or extreme cold when venturing outdoors.

FIRST AIDE KITCHEN ESSENTIALS:

ADHESIVE BANDAGES (ASSORTED SIZES)
For covering small cuts and scrapes.

STERILE GAUZE PADS
To dress larger wounds or burns.

ADHESIVE TAPE
To secure gauze or bandages in place.

ANTISEPTIC WIPES OR ALCOHOL PADS
For cleaning and disinfecting wounds.

ANTIBIOTIC OINTMENT
To prevent infection in minor cuts and burns.

BURN GEL OR BURN DRESSING
Specifically designed for treating burns from heat or hot surfaces.

DISPOSABLE GLOVES
To protect against contamination when administering first aid.

SCISSORS
For cutting tape, gauze, or clothing if needed.

INSTANT COLD PACKS
To reduce swelling or soothe minor burns.

PAIN RELIEVERS
Such as acetaminophen or ibuprofen, for minor aches and pains.

EMERGENCY CONTACT NUMBERS
Including local emergency services and poison control.

Ensure that your first aid kit is stored in a dry, easily accessible location in your kitchen, away from heat and moisture.

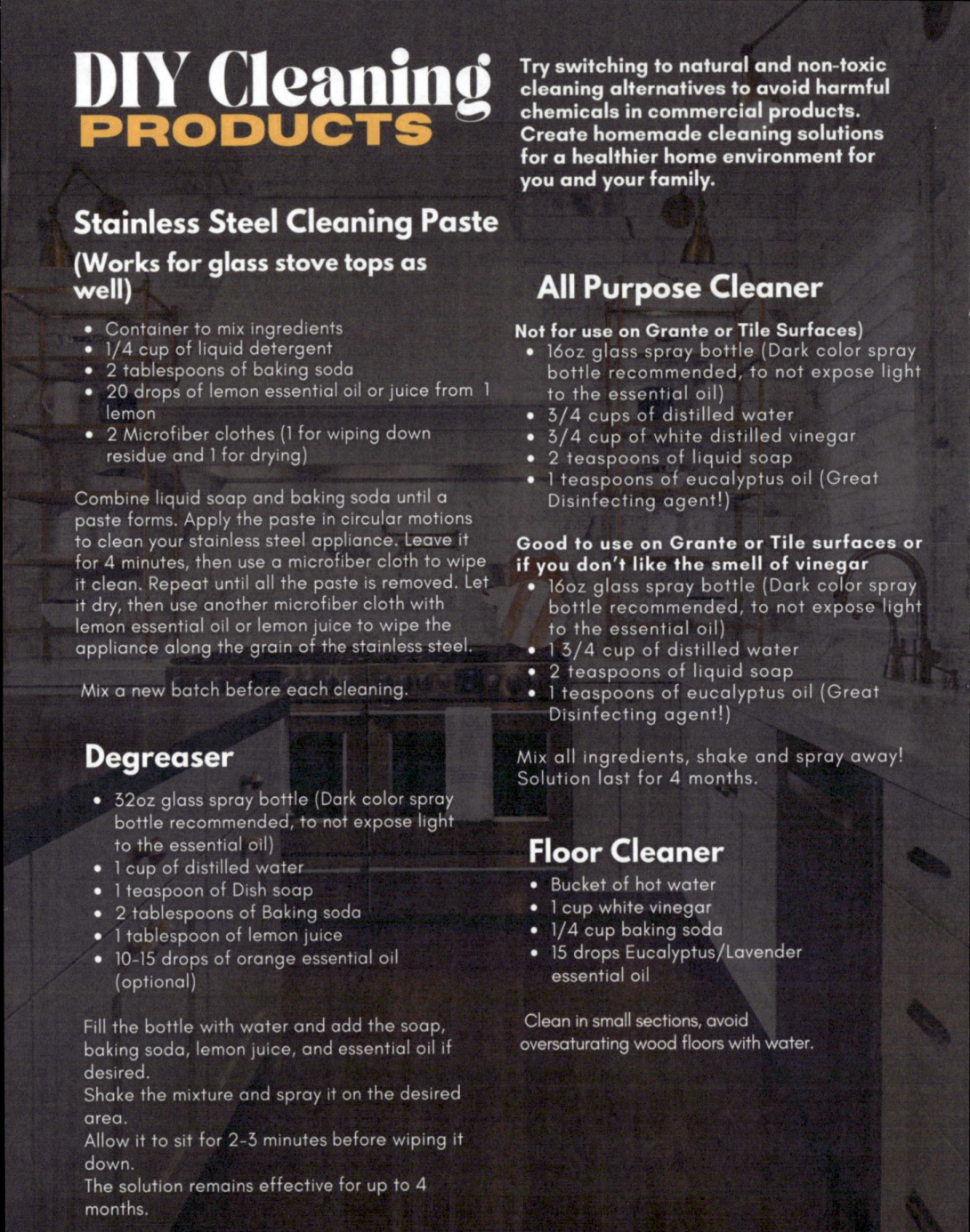

Closing the Kitchen
CHECKLIST

After a tiring day, preparing dinner and then tidying up can feel overwhelming, but it's all about perspective. By adopting the food service concept of "closing" in your kitchen, you can view cleaning as a means to set up the next shift (yourself in the morning) for a fresh start with a clean workspace (your kitchen).

- Declutter countertop, putting away any items that dont belong.
- Remove Items & clean and sanitize countertops & table.
- Sweep and Mop Floors.
- Wipe Down Sink & Faucet.
- Take Out Trash.
- Wipe Down Backsplash and Walls.
- Wipe Down Stove.
- Wipe down the inside & outside of microwave.
- Wipe down the refrigerator handles and the exterior surfaces.
- Clean all dishes, pots, pans, and utensils. Dry and put them away or load the dishwasher and run it.
- Put away any leftovers in appropriate containers and store them in the refrigerator.
- Look through fruits and vegetables for anything that needs to be used soon or discarded.
- Disinfect handles, knobs, light switches, and other frequently touched surfaces.

QUICK CLEANING FOR THOSE BUSY NIGHTS

- Declutter countertop, putting away any items that dont belong.
- Remove Items & clean and sanitize countertops & table.
- Sweep the Floor.
- Clean Sink & Faucet.
- Take Out Trash.
- Wipe Down Stove.
- Clean all dishes, pots, pans, and utensils. Dry and put them away or load the dishwasher and run it.
- Put away any leftovers in appropriate containers and store them in the refrigerator.

SET UP FOR MORNING

- Prepare anything needed for the next morning, like setting up the coffee maker or laying out breakfast items
- Take out any frozen prep food needed for the next day and store in refrigerator.

Measurements CONVERSION

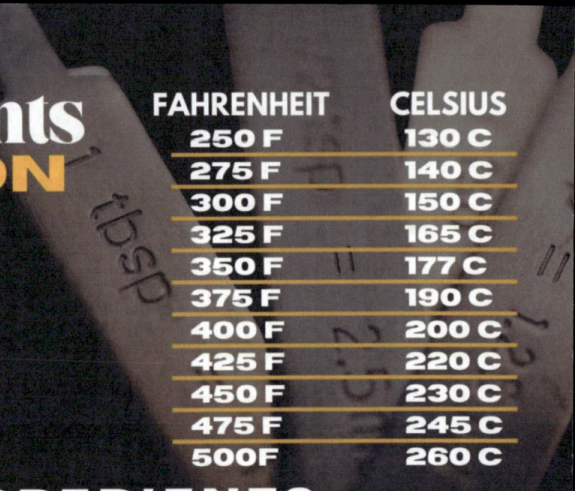

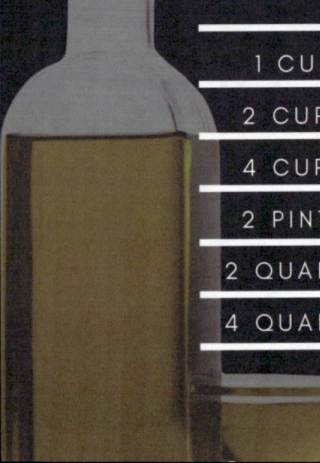

FAHRENHEIT	CELSIUS
250 F	130 C
275 F	140 C
300 F	150 C
325 F	165 C
350 F	177 C
375 F	190 C
400 F	200 C
425 F	220 C
450 F	230 C
475 F	245 C
500F	260 C

DRY INGREDIENTS

3 TEASPOONS	1 TABLESPOON	1/2 OUNCE	14.3 GRAMS
2 TABLESPOONS	1/8 CUP	1 OUNCE	28.3 GRAMS
4 TABLESPOONS	1/4 CUP	2 OUNCES	56.7 GRAMS
51/3 TABLESPOONS	1/3 CUP	2.6 OUNCES	75.6 GRAMS
8 TABLESPOONS	1/2 CUP	4 OUNCES	113.4 GRAMS
12 TABLESPOONS	3/4 CUP	6 OUNCES	.375 POUNDS
32 TABLESPOONS	2CUPS	16 OUNCES	1 POUND
64 TABLESPOONS	4 CUPS	32 OUNCES	2 POUNDS

LIQUID

1 CUP	8 OUNCES	1/2 PINT	237 ML
2 CUPS	16 OUNCES	1 PINT	474 ML
4 CUPS	32 OUNCES	1 QUARTS	946 ML
2 PINTS	32 OUNCES	1 QUARTS	946 ML
2 QUARTS	64 OUNCES	1/2 GALLON	1.89 LITERS
4 QUARTS	128 OUNCES	1 GALLON	3.784 LITERS

Common Cooking
TERMS & TECHNIQUES

AL DENTE
An Italian term meaning "to the tooth," used to describe pasta that is cooked until it offers a slight resistance when bitten.

BAKE
To cook food by surrounding it with dry heat in an oven.

BLANCH
To briefly boil food and then plunge it into ice water to stop the cooking process, often used to loosen skins or prepare vegetables for freezing.

BRAISE
To cook food slowly in a small amount of liquid in a covered pot, typically after browning it.

BROIL
To cook food directly under a heat source at high temperature.

CHOP
To cut food into bite-sized pieces using a knife.

CREAM
To beat ingredients (typically butter and sugar) together until they become light and fluffy.

DEGLAZE
To add liquid (such as wine or broth) to a hot pan to release and dissolve the flavorful bits stuck to the bottom.

DICE
To cut food into small, uniform cubes.

FOLD
To gently mix ingredients by lifting and turning them with a spatula or spoon, often used to incorporate air into batters or to mix delicate ingredients.

JULIENNE
To cut food into thin, matchstick-sized strips.

KNEAD
To work dough by pressing, folding, and stretching it to develop the gluten.

POACH
To cook food gently in simmering liquid.

REDUCE
To cook a liquid until it decreases in volume, intensifying its flavor.

SAUTÉ
To cook food quickly in a small amount of oil or butter over medium-high heat.

SIMMER
To cook food gently in liquid at a temperature just below boiling.

STEAM
To cook food with the steam generated by boiling water.

WHISK
To beat ingredients together using a wire whisk or fork to incorporate air and produce a smooth mixture.

Understanding
BEHIND BAKING

FLOUR
Purpose: Provides structure.
Chemistry: Contains proteins (glutenin and gliadin) that form gluten when mixed with water. Gluten provides elasticity and strength, trapping air bubbles and allowing dough to rise.

SUGAR
Purpose: Sweetens, tenderizes, and aids in browning.
Chemistry: Sugar is hygroscopic, meaning it attracts and retains moisture, which helps keep baked goods moist. It also caramelizes at high temperatures, contributing to browning and flavor.

BAKING POWDER
Purpose: Leavening agent.
Chemistry: Baking powder is a combination of an acid (usually cream of tartar) and a base (baking soda). It releases carbon dioxide gas when it reacts with moisture and heat, causing dough to rise and become light and fluffy.

BAKING SODA
Purpose: Leavening agent.
Chemistry: Baking soda (sodium bicarbonate) needs an acidic component to activate and produce carbon dioxide gas. This gas helps the dough rise. Without acid, it won't work effectively and may leave a bitter taste.

EGGS
Purpose: Provide structure, moisture, and leavening.
Chemistry: Eggs coagulate when heated, helping to set the structure of baked goods. They also trap air when beaten, contributing to leavening. Yolks add fat and emulsify ingredients, creating a smooth and creamy texture.

BUTTER (OR FATS)
Purpose: Adds moisture, richness, and flavor; aids in leavening.
Chemistry: Fat coats flour proteins, limiting gluten development and resulting in tender baked goods. It also traps air when creamed with sugar, aiding in leavening.

MILK (OR OTHER LIQUIDS)
Purpose: Adds moisture, helps dissolve sugar and salt, and activates leavening agents.
Chemistry: Liquids hydrate proteins and starches, initiating gluten formation and gelatinization. They also create steam during baking, contributing to leavening.

SALT
Purpose: Enhances flavor and controls yeast fermentation.
Chemistry: Salt strengthens gluten structure and enhances flavor by balancing sweetness. In yeast breads, it regulates yeast activity, preventing over-rising and ensuring a consistent texture.

YEAST
Purpose: Leavening agent in bread and other yeast-based products.
Chemistry: Yeast ferments sugars, producing carbon dioxide and ethanol. The gas gets trapped in the dough, causing it to rise. Yeast also contributes to the flavor and aroma of baked goods.

CREAM OF TARTAR
Purpose: Stabilizes beaten egg whites and acts as an acid in baking powder.
Chemistry: Cream of tartar (potassium bitartrate) stabilizes egg whites by increasing the acidity, which helps to maintain their volume and texture. It also reacts with baking soda in baking powder to produce carbon dioxide gas.

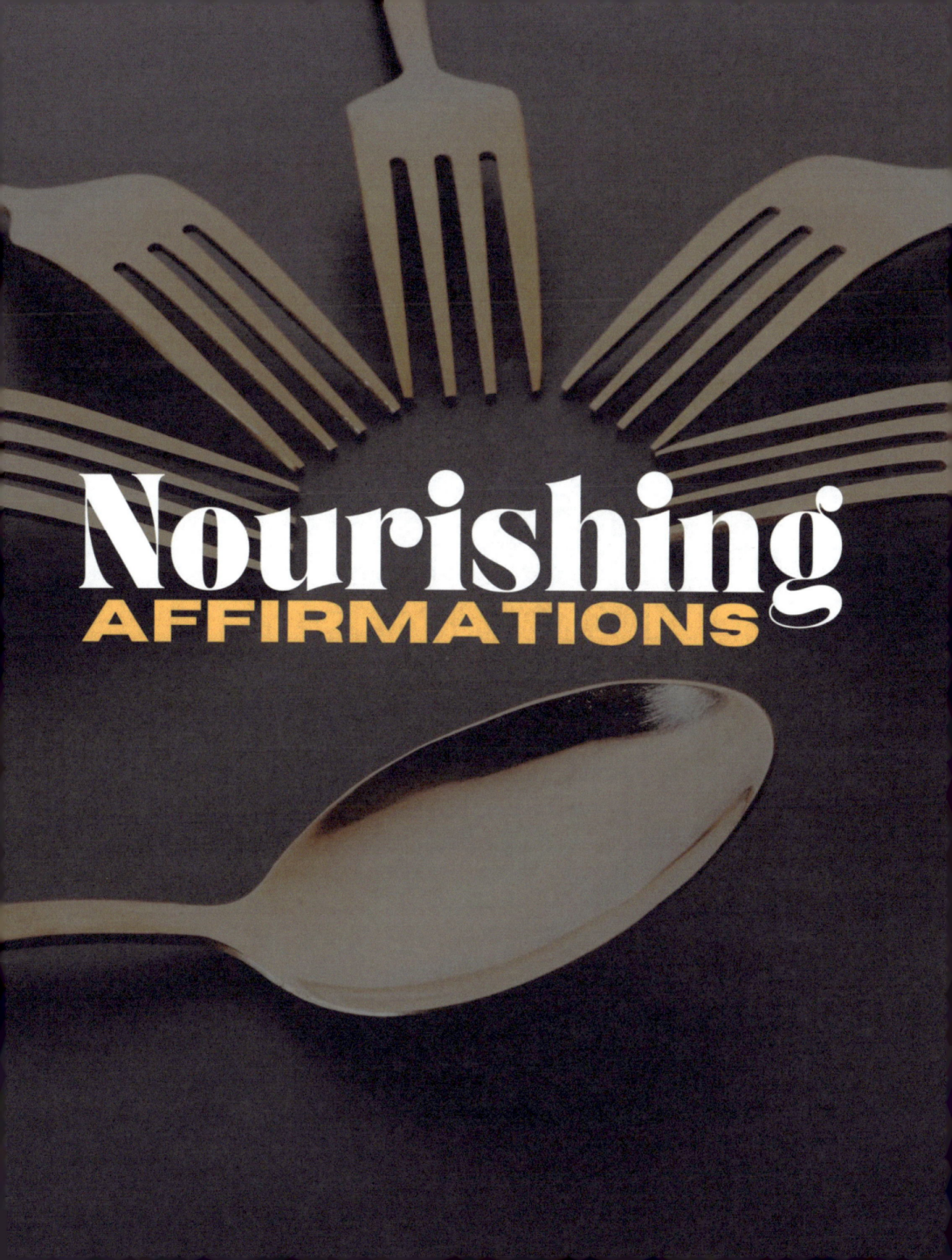

YOUR Mindset

behind cooking can make it an enjoyable creative process or a stressful kitchen nightmare. By maintaining a positive mindset and using these affirmations, you can turn cooking into a delightful and rewarding part of your day. Embrace the idea that cooking is a journey of exploration and learning, where mistakes are just opportunities for growth. So next time you step into the kitchen, take a deep breath, smile, and remember that you have the power to create something wonderful.

- **Confidence in the Kitchen**
- **Healthy Habits**
- **Picky Eaters**
- **Meal Planning Exhaustion**
- **Doing Dishes**

Confidence In THE KITCHEN

When you need a pep talk to feel like the ultimate kitchen queen!

"I enjoy the act of nourishing my family without tying my self-worth to their reactions."

"I am proud of myself for all I do, inside and outside the kitchen."

"I let go of the pressure to please everyone with every meal."

"I am at peace with my efforts, knowing I am enough as I am."

"I honor my efforts, knowing I do my best every day."

"I am confident in my ability to create balanced and delicious meals."

"I am confident in my kitchen, and my food choices reflect my family's unique tastes and preferences."

"Every meal I make, whether simple or elaborate, is an expression of my love and care."

"I trust that my efforts in the kitchen contribute to my family's happiness and health."

"As I continue to learn and experiment with cooking, my confidence grows, making every meal an opportunity for growth and success."

Healthy HABITS

When you have an unhealthy relationship with food

"I let go of any food rules or restrictions that no longer serve me, and I embrace a flexible and intuitive approach to eating."

"I am redefining what it means to nourish my body, focusing on self-care and compassion in my relationship with food."

"I release any shame attached to my body and embrace it with love and acceptance."

"I listen to my body's hunger and fullness cues, honoring its needs with compassion."

"I forgive myself for any negative beliefs or behaviors around food, and I choose to cultivate a positive relationship with it."

"I choose foods that nourish my body and support my overall health and well-being."

"I am worthy of enjoying food without guilt or shame."

"I am worthy of pleasure and enjoyment in eating, free from judgment or criticism."

"I release any past trauma related to food and eating, and I embrace a future filled with nourishment and joy."

"I am grateful for the opportunity to learn and grow in my journey towards a healthy and loving relationship with food."

Picky EATERS

When introducing a variety of foods to your child feels overwhelming.

"I am doing my best to provide nutritious meals for my children, even if they are picky eaters."

"I release feelings of guilt and trust that my children's eating habits will improve over time with patience and consistency."

"I offer a variety of healthy food options for my children and encourage them to explore new flavors and textures at their own pace."

"I am not alone in facing the challenges of picky eating, and there are resources and support available to help me navigate this journey."

"I focus on creating a positive mealtime environment filled with love and encouragement, rather than stress and pressure."

"I celebrate the small victories and progress my children make towards trying new foods, knowing that change takes time."

"I am a loving and caring parent, and my children's well-being goes beyond their diet."

"I prioritize balance and flexibility in my approach to feeding my family, knowing that occasional indulgences are part of a healthy lifestyle."

"I model healthy eating habits and positive attitudes towards food, knowing that my actions speak louder than words."

"I choose to focus on the nutrients my children do consume rather than fixating on what they don't."

Meal Planning EXHAUSTION

When the chaos in the kitchen becomes overwhelming.

I release any guilt or pressure to create perfect meal plans and embrace flexibility and creativity in my approach."

"I am capable of creating healthy and delicious meal plans that nourish my family and simplify my life."

"Meal planning brings order and efficiency to my busy schedule, allowing me to prioritize self-care and family time."

"Meal planning empowers me to make healthier choices and save time and money in the kitchen."

"I am organized and focused, and I approach meal planning with a positive mindset and determination."

"I celebrate my successes and learn from my challenges, continuously improving my meal planning skills."

"I honor my commitment to meal planning as a form of self-care and an investment in my family's well-being."

"I release any fear of failure and embrace imperfection in my meal planning journey."

"I am resourceful and adaptable, finding creative solutions to obstacles that arise in meal planning."

"I prioritize simplicity and efficiency in my meal plans, focusing on nutritious and easy-to-prepare meals."

"I am patient with myself as I develop the habit of meal planning, knowing that consistency is key to success."

Doing DISHES

When the idea of cleaning up after cooking at home seems daunting.

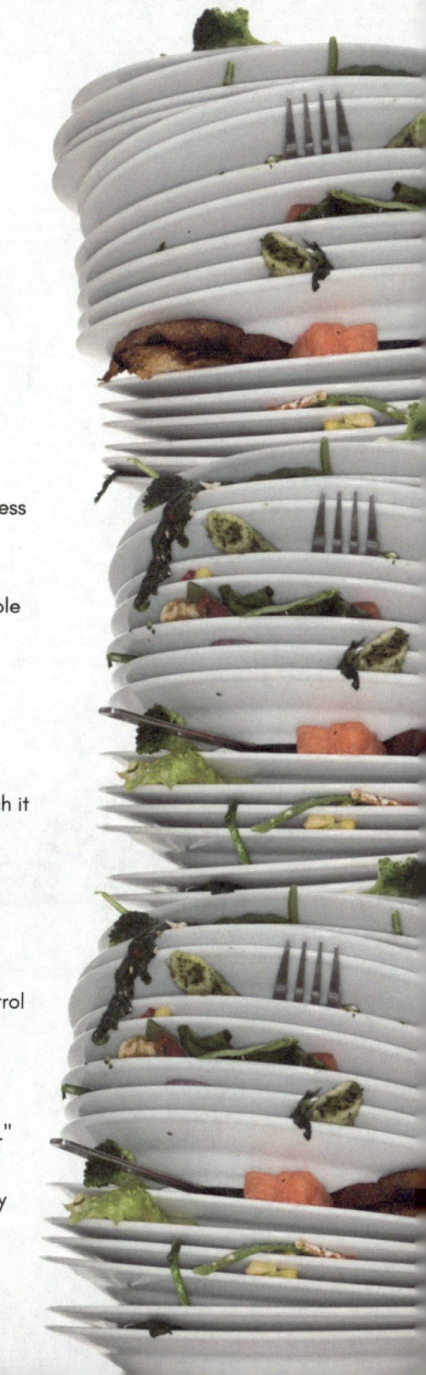

"I am grateful for the abundance represented by the dishes, as it means my family is well-fed and cared for."

"I tackle the dishes with patience and grace, knowing that I am creating a clean and welcoming home for my family."

"I embrace the rhythm of washing dishes as a moment of mindfulness and self-care."

"I appreciate the opportunity to nurture my family through the simple act of cleaning dishes."

"I choose to maintain a clean and organized space to promote peace and tranquility in my home."

"I release any negative feelings towards dishwashing and approach it with a positive attitude and sense of purpose."

"I honor my efforts in maintaining a clean and organized home, knowing that it brings comfort and stability to my family."

"Choosing to tackle chores promptly empowers me to reclaim control over my environment and mindset."

"I remind myself that even mundane tasks like washing dishes are opportunities to practice mindfulness and presence in the moment."

"Prioritizing chores like doing dishes promptly is an investment in my mental well-being."

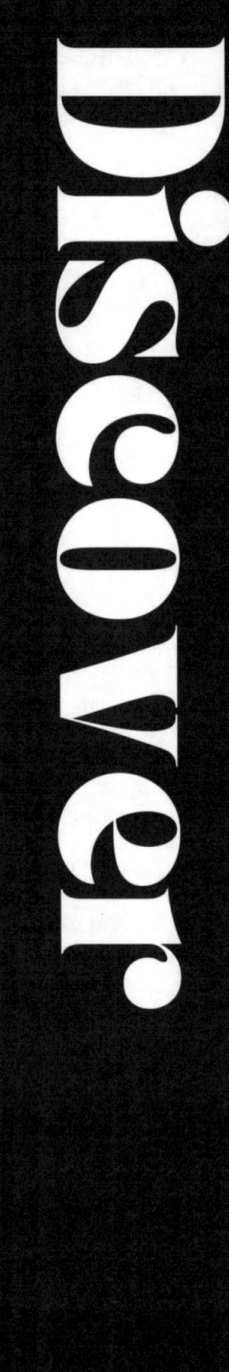

the joy of cooking! This collection is designed to inspire and empower you in the kitchen, showing that creating delicious meals can be simple and enjoyable. Each recipe is crafted to be easy to follow, making cooking feel less like a chore and more like an adventure. To make your cooking experience even more personalized, each recipe includes a section for you to note any alternate changes or adaptations that suit your preferences and dietary needs. Welcome to a world where cooking is fun, rewarding, and accessible to everyone.

- Pancake Mix
- Pancake Syrup
- Granola/Granola Bars
- High Fiber Whole Wheat Bread
- Versatile Dough
- Seasoning Mixtures
- Ketchup
- Mayonnaise
- BBQ Sauce
- Honey Mustard
- Salad Dressings
- Pasta Sauce
- Pesto Sauce
- Alfredo Sauce
- Peanut Butter
- High Iron Dark Chocolate
- Nut Milk
- Smoothie Café
- Infused Water

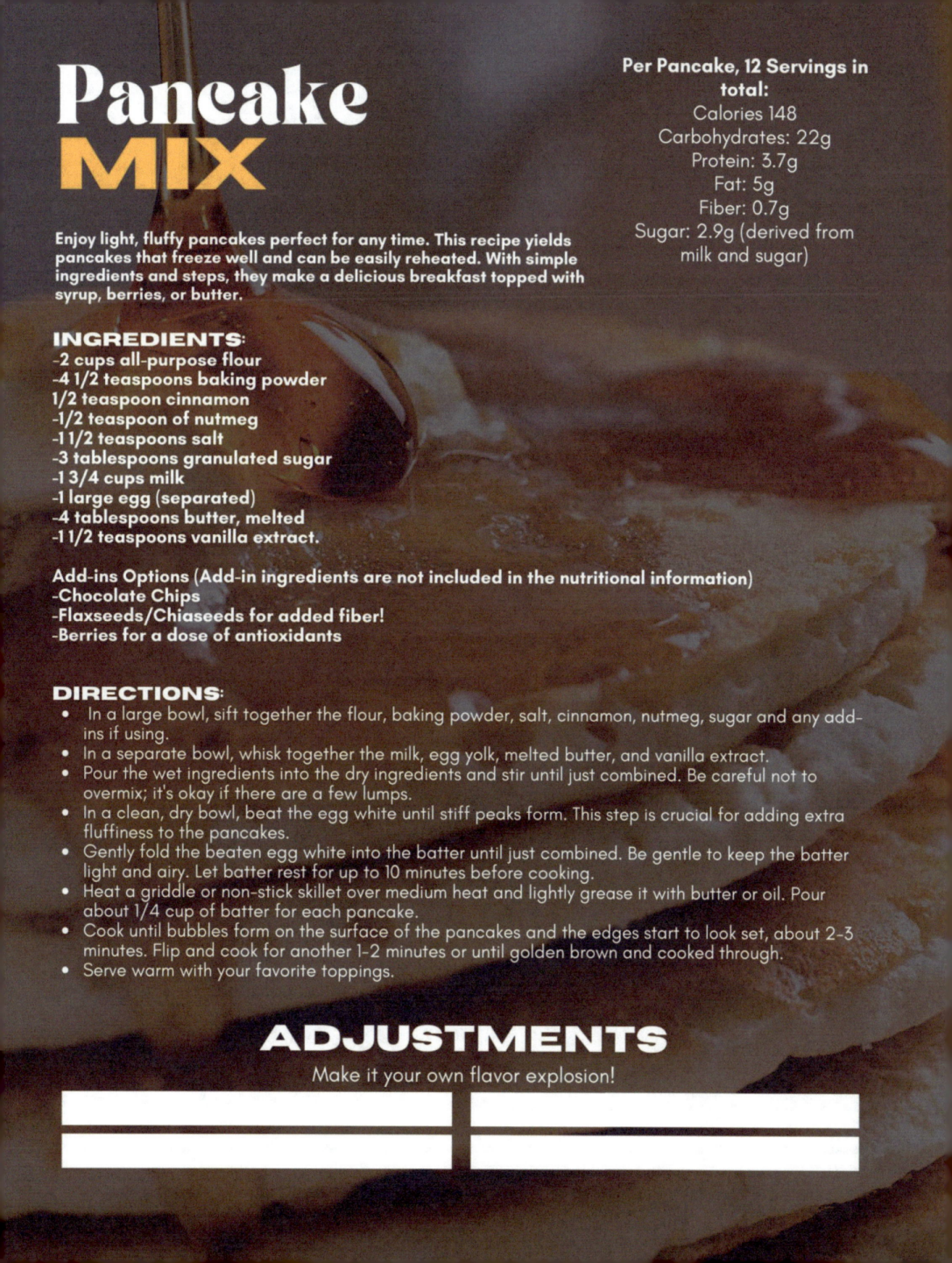

Pancake MIX

Per Pancake, 12 Servings in total:
Calories 148
Carbohydrates: 22g
Protein: 3.7g
Fat: 5g
Fiber: 0.7g
Sugar: 2.9g (derived from milk and sugar)

Enjoy light, fluffy pancakes perfect for any time. This recipe yields pancakes that freeze well and can be easily reheated. With simple ingredients and steps, they make a delicious breakfast topped with syrup, berries, or butter.

INGREDIENTS:
- 2 cups all-purpose flour
- 4 1/2 teaspoons baking powder
- 1/2 teaspoon cinnamon
- 1/2 teaspoon of nutmeg
- 1 1/2 teaspoons salt
- 3 tablespoons granulated sugar
- 1 3/4 cups milk
- 1 large egg (separated)
- 4 tablespoons butter, melted
- 1 1/2 teaspoons vanilla extract.

Add-ins Options (Add-in ingredients are not included in the nutritional information)
- Chocolate Chips
- Flaxseeds/Chiaseeds for added fiber!
- Berries for a dose of antioxidants

DIRECTIONS:
- In a large bowl, sift together the flour, baking powder, salt, cinnamon, nutmeg, sugar and any add-ins if using.
- In a separate bowl, whisk together the milk, egg yolk, melted butter, and vanilla extract.
- Pour the wet ingredients into the dry ingredients and stir until just combined. Be careful not to overmix; it's okay if there are a few lumps.
- In a clean, dry bowl, beat the egg white until stiff peaks form. This step is crucial for adding extra fluffiness to the pancakes.
- Gently fold the beaten egg white into the batter until just combined. Be gentle to keep the batter light and airy. Let batter rest for up to 10 minutes before cooking.
- Heat a griddle or non-stick skillet over medium heat and lightly grease it with butter or oil. Pour about 1/4 cup of batter for each pancake.
- Cook until bubbles form on the surface of the pancakes and the edges start to look set, about 2-3 minutes. Flip and cook for another 1-2 minutes or until golden brown and cooked through.
- Serve warm with your favorite toppings.

ADJUSTMENTS

Make it your own flavor explosion!

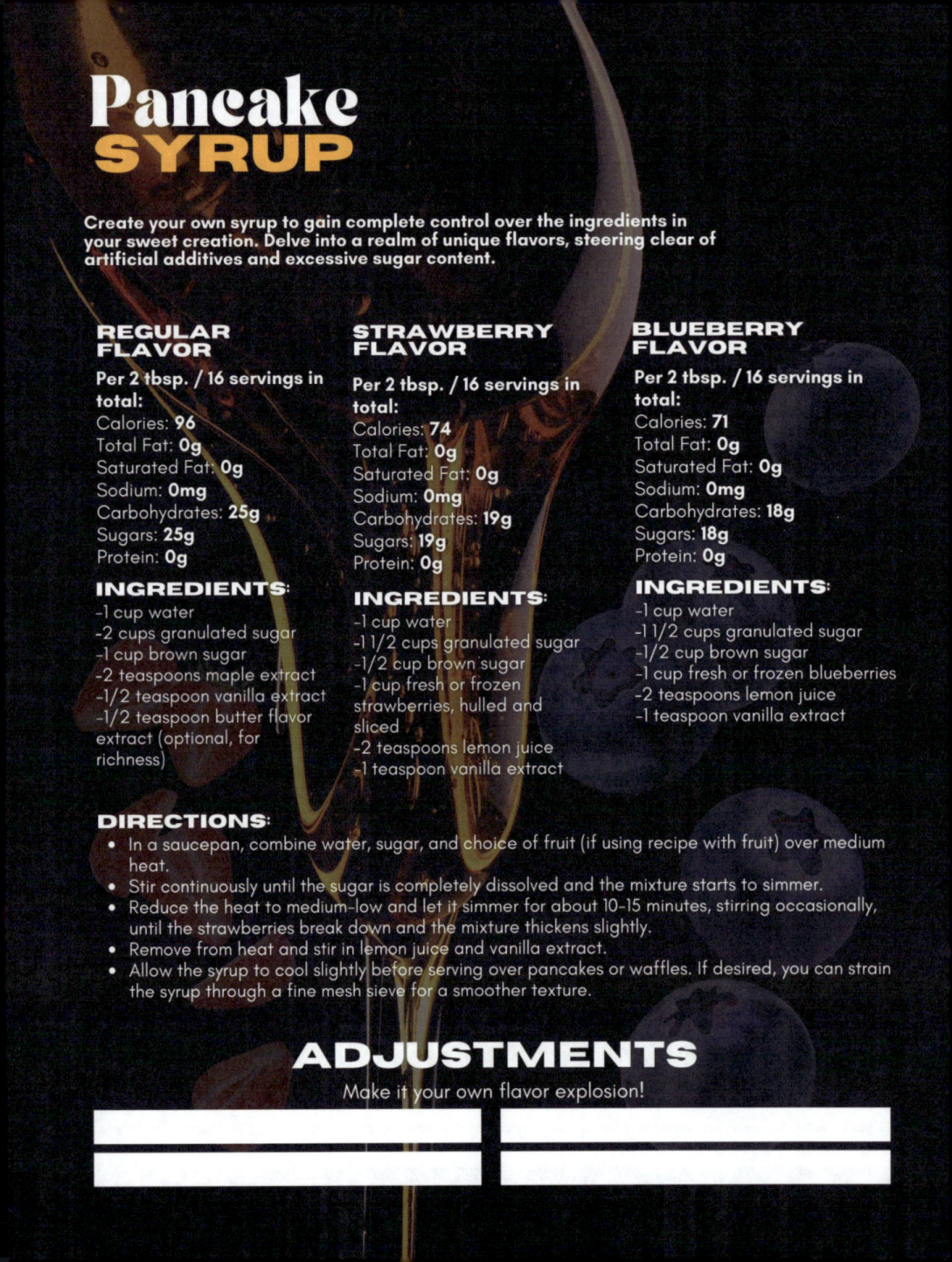

Pancake SYRUP

Create your own syrup to gain complete control over the ingredients in your sweet creation. Delve into a realm of unique flavors, steering clear of artificial additives and excessive sugar content.

REGULAR FLAVOR

Per 2 tbsp. / 16 servings in total:
Calories: **96**
Total Fat: **0g**
Saturated Fat: **0g**
Sodium: **0mg**
Carbohydrates: **25g**
Sugars: **25g**
Protein: **0g**

INGREDIENTS:
- 1 cup water
- 2 cups granulated sugar
- 1 cup brown sugar
- 2 teaspoons maple extract
- 1/2 teaspoon vanilla extract
- 1/2 teaspoon butter flavor extract (optional, for richness)

STRAWBERRY FLAVOR

Per 2 tbsp. / 16 servings in total:
Calories: **74**
Total Fat: **0g**
Saturated Fat: **0g**
Sodium: **0mg**
Carbohydrates: **19g**
Sugars: **19g**
Protein: **0g**

INGREDIENTS:
- 1 cup water
- 1 1/2 cups granulated sugar
- 1/2 cup brown sugar
- 1 cup fresh or frozen strawberries, hulled and sliced
- 2 teaspoons lemon juice
- 1 teaspoon vanilla extract

BLUEBERRY FLAVOR

Per 2 tbsp. / 16 servings in total:
Calories: **71**
Total Fat: **0g**
Saturated Fat: **0g**
Sodium: **0mg**
Carbohydrates: **18g**
Sugars: **18g**
Protein: **0g**

INGREDIENTS:
- 1 cup water
- 1 1/2 cups granulated sugar
- 1/2 cup brown sugar
- 1 cup fresh or frozen blueberries
- 2 teaspoons lemon juice
- 1 teaspoon vanilla extract

DIRECTIONS:

- In a saucepan, combine water, sugar, and choice of fruit (if using recipe with fruit) over medium heat.
- Stir continuously until the sugar is completely dissolved and the mixture starts to simmer.
- Reduce the heat to medium-low and let it simmer for about 10-15 minutes, stirring occasionally, until the strawberries break down and the mixture thickens slightly.
- Remove from heat and stir in lemon juice and vanilla extract.
- Allow the syrup to cool slightly before serving over pancakes or waffles. If desired, you can strain the syrup through a fine mesh sieve for a smoother texture.

ADJUSTMENTS

Make it your own flavor explosion!

Granola/ GRANOLA BARS

Per 1/2 cup / 10 servings in total:
Calories: 320
Total Fat: 15g
Saturated Fat: 9g
Cholesterol: 0mg
Sodium: 200mg
Total Carbohydrates: 38g
Dietary Fiber: 4g
Sugars: 15g
Protein: 7.6g

INGREDIENTS:

- 4 cups rolled oats
- 1/2 cup hemp seeds (optional)
- 1/2 cup honey or maple syrup
- 3 Tablespoons Turbinado Sugar (brown sugar can be substituted)
- 1/2 cup of coconut oil
- 1 tablespoon vanilla extract
- 1/2 teaspoon ground cinnamon
- 1 teaspoon of salt

Optional add-ins: 1/2 cup of nuts, seeds, cheerios, dried fruis, or shredded coconut

DIRECTIONS:

- Preheat your oven to 325°F.
- Line a baking sheet with parchment paper.
- In a large bowl, combine the oats, optional add-ins, cinnamon, and salt.
- On low heat, warm the honey or maple syrup and oil. Stir in the vanilla extract.
- Pour the wet ingredients over the dry ingredients and mix well until all the dry ingredients are coated.
- Spread the mixture evenly on the prepared baking sheet.
- Bake for 20-25 minutes, stirring halfway through, until golden brown.
- Let the granola cool completely on the baking sheet. Once cool, it will become crunchy. Store in an airtight container for up to 4-5 weeks.

Whipping up your own batch of granola and granola bars is like being a taste wizard, creating snacks that match your cravings and dietary needs. It's a delicious and satisfying adventure!

PEANUT BUTTER & CHIP CHOCOLATE BARS

1 bar / 12 servings in total:
Calories: 275
Total Fat: 14g
Saturated Fat: 7g
Cholesterol: 0mg
Sodium: 48mg
Total Carbohydrates: 32g
Dietary Fiber: 3g
Sugars: 14g
Protein: 9g

INGREDIENTS:

- 3 cups prepared granola
- 1 cup creamy peanut butter
- 1 teaspoon of vanilla
- 1/4 teaspoon of salt
- 1/2 cup honey or maple syrup
- 1/2 cup mini chocolate chips

DIRECTIONS:

- Line an 8x8-inch baking dish with parchment paper.
- In a medium saucepan over low heat, combine the peanut butter and honey/maple syrup. Stir until the mixture is smooth and well combined. Remove from heat and add vanilla and salt.
- Allow the mixture to cool for about 5 minutes to prevent the chocolate chips from melting too much when added in.
- Mix together the granola and the melted peanut butter until the granola is well coated.
- Add in chocolate chips & stir til well combined.
- Press mixture firmly into an even layer using the back of a spoon or a spatula.
- Take another sheet of parchment paper and lay it on top of the mixture and press firmly. Leave top parchment paper to help remove bars from pan.
- Refrigerate the bars for at least 2 hours.
- Once set, lift the granola out of the pan using the parchment paper.
- Cut & store the bars in an airtight container in the refrigerator.

ADJUSTMENTS

Make it your own flavor explosion!

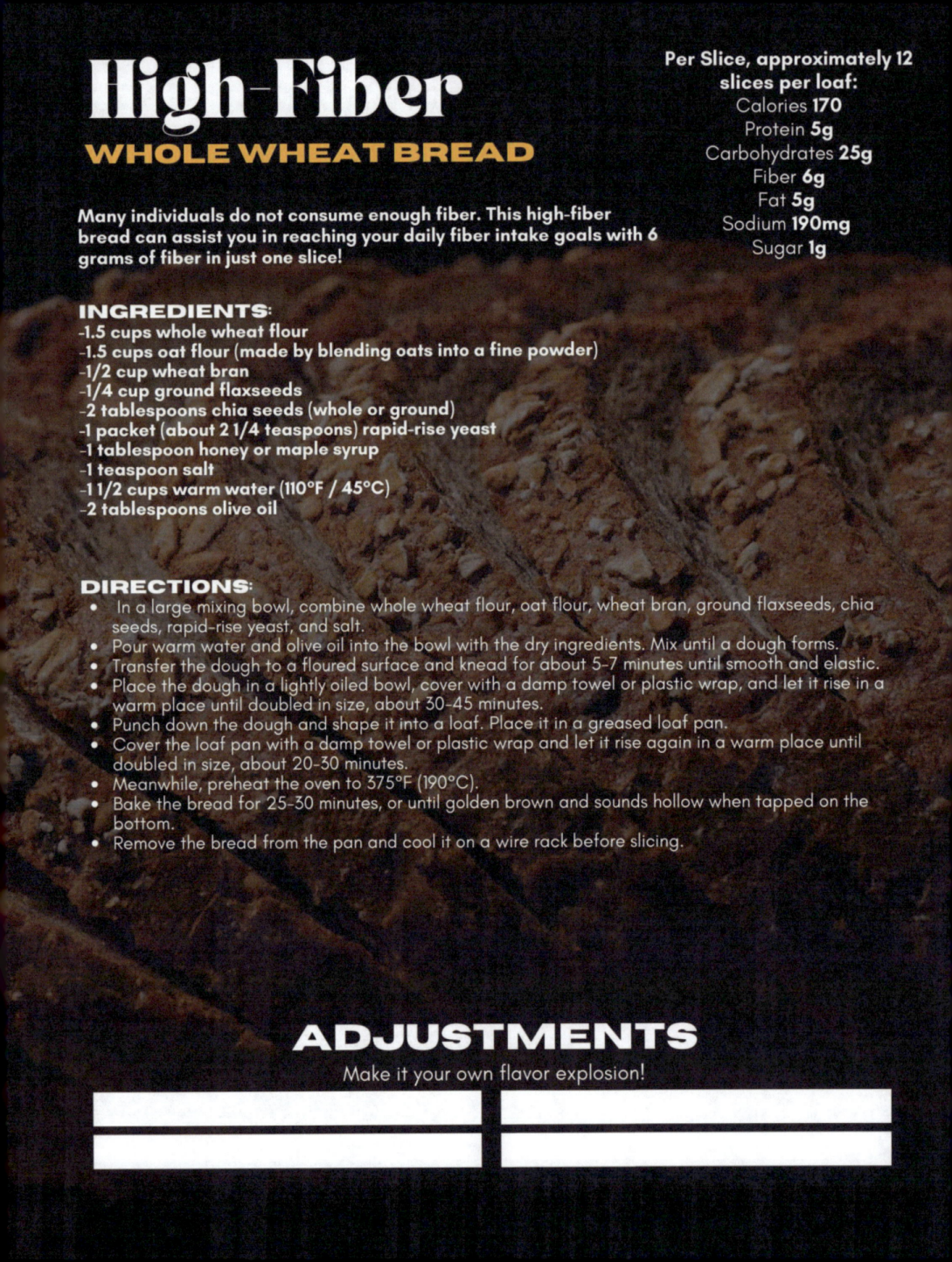

High-Fiber

WHOLE WHEAT BREAD

Per Slice, approximately 12 slices per loaf:
Calories **170**
Protein **5g**
Carbohydrates **25g**
Fiber **6g**
Fat **5g**
Sodium **190mg**
Sugar **1g**

Many individuals do not consume enough fiber. This high-fiber bread can assist you in reaching your daily fiber intake goals with 6 grams of fiber in just one slice!

INGREDIENTS:

- 1.5 cups whole wheat flour
- 1.5 cups oat flour (made by blending oats into a fine powder)
- 1/2 cup wheat bran
- 1/4 cup ground flaxseeds
- 2 tablespoons chia seeds (whole or ground)
- 1 packet (about 2 1/4 teaspoons) rapid-rise yeast
- 1 tablespoon honey or maple syrup
- 1 teaspoon salt
- 1 1/2 cups warm water (110°F / 45°C)
- 2 tablespoons olive oil

DIRECTIONS:

- In a large mixing bowl, combine whole wheat flour, oat flour, wheat bran, ground flaxseeds, chia seeds, rapid-rise yeast, and salt.
- Pour warm water and olive oil into the bowl with the dry ingredients. Mix until a dough forms.
- Transfer the dough to a floured surface and knead for about 5-7 minutes until smooth and elastic.
- Place the dough in a lightly oiled bowl, cover with a damp towel or plastic wrap, and let it rise in a warm place until doubled in size, about 30-45 minutes.
- Punch down the dough and shape it into a loaf. Place it in a greased loaf pan.
- Cover the loaf pan with a damp towel or plastic wrap and let it rise again in a warm place until doubled in size, about 20-30 minutes.
- Meanwhile, preheat the oven to 375°F (190°C).
- Bake the bread for 25-30 minutes, or until golden brown and sounds hollow when tapped on the bottom.
- Remove the bread from the pan and cool it on a wire rack before slicing.

ADJUSTMENTS

Make it your own flavor explosion!

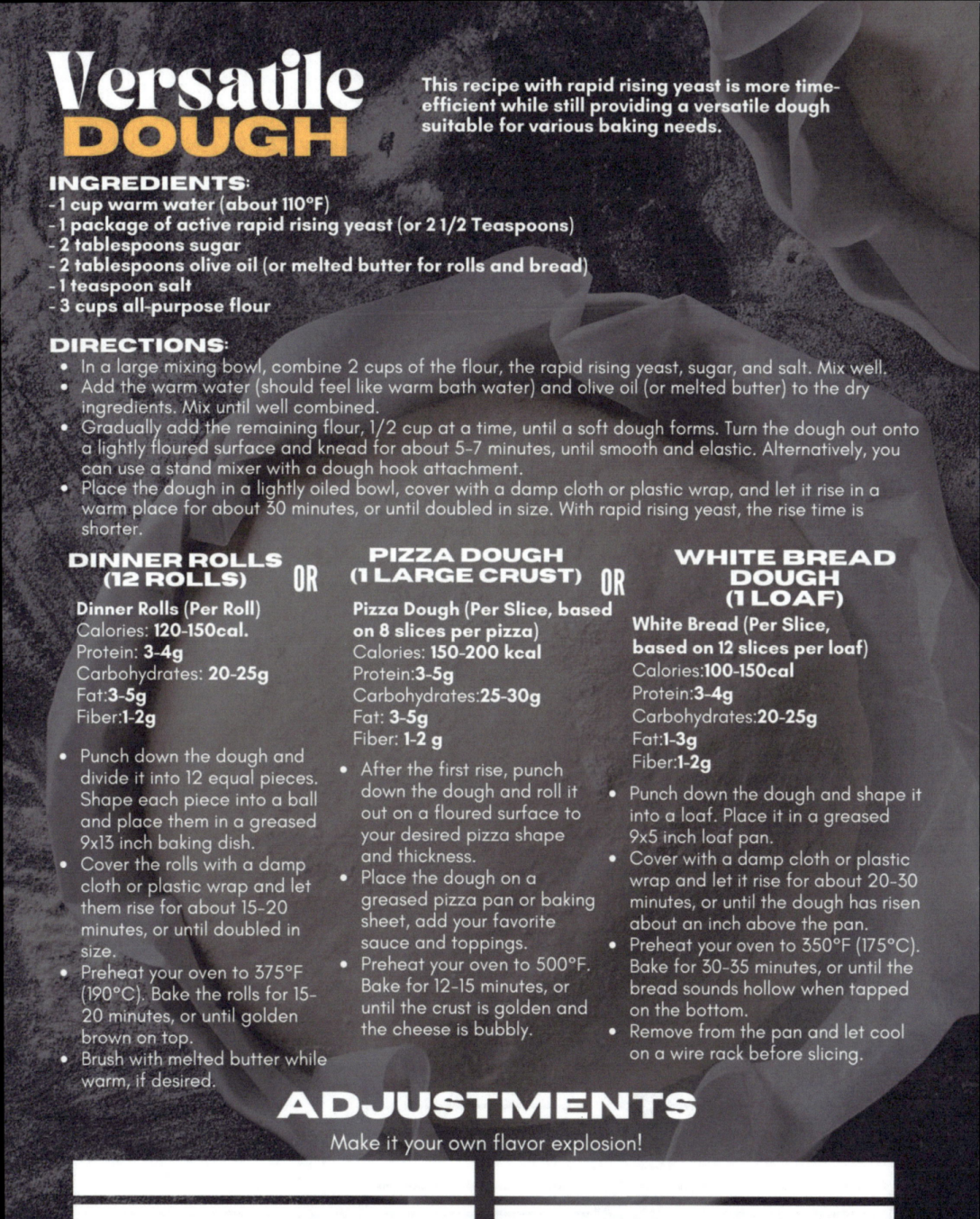

Versatile DOUGH

This recipe with rapid rising yeast is more time-efficient while still providing a versatile dough suitable for various baking needs.

INGREDIENTS:

- 1 cup warm water (about 110°F)
- 1 package of active rapid rising yeast (or 2 1/2 Teaspoons)
- 2 tablespoons sugar
- 2 tablespoons olive oil (or melted butter for rolls and bread)
- 1 teaspoon salt
- 3 cups all-purpose flour

DIRECTIONS:

- In a large mixing bowl, combine 2 cups of the flour, the rapid rising yeast, sugar, and salt. Mix well.
- Add the warm water (should feel like warm bath water) and olive oil (or melted butter) to the dry ingredients. Mix until well combined.
- Gradually add the remaining flour, 1/2 cup at a time, until a soft dough forms. Turn the dough out onto a lightly floured surface and knead for about 5-7 minutes, until smooth and elastic. Alternatively, you can use a stand mixer with a dough hook attachment.
- Place the dough in a lightly oiled bowl, cover with a damp cloth or plastic wrap, and let it rise in a warm place for about 30 minutes, or until doubled in size. With rapid rising yeast, the rise time is shorter.

DINNER ROLLS (12 ROLLS)

OR

PIZZA DOUGH (1 LARGE CRUST)

OR

WHITE BREAD DOUGH (1 LOAF)

Dinner Rolls (Per Roll)
Calories: **120-150cal.**
Protein: **3-4g**
Carbohydrates: **20-25g**
Fat:**3-5g**
Fiber:**1-2g**

- Punch down the dough and divide it into 12 equal pieces. Shape each piece into a ball and place them in a greased 9x13 inch baking dish.
- Cover the rolls with a damp cloth or plastic wrap and let them rise for about 15-20 minutes, or until doubled in size.
- Preheat your oven to 375°F (190°C). Bake the rolls for 15-20 minutes, or until golden brown on top.
- Brush with melted butter while warm, if desired.

Pizza Dough (Per Slice, based on 8 slices per pizza)
Calories: **150-200 kcal**
Protein:**3-5g**
Carbohydrates:**25-30g**
Fat: **3-5g**
Fiber: **1-2 g**

- After the first rise, punch down the dough and roll it out on a floured surface to your desired pizza shape and thickness.
- Place the dough on a greased pizza pan or baking sheet, add your favorite sauce and toppings.
- Preheat your oven to 500°F. Bake for 12-15 minutes, or until the crust is golden and the cheese is bubbly.

White Bread (Per Slice, based on 12 slices per loaf)
Calories:**100-150cal**
Protein:**3-4g**
Carbohydrates:**20-25g**
Fat:**1-3g**
Fiber:**1-2g**

- Punch down the dough and shape it into a loaf. Place it in a greased 9x5 inch loaf pan.
- Cover with a damp cloth or plastic wrap and let it rise for about 20-30 minutes, or until the dough has risen about an inch above the pan.
- Preheat your oven to 350°F (175°C). Bake for 30-35 minutes, or until the bread sounds hollow when tapped on the bottom.
- Remove from the pan and let cool on a wire rack before slicing.

ADJUSTMENTS

Make it your own flavor explosion!

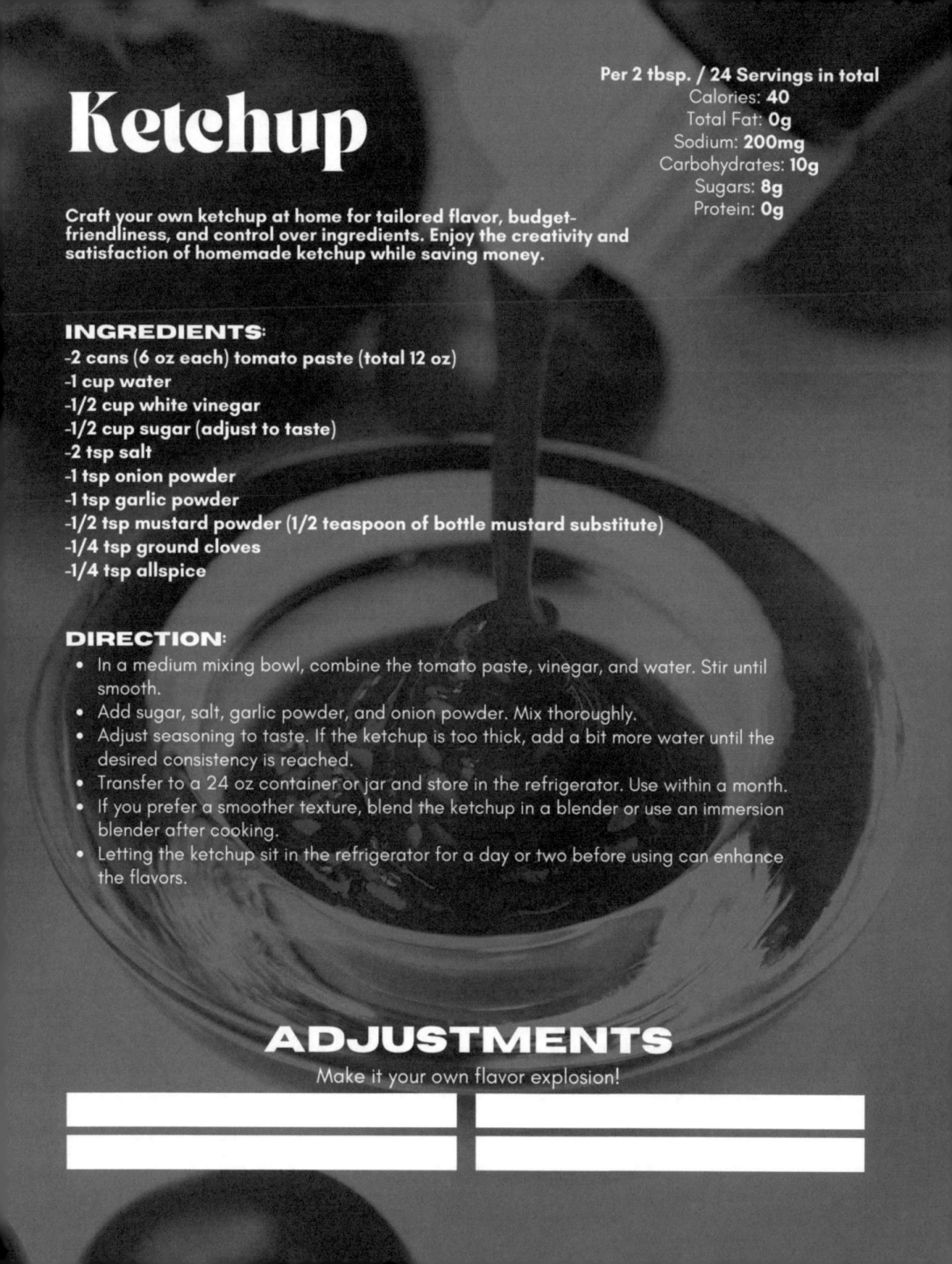

Ketchup

Per 2 tbsp. / 24 Servings in total
Calories: **40**
Total Fat: **0g**
Sodium: **200mg**
Carbohydrates: **10g**
Sugars: **8g**
Protein: **0g**

Craft your own ketchup at home for tailored flavor, budget-friendliness, and control over ingredients. Enjoy the creativity and satisfaction of homemade ketchup while saving money.

INGREDIENTS:

- 2 cans (6 oz each) tomato paste (total 12 oz)
- 1 cup water
- 1/2 cup white vinegar
- 1/2 cup sugar (adjust to taste)
- 2 tsp salt
- 1 tsp onion powder
- 1 tsp garlic powder
- 1/2 tsp mustard powder (1/2 teaspoon of bottle mustard substitute)
- 1/4 tsp ground cloves
- 1/4 tsp allspice

DIRECTION:

- In a medium mixing bowl, combine the tomato paste, vinegar, and water. Stir until smooth.
- Add sugar, salt, garlic powder, and onion powder. Mix thoroughly.
- Adjust seasoning to taste. If the ketchup is too thick, add a bit more water until the desired consistency is reached.
- Transfer to a 24 oz container or jar and store in the refrigerator. Use within a month.
- If you prefer a smoother texture, blend the ketchup in a blender or use an immersion blender after cooking.
- Letting the ketchup sit in the refrigerator for a day or two before using can enhance the flavors.

ADJUSTMENTS

Make it your own flavor explosion!

Mayonnaise

Making homemade mayonnaise provides a healthier option without additives, allows customization of ingredients and flavors, and offers a rewarding culinary experience.

Per 2 tbsp. / 8 servings in total:
Calories: **197**
Total Fat: **22g**
Saturated Fat: **2g**
Sodium: **69mg**
Total Carbohydrates: **0g**
Protein: **0g**

INGREDIENTS

- 1 egg yolk
- 1 tablespoon Dijon mustard
- 1 tablespoon lemon juice or white vinegar
- 1 cup neutral-flavored oil (such as vegetable or canola oil)
- Salt and pepper to taste

DIRECTIONS:

In a mixing bowl, whisk together the egg yolk, Dijon mustard, and lemon juice or vinegar until well combined.
Slowly drizzle in the oil while whisking continuously, starting with just a few drops at a time and gradually increasing to a thin stream, until the mixture begins to thicken and emulsify.
Continue whisking until all of the oil is incorporated and the mayo is thick and creamy.
Season with salt and pepper to taste.
Transfer the homemade mayo to a clean jar or container and store it in the refrigerator for up to 1 week.

VEGAN OPTION

Per 2 tbsp. / 8 servings in total:
Calories: **126**
Total Fat: **14g**
Saturated Fat: **1g**
Sodium: **120mg**
Carbohydrates: **0.5g**
Protein: **0g**

INGREDIENTS

- 1 cup unsweetened soy milk or almond milk
- 1 tablespoon apple cider vinegar or lemon juice
- 1 teaspoon Dijon mustard
- 1/2 teaspoon salt
- 1 cup neutral-flavored oil (such as vegetable or canola oil)
- Optional: 1-2 teaspoons agave syrup or maple syrup for sweetness (adjust to taste)

DIRECTIONS:

In a blender, combine the soy milk or almond milk, apple cider vinegar or lemon juice, Dijon mustard, and salt.
Blend on low speed until well combined.
With the blender running on low speed, slowly drizzle in the neutral-flavored oil in a thin, steady stream. It's important to add the oil slowly to allow the mixture to emulsify and thicken properly.
Continue blending until the mixture thickens to a creamy mayo consistency. This may take a few minutes.
Once the mayo is thick and creamy, taste and adjust the seasoning as needed. If you prefer a slightly sweeter mayo, you can add 1-2 teaspoons of agave syrup or maple syrup and blend again until well combined.
Transfer the vegan mayo to a clean jar or container and store it in the refrigerator for up to 1 week.

ADJUSTMENTS

Make it your own flavor explosion!

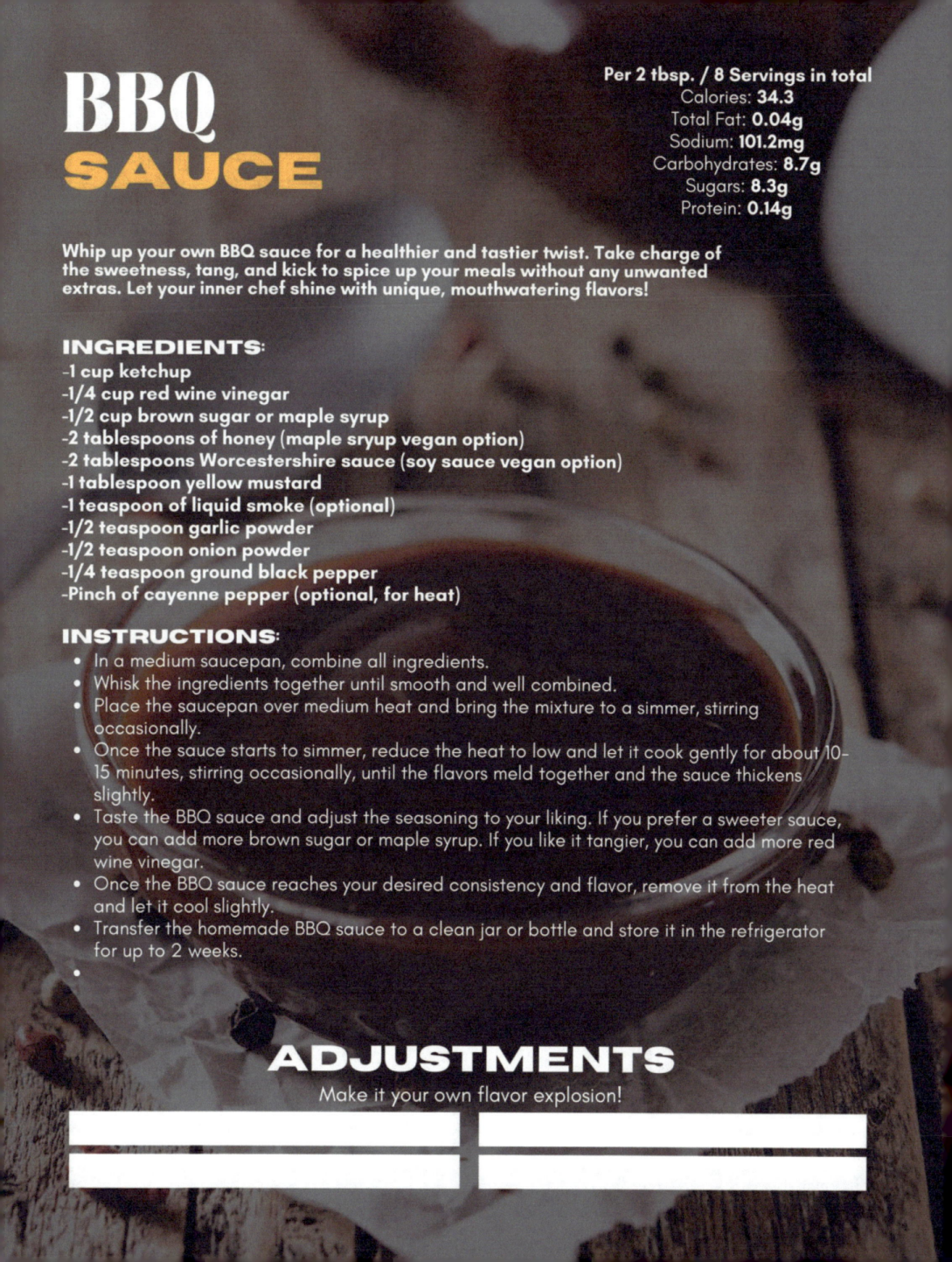

BBQ SAUCE

Per 2 tbsp. / 8 Servings in total
Calories: **34.3**
Total Fat: **0.04g**
Sodium: **101.2mg**
Carbohydrates: **8.7g**
Sugars: **8.3g**
Protein: **0.14g**

Whip up your own BBQ sauce for a healthier and tastier twist. Take charge of the sweetness, tang, and kick to spice up your meals without any unwanted extras. Let your inner chef shine with unique, mouthwatering flavors!

INGREDIENTS:

- 1 cup ketchup
- 1/4 cup red wine vinegar
- 1/2 cup brown sugar or maple syrup
- 2 tablespoons of honey (maple sryup vegan option)
- 2 tablespoons Worcestershire sauce (soy sauce vegan option)
- 1 tablespoon yellow mustard
- 1 teaspoon of liquid smoke (optional)
- 1/2 teaspoon garlic powder
- 1/2 teaspoon onion powder
- 1/4 teaspoon ground black pepper
- Pinch of cayenne pepper (optional, for heat)

INSTRUCTIONS:

- In a medium saucepan, combine all ingredients.
- Whisk the ingredients together until smooth and well combined.
- Place the saucepan over medium heat and bring the mixture to a simmer, stirring occasionally.
- Once the sauce starts to simmer, reduce the heat to low and let it cook gently for about 10-15 minutes, stirring occasionally, until the flavors meld together and the sauce thickens slightly.
- Taste the BBQ sauce and adjust the seasoning to your liking. If you prefer a sweeter sauce, you can add more brown sugar or maple syrup. If you like it tangier, you can add more red wine vinegar.
- Once the BBQ sauce reaches your desired consistency and flavor, remove it from the heat and let it cool slightly.
- Transfer the homemade BBQ sauce to a clean jar or bottle and store it in the refrigerator for up to 2 weeks.

ADJUSTMENTS

Make it your own flavor explosion!

Honey MUSTARD

Per 2 tbsp. / 8 Servings in total
Calories: **70**
Total Fat: **3g**
Saturated Fat: **0.5g**
Sodium: **175mg**
Total Carbohydrates: **10g**
Dietary Fiber: **0.25g**
Sugars: **9g**
Protein: **0.5g**

Making honey mustard sauce at home allows customization of flavors and promotes healthier eating by controlling ingredients. It adds a homemade touch to dishes without unnecessary additives.

INGREDIENTS:

- 1/2 cup Dijon mustard (yellow mustard works too)
- 1/4 cup honey
- 2 tablespoons mayonnaise
- 1 tablespoon lemon juice or apple cider vinegar (optional)

DIRECTIONS:

- In a small bowl, combine the Dijon mustard and honey. Mix well until fully integrated.
- Add the mayonnaise to the bowl and stir until the mixture is smooth and creamy.
- If you like a tangier taste, add the lemon juice or apple cider vinegar and mix well.
- Taste and adjust the sweetness or tanginess by adding more honey or mustard as needed.
- Serve immediately or refrigerate in an airtight container until ready to use.

ADJUSTMENTS

Make it your own flavor explosion!

Salad

DRESSINGS

Homemade salad dressings offer control over ingredients, using fresh herbs, quality oils, and natural sweeteners for nutritious options.

RANCH DRESSING

Per 2 tbsp. / 8 servings in total:
Calories: **163**
Total Fat: **17g**
Saturated Fat: **4g**
Cholesterol: **17mg**
Sodium: **211mg**
Total Carbohydrates: **1g**
Protein: **1g**

INGREDIENTS:
- 1/2 cup mayonnaise
- 1/2 cup sour cream
- 1 teaspoon dried parsley
- 1/2 teaspoon dried dill weed
- 1/2 teaspoon garlic powder
- 1/4 teaspoon onion powder
- 1/4 teaspoon salt
- 1/4 teaspoon black pepper
- 1 tablespoon lemon juice
- 1/4 cup milk (adjust consistency to your liking)

ITALIAN DRESSING

Per 2 tbsp. / 8 servings in total:
Calories: **120 cal**
Total Fat: **14g**
Saturated Fat: **2g**
Sodium: **150mg**
Total Carbohydrates: **1g**
Dietary Fiber: **0g**
Sugars: **0g (1g if sugar is added)**
Protein: **0g**

INGREDIENTS:
- 1/2 cup extra virgin olive oil
- 1/4 cup red wine vinegar
- 1 teaspoon dried oregano
- 1 teaspoon dried basil
- 1 teaspoon garlic powder
- 1 teaspoon onion powder
- 1 teaspoon Dijon mustard (optional)
- 1/2 teaspoon salt
- 1/4 teaspoon black pepper
- 1/4 teaspoon sugar (optional)

CAESAR DRESSING:

Per 2 tbsp. / 8 servings in total:
Calories: **166**
Total Fat: **18g**
Saturated Fat: **3g**
Cholesterol: **8mg**
Sodium: **184mg**
Total Carbohydrates: **1g**
Protein: **1g**

INGREDIENTS:
- 1/2 cup mayonnaise
- 1/4 cup grated Parmesan cheese
- 2 tablespoons lemon juice
- 1 tablespoon Dijon mustard
- 1 clove garlic, minced
- 1/4 teaspoon Worcestershire sauce
- Salt and pepper to taste
- 1/4 cup olive oil

DIRECTIONS:

- In a bowl or jar, combine all ingredient.
- Whisk together until well combined, or if using a jar, screw on the lid and shake vigorously until the ingredients are well mixed.
- Taste and adjust the seasoning as needed. You can add more salt, pepper, or herbs according to your preference.
- Store the dressing in an airtight container in the refrigerator. Shake well before each use as the ingredients may separate.

ADJUSTMENTS

Make it your own flavor explosion!

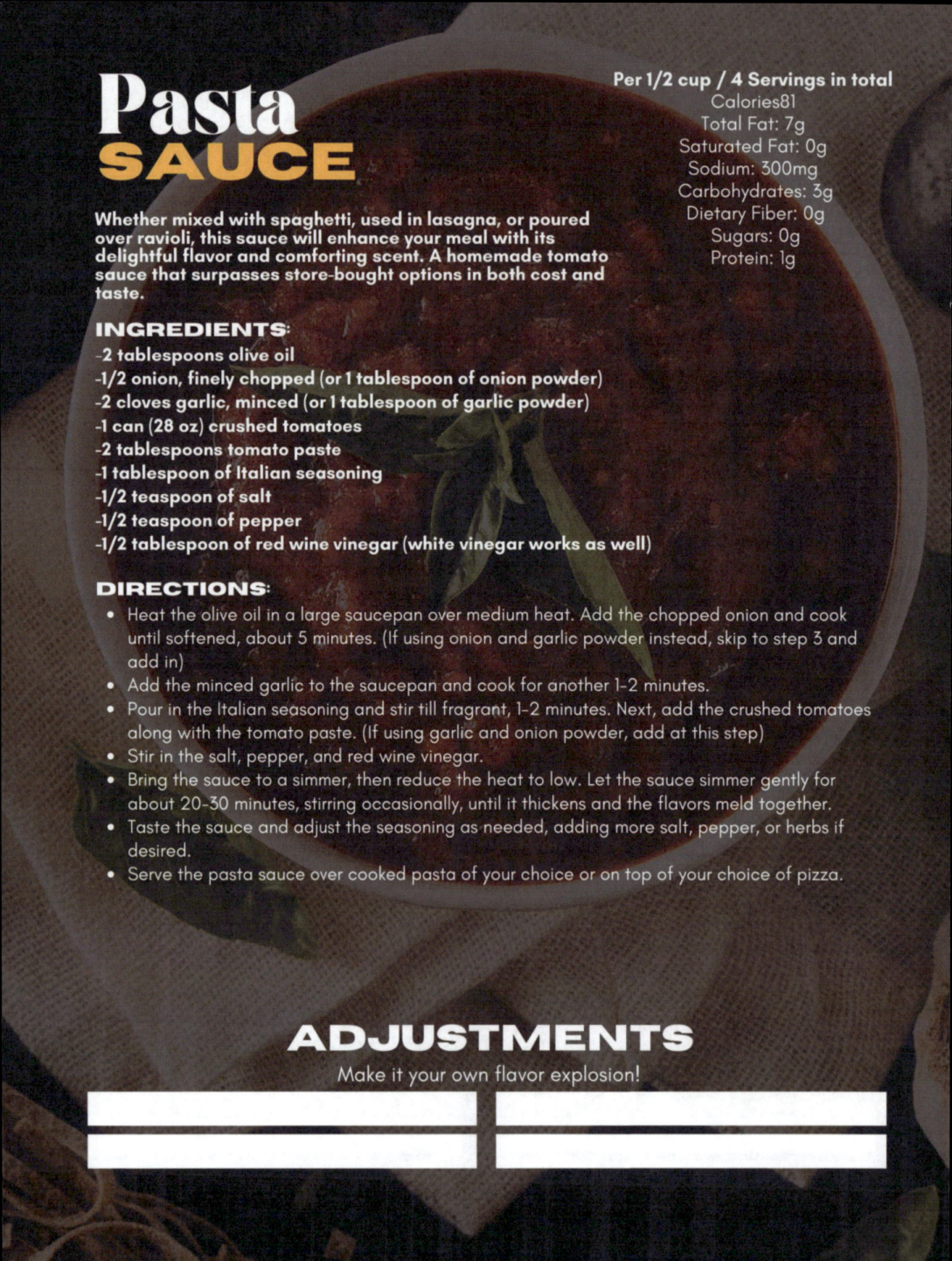

Pasta SAUCE

Per 1/2 cup / 4 Servings in total
Calories81
Total Fat: 7g
Saturated Fat: 0g
Sodium: 300mg
Carbohydrates: 3g
Dietary Fiber: 0g
Sugars: 0g
Protein: 1g

Whether mixed with spaghetti, used in lasagna, or poured over ravioli, this sauce will enhance your meal with its delightful flavor and comforting scent. A homemade tomato sauce that surpasses store-bought options in both cost and taste.

INGREDIENTS:

- 2 tablespoons olive oil
- 1/2 onion, finely chopped (or 1 tablespoon of onion powder)
- 2 cloves garlic, minced (or 1 tablespoon of garlic powder)
- 1 can (28 oz) crushed tomatoes
- 2 tablespoons tomato paste
- 1 tablespoon of Italian seasoning
- 1/2 teaspoon of salt
- 1/2 teaspoon of pepper
- 1/2 tablespoon of red wine vinegar (white vinegar works as well)

DIRECTIONS:

- Heat the olive oil in a large saucepan over medium heat. Add the chopped onion and cook until softened, about 5 minutes. (If using onion and garlic powder instead, skip to step 3 and add in)
- Add the minced garlic to the saucepan and cook for another 1-2 minutes.
- Pour in the Italian seasoning and stir till fragrant, 1-2 minutes. Next, add the crushed tomatoes along with the tomato paste. (If using garlic and onion powder, add at this step)
- Stir in the salt, pepper, and red wine vinegar.
- Bring the sauce to a simmer, then reduce the heat to low. Let the sauce simmer gently for about 20-30 minutes, stirring occasionally, until it thickens and the flavors meld together.
- Taste the sauce and adjust the seasoning as needed, adding more salt, pepper, or herbs if desired.
- Serve the pasta sauce over cooked pasta of your choice or on top of your choice of pizza.

ADJUSTMENTS

Make it your own flavor explosion!

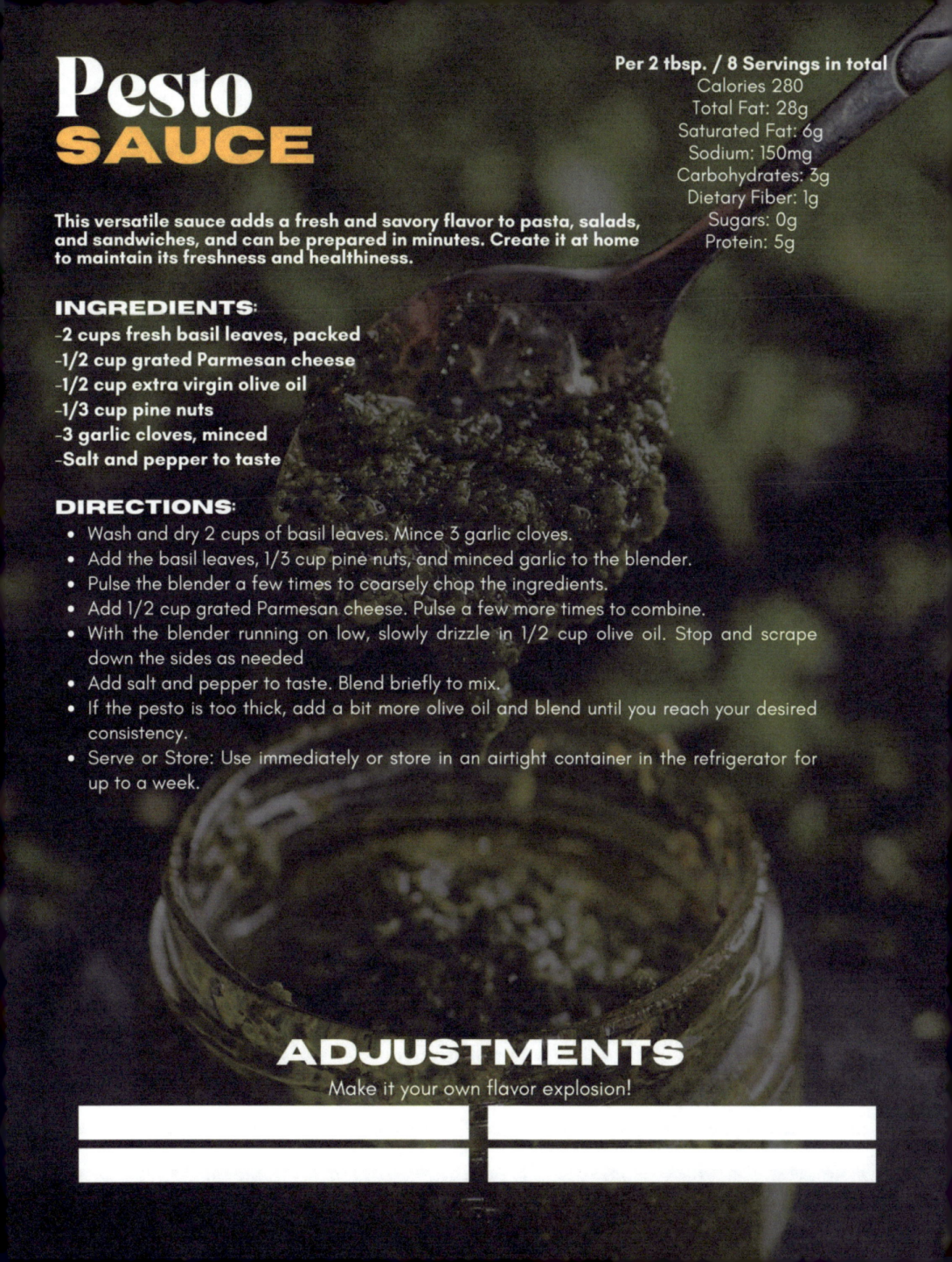

Pesto SAUCE

Per 2 tbsp. / 8 Servings in total
Calories 280
Total Fat: 28g
Saturated Fat: 6g
Sodium: 150mg
Carbohydrates: 5g
Dietary Fiber: 1g
Sugars: 0g
Protein: 5g

This versatile sauce adds a fresh and savory flavor to pasta, salads, and sandwiches, and can be prepared in minutes. Create it at home to maintain its freshness and healthiness.

INGREDIENTS:

- 2 cups fresh basil leaves, packed
- 1/2 cup grated Parmesan cheese
- 1/2 cup extra virgin olive oil
- 1/3 cup pine nuts
- 3 garlic cloves, minced
- Salt and pepper to taste

DIRECTIONS:

- Wash and dry 2 cups of basil leaves. Mince 3 garlic cloves.
- Add the basil leaves, 1/3 cup pine nuts, and minced garlic to the blender.
- Pulse the blender a few times to coarsely chop the ingredients.
- Add 1/2 cup grated Parmesan cheese. Pulse a few more times to combine.
- With the blender running on low, slowly drizzle in 1/2 cup olive oil. Stop and scrape down the sides as needed
- Add salt and pepper to taste. Blend briefly to mix.
- If the pesto is too thick, add a bit more olive oil and blend until you reach your desired consistency.
- Serve or Store: Use immediately or store in an airtight container in the refrigerator for up to a week.

ADJUSTMENTS

Make it your own flavor explosion!

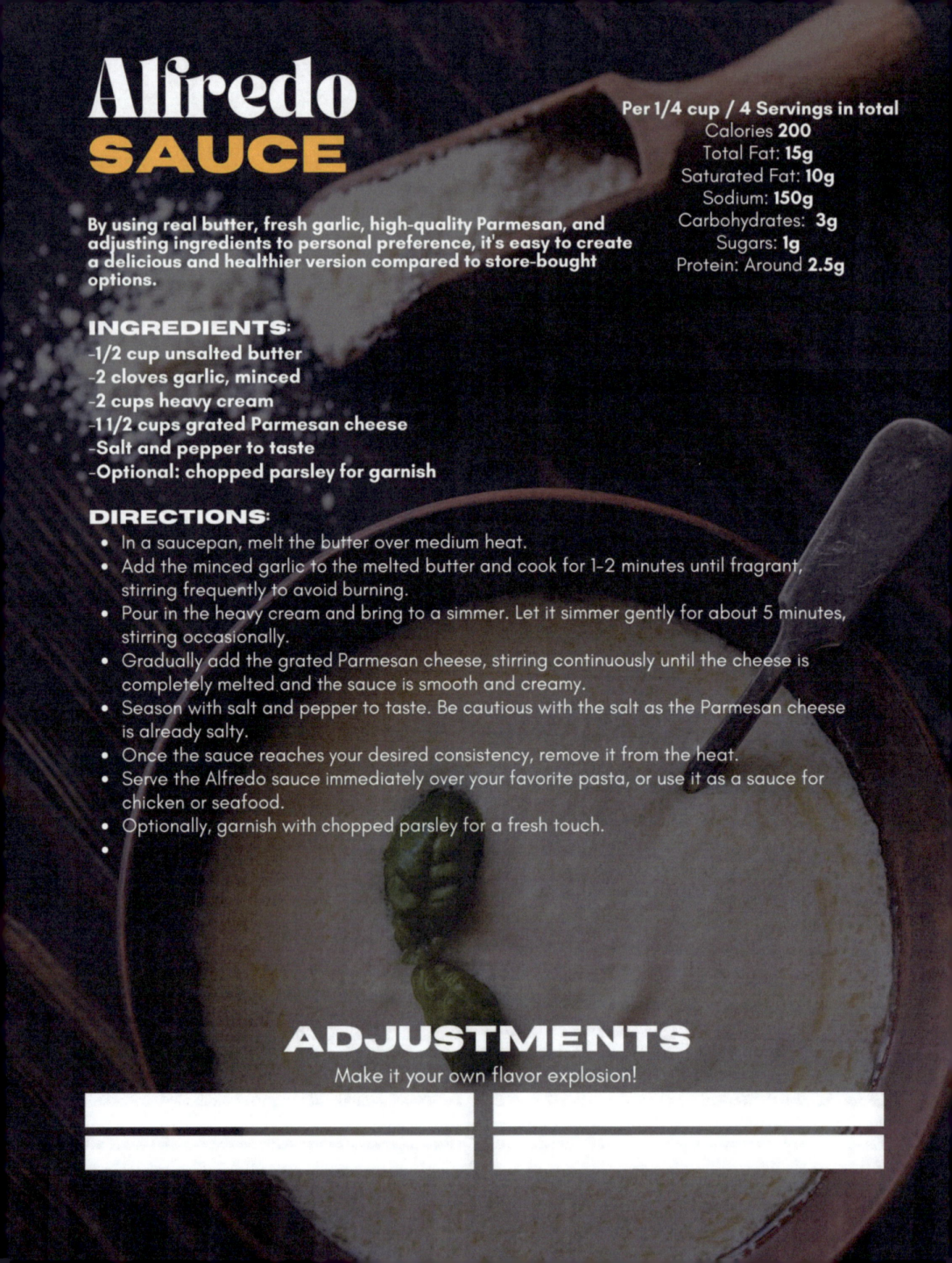

Alfredo
SAUCE

Per 1/4 cup / 4 Servings in total
Calories **200**
Total Fat: **15g**
Saturated Fat: **10g**
Sodium: **150g**
Carbohydrates: **3g**
Sugars: **1g**
Protein: Around **2.5g**

By using real butter, fresh garlic, high-quality Parmesan, and adjusting ingredients to personal preference, it's easy to create a delicious and healthier version compared to store-bought options.

INGREDIENTS:

- 1/2 cup unsalted butter
- 2 cloves garlic, minced
- 2 cups heavy cream
- 1 1/2 cups grated Parmesan cheese
- Salt and pepper to taste
- Optional: chopped parsley for garnish

DIRECTIONS:

- In a saucepan, melt the butter over medium heat.
- Add the minced garlic to the melted butter and cook for 1-2 minutes until fragrant, stirring frequently to avoid burning.
- Pour in the heavy cream and bring to a simmer. Let it simmer gently for about 5 minutes, stirring occasionally.
- Gradually add the grated Parmesan cheese, stirring continuously until the cheese is completely melted and the sauce is smooth and creamy.
- Season with salt and pepper to taste. Be cautious with the salt as the Parmesan cheese is already salty.
- Once the sauce reaches your desired consistency, remove it from the heat.
- Serve the Alfredo sauce immediately over your favorite pasta, or use it as a sauce for chicken or seafood.
- Optionally, garnish with chopped parsley for a fresh touch.

ADJUSTMENTS

Make it your own flavor explosion!

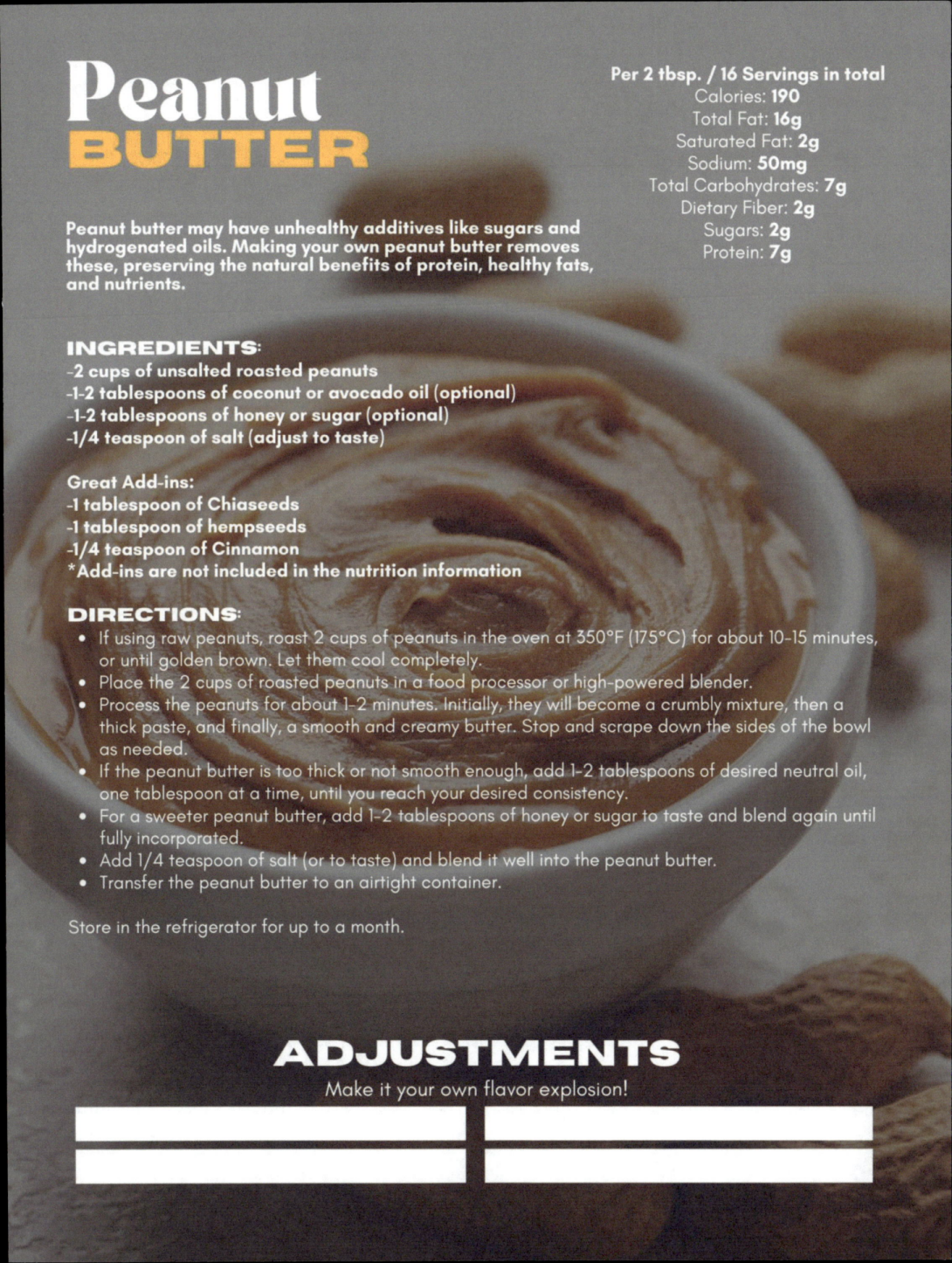

Peanut BUTTER

Per 2 tbsp. / 16 Servings in total
Calories: **190**
Total Fat: **16g**
Saturated Fat: **2g**
Sodium: **50mg**
Total Carbohydrates: **7g**
Dietary Fiber: **2g**
Sugars: **2g**
Protein: **7g**

Peanut butter may have unhealthy additives like sugars and hydrogenated oils. Making your own peanut butter removes these, preserving the natural benefits of protein, healthy fats, and nutrients.

INGREDIENTS:

- 2 cups of unsalted roasted peanuts
- 1-2 tablespoons of coconut or avocado oil (optional)
- 1-2 tablespoons of honey or sugar (optional)
- 1/4 teaspoon of salt (adjust to taste)

Great Add-ins:
- 1 tablespoon of Chiaseeds
- 1 tablespoon of hempseeds
- 1/4 teaspoon of Cinnamon

*Add-ins are not included in the nutrition information

DIRECTIONS:

- If using raw peanuts, roast 2 cups of peanuts in the oven at 350°F (175°C) for about 10-15 minutes, or until golden brown. Let them cool completely.
- Place the 2 cups of roasted peanuts in a food processor or high-powered blender.
- Process the peanuts for about 1-2 minutes. Initially, they will become a crumbly mixture, then a thick paste, and finally, a smooth and creamy butter. Stop and scrape down the sides of the bowl as needed.
- If the peanut butter is too thick or not smooth enough, add 1-2 tablespoons of desired neutral oil, one tablespoon at a time, until you reach your desired consistency.
- For a sweeter peanut butter, add 1-2 tablespoons of honey or sugar to taste and blend again until fully incorporated.
- Add 1/4 teaspoon of salt (or to taste) and blend it well into the peanut butter.
- Transfer the peanut butter to an airtight container.

Store in the refrigerator for up to a month.

ADJUSTMENTS

Make it your own flavor explosion!

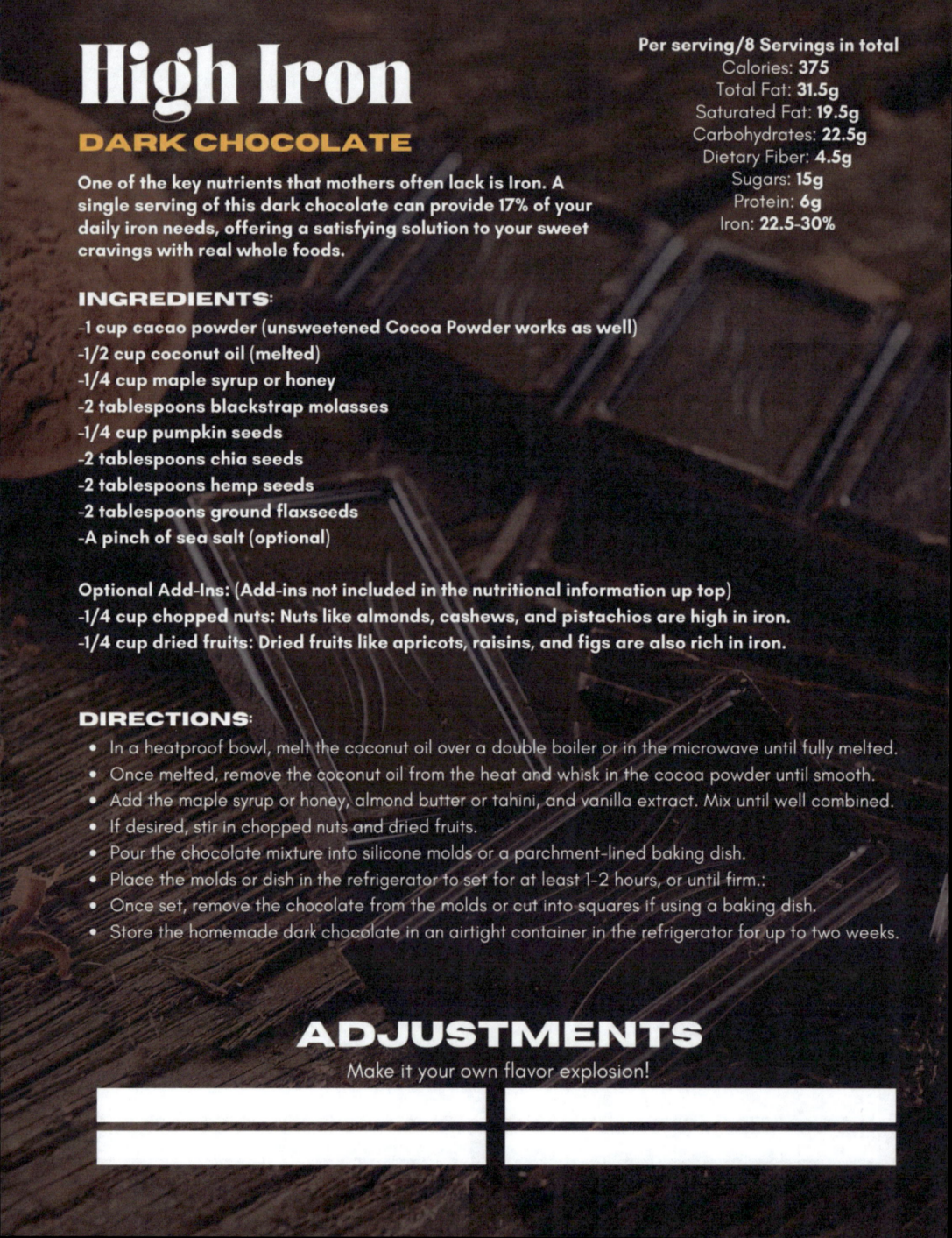

High Iron

DARK CHOCOLATE

One of the key nutrients that mothers often lack is Iron. A single serving of this dark chocolate can provide 17% of your daily iron needs, offering a satisfying solution to your sweet cravings with real whole foods.

Per serving/8 Servings in total
Calories: **375**
Total Fat: **31.5g**
Saturated Fat: **19.5g**
Carbohydrates: **22.5g**
Dietary Fiber: **4.5g**
Sugars: **15g**
Protein: **6g**
Iron: **22.5-30%**

INGREDIENTS:

- 1 cup cacao powder (unsweetened Cocoa Powder works as well)
- 1/2 cup coconut oil (melted)
- 1/4 cup maple syrup or honey
- 2 tablespoons blackstrap molasses
- 1/4 cup pumpkin seeds
- 2 tablespoons chia seeds
- 2 tablespoons hemp seeds
- 2 tablespoons ground flaxseeds
- A pinch of sea salt (optional)

Optional Add-Ins: (Add-ins not included in the nutritional information up top)
- 1/4 cup chopped nuts: Nuts like almonds, cashews, and pistachios are high in iron.
- 1/4 cup dried fruits: Dried fruits like apricots, raisins, and figs are also rich in iron.

DIRECTIONS:

- In a heatproof bowl, melt the coconut oil over a double boiler or in the microwave until fully melted.
- Once melted, remove the coconut oil from the heat and whisk in the cocoa powder until smooth.
- Add the maple syrup or honey, almond butter or tahini, and vanilla extract. Mix until well combined.
- If desired, stir in chopped nuts and dried fruits.
- Pour the chocolate mixture into silicone molds or a parchment-lined baking dish.
- Place the molds or dish in the refrigerator to set for at least 1-2 hours, or until firm.
- Once set, remove the chocolate from the molds or cut into squares if using a baking dish.
- Store the homemade dark chocolate in an airtight container in the refrigerator for up to two weeks.

ADJUSTMENTS

Make it your own flavor explosion!

Nut MILK

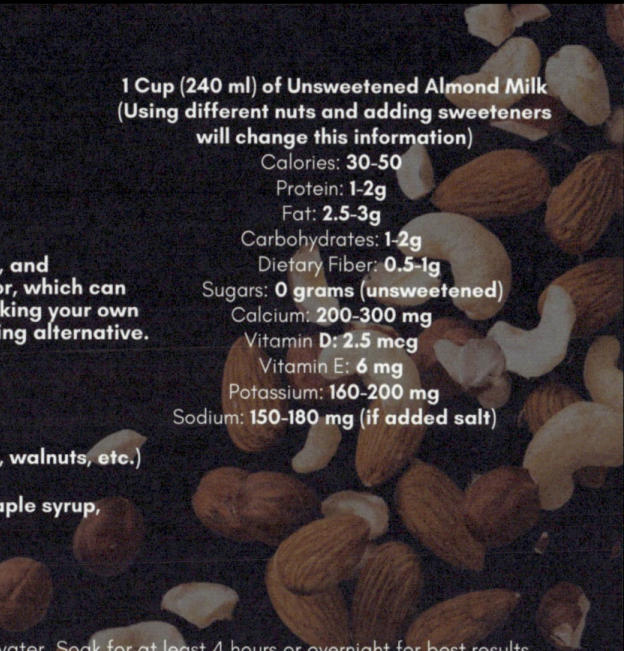

1 Cup (240 ml) of Unsweetened Almond Milk (Using different nuts and adding sweeteners will change this information)

Calories: **30-50**
Protein: **1-2g**
Fat: **2.5-3g**
Carbohydrates: **1-2g**
Dietary Fiber: **0.5-1g**
Sugars: **0 grams (unsweetened)**
Calcium: **200-300 mg**
Vitamin **D: 2.5 mcg**
Vitamin E: **6 mg**
Potassium: **160-200 mg**
Sodium: **150-180 mg (if added salt)**

Many brands add thickeners, stabilizers, and sweeteners to enhance texture and flavor, which can dilute the nutritional value. However, making your own nut milk at home is a simple and rewarding alternative.

INGREDIENTS:

- 1 cup nuts (almonds, cashews, hazelnuts, walnuts, etc.)
- 4 cups water (plus more for soaking)
- Optional: 1-2 tablespoons sweetener (maple syrup, honey, dates, etc.)
- Optional: 1 teaspoon vanilla extract
- Optional: a pinch of salt

DIRECTIONS:

- Place the nuts in a bowl and cover with water. Soak for at least 4 hours or overnight for best results. Drain and rinse the soaked nuts thoroughly.
- Add the soaked nuts and 4 cups of fresh water to a blender. Blend on high speed for 1-2 minutes until the mixture is smooth and creamy.
- Place a nut milk bag, cheesecloth, or a fine mesh strainer over a large bowl or pitcher. Pour the blended mixture into the strainer and let the liquid drain through. Squeeze or press to extract as much milk as possible from the nut pulp.
- If desired, return the milk to the blender and add sweetener, vanilla extract, and a pinch of salt. Blend again for a few seconds to combine.

Transfer the nut milk to a clean bottle or jar and refrigerate. Nut milk will keep for about 3-5 days in the refrigerator. Shake well before each use, as it may separate over time.

The leftover nut pulp can be used in baking, smoothies, or as a base for homemade granola.

Enjoy your homemade nut milk!

ADJUSTMENTS

Make it your own flavor explosion!

a meal planning system can feel overwhelming without clear guidance on where to begin. To help you establish an effective and sustainable meal planning routine, this chapter breaks down the process into three parts. By following these steps, you'll be a meal prep pro in no time, cooking up a storm that fits your vibe effortlessly!

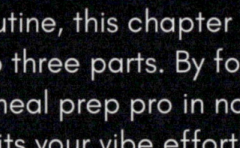

- Staples List (Dry Goods List)
- Staples List (Refrigeration List)
- Family Favors
- Family Meal Rotation Lists (3 pages)
- Toddler Nutritional Needs
- Theme Meal Ideas
- Ways To Stretch Your Meals
- Busy Days Meal Ideas
- 5 Minutes or Less Snack Ideas
- Alternative Ingredients (Gluten Free/Dairy-Free)
- Alternative Ingredients (Refined Sugar Free)
- Glycemic Index List
- Macro-nutrients Food List

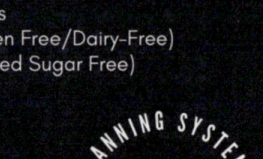

- Month Overview Guide
- Month Overview
- Batch Planner Guide
- Batch Planner (30 planners)
- Meal Planning Reflection (30
- Inventory Checklist Guide
- Inventory Checkkist (30 Checklist)

- Avoiding Store Tactics
- Produce Shopping Guide
- Produce In Season
- Storage Guide (Fruits)
- Storage Guide (Vegetables)
- Storage Guide (Proteins & Carbs)
- Shopping List (25 pages)
- Events & Parties Planners (15 pages)

Section ONE

This section provides resources to assist you in mastering efficient meal planning techniques.

- Staples List (Dry Goods List)
- Staples List (Refrigeration List)
- Family Favors
- Family Meal Rotation Lists (3 pages)
- Toddler Nutritional Needs
- Theme Meal Ideas
- Ways To Stretch Your Meals
- Busy Days Meal Ideas
- 5 Minutes or Less Snack Ideas
- Alternative Ingredients (Gluten Free/Dairy-Free)
- Alternative Ingredients (Refined Sugar Free)
- Glycemic Index List
- Macro-nutrients Food List

Staples LIST

(DRY GOODS LIST)

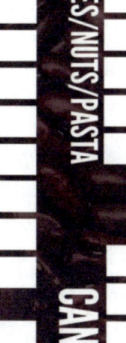

SEASONINGS

	QTY FOR THE MONTH	SIZE	TOTAL PRICE
TOTAL			

NON-PERISHABLE FRUITS & VEGGIES

	QTY FOR THE MONTH	SIZE	TOTAL PRICE
TOTAL			

BAKING ESSENTIAL

	QTY FOR THE MONTH	SIZE	TOTAL PRICE
TOTAL			

BULK GRAINS/LEGUMES/NUTS/PASTA

	QTY FOR THE MONTH	SIZE	TOTAL PRICE
TOTAL			

CANNED GOODS

	QTY FOR THE MONTH	SIZE	TOTAL PRICE
TOTAL			

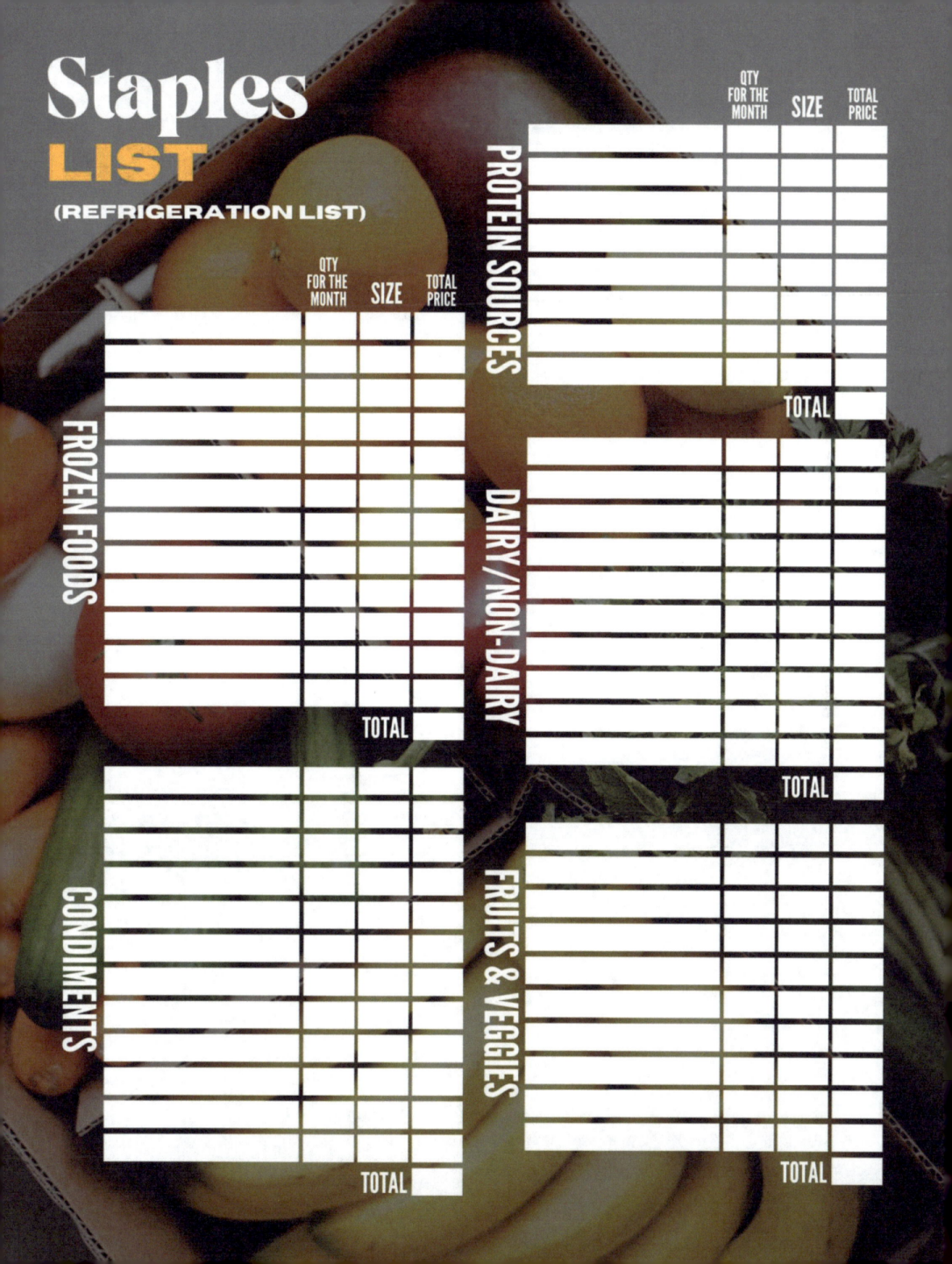

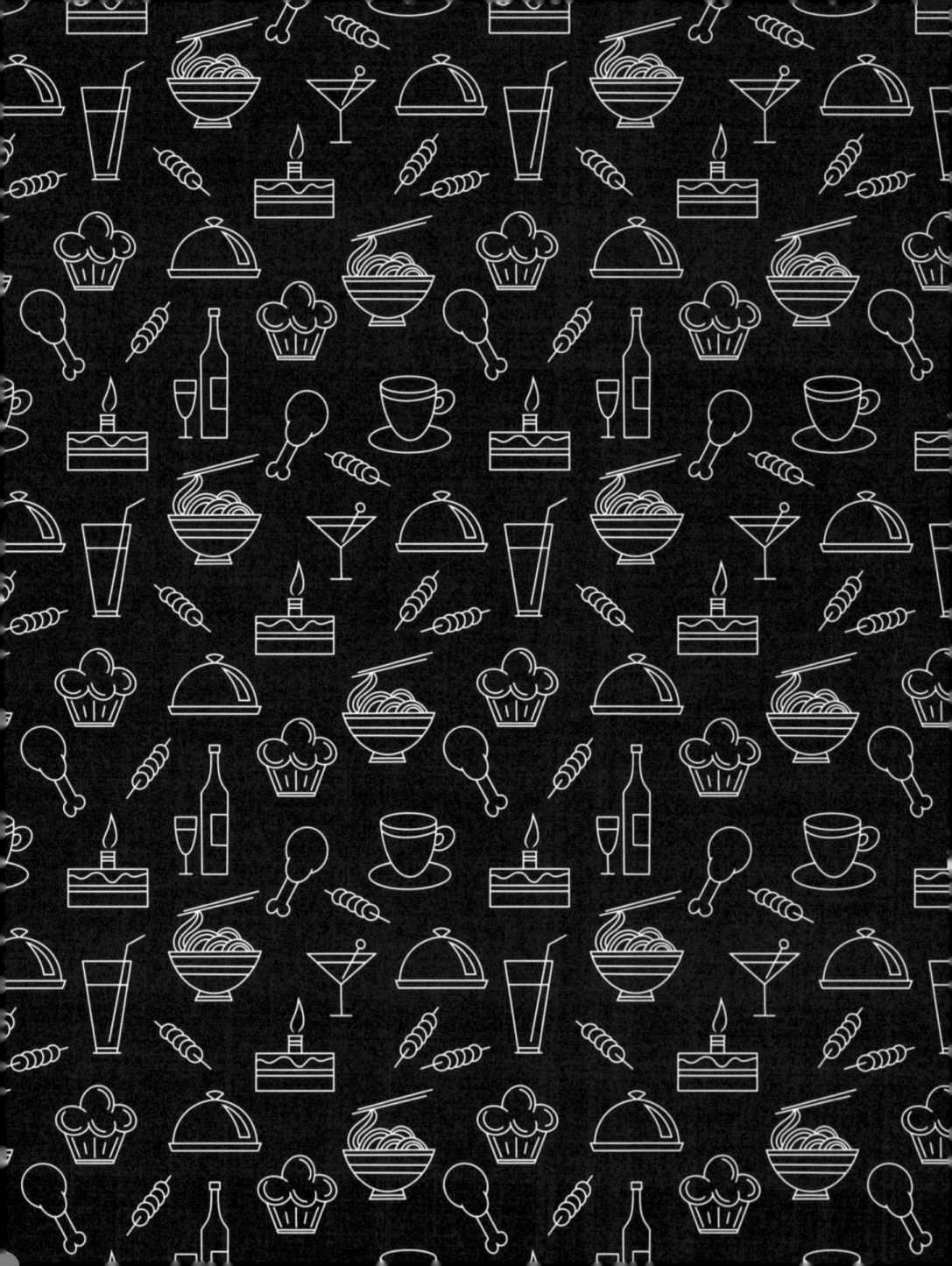

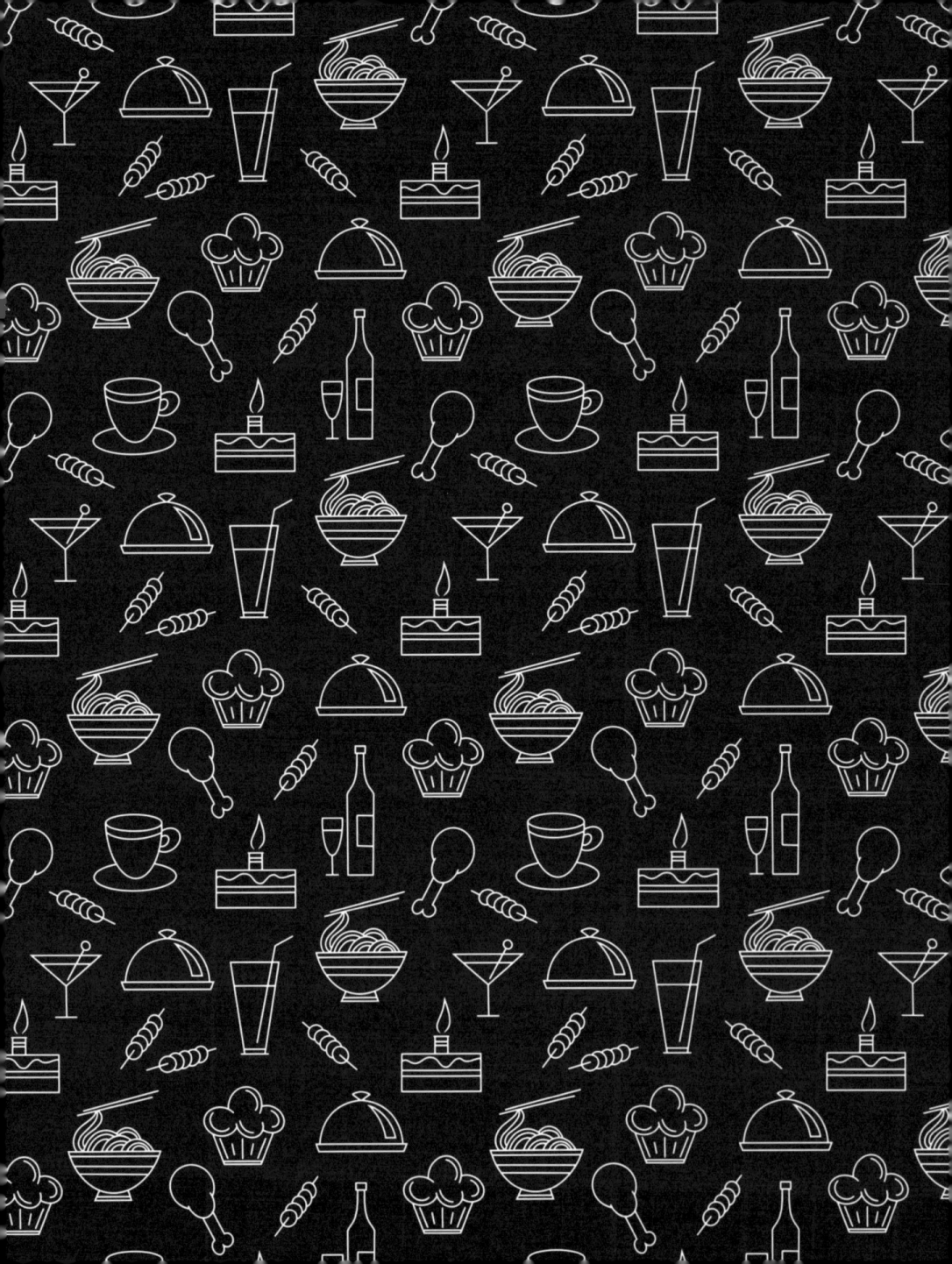

Toddler Nutritional NEEDS

Ah, the toddler years – a wild adventure filled with tiny food critics! The daily puzzle of wondering if your little one is getting enough nutrients can be a real head-scratcher. Having a handy roadmap for toddler nutrition can be a lifesaver, making sure that even on those super picky days, you can balance out the snack attacks with some wholesome goodies.

For precise needs, especially if there are health concerns or dietary restrictions, consulting a pediatrician or a registered dietitian is recommended. They can provide tailored advice based on the individual child's needs.

CALORIES:
Toddlers (1-3 years old) **1,000 to 1,400 calories per day**

CARBOHYDRATES:
- Recommended Intake: **45-65% of total daily calories**
- Approximate Amount: **130-210 grams of carbohydrates per day (based on a 1,200-calorie diet)**

PROTEIN:
- Recommended Intake: **5-20% of total daily calories**
- Approximate Amount: **13-20 grams of protein per day (based on a 1,200-calorie diet)**

FAT:
- Recommended Intake: **30-40% of total daily calories**
- Approximate Amount: **33-47 grams of fat per day (based on a 1,200-calorie diet)**
- Essential Fatty Acids:
- Omega-6: **7 grams per day**
- Omega-3): **0.7 grams per day**

FIBER:
19 grams per day

SUGAR:
25 grams added sugars per day

VITAMINS AND MINERALS
While this list focuses on macronutrients, toddlers also need adequate vitamins and minerals for proper growth and development. Here are some key one

- Calcium: **700 mg per day**
- Iron: **7 mg per day**
- Vitamin D: **600 IU (15 mcg) per day**
- Vitamin A: **300 mcg per day**
- Vitamin C: **15 mg per day**

HYDRATION:
Water: Toddlers should drink about **1.3 liters (5.5 cups) of fluids per day.**

Theme Meal IDEAS

- **Slow Cooker Night:** Pulled pork sandwiches, beef stew, or chicken curry cooked low and slow.
- **Insta Pot Night:** Quick and easy meals like beef and broccoli, chicken tikka masala, or vegetable risotto made in the Instant Pot.
- **One Pot Delight:** Hearty soups, chili, or stews made in a single pot for easy cleanup.
- **Casserole Night:** Classic casseroles like lasagna, shepherd's pie, or tuna noodle casserole.
- **Pasta Night:** Choose from various pasta dishes like spaghetti carbonara, fettuccine alfredo, or pesto pasta.
- **Pizza Party:** Homemade pizza with various toppings, garlic knots, and Caesar salad.
- **Spanish Flavors Night:** Paella, patatas bravas, or Spanish omelette (tortilla española).
- **Breakfast for Dinner:** Pancakes, waffles, scrambled eggs, and bacon served with syrup or fresh fruit.
- **Asian Fusion:** Stir-fry dishes, orange chicken, potstickers, or ramen noodles.
- **Appetizer Night:** A variety of appetizers like bruschetta, stuffed mushrooms, or buffalo chicken dip.
- **Diner Classics:** Cheeseburgers, fries, onion rings, and milkshakes.
- **Comfort Food Classics:** Meatloaf, mashed potatoes, green beans, and gravy.
- **Taco Tuesday:** Build-your-own taco bar with a variety of toppings and fillings like seasoned ground beef, grilled chicken, black beans, salsa, cheese, lettuce, and sour cream.
- **Salad Night:** Create custom salads with a variety of fresh greens, vegetables, proteins (such as grilled chicken, shrimp, or tofu), nuts, seeds, and dressings.
- **Soup and Sandwich Night:** Pair hearty soups like tomato basil, chicken noodle, or broccoli cheddar with classic sandwiches like grilled cheese, BLT, or turkey club.
- **Meatless Monday:** Explore vegetarian and vegan cuisine with dishes like vegetable stir-fry, lentil curry, chickpea salad wraps, or spinach and feta stuffed peppers.
- **Mediterranean Feast:** Grilled chicken kebabs, tabbouleh salad, hummus, and pita bread.
- **BBQ Bash:** Grilled burgers, hot dogs, corn on the cob, and coleslaw.
- **Hawaiian Luau:** Teriyaki chicken, pineapple fried rice, and macaroni salad.
- **Seafood Extravaganza:** Grilled shrimp skewers, seafood paella, and garlic bread.
- **Vegetarian Delight:** Stuffed bell peppers, quinoa salad, and roasted vegetables.
- **Southern Soul Food:** Fried chicken, collard greens, cornbread, and black-eyed peas.
- **French Bistro:** Beef bourguignon, ratatouille, baguette, and cheese plate.
- **Greek Getaway:** Gyros, Greek salad, tzatziki sauce, and spanakopita.
- **Tex-Mex Treats:** Enchiladas, refried beans, Mexican rice, and churros for dessert.
- **Sushi Night:** Assorted sushi rolls, miso soup, edamame, and seaweed salad.
- **Picnic in the Park:** Sandwiches, pasta salad, fruit skewers, and lemonade.
- **Caribbean Cruise:** Jerk chicken, rice and peas, plantains, and mango salsa.
- **Cajun Cookout:** Jambalaya, gumbo, cornbread, and bread pudding.
- **Bollywood Buffet:** Chicken tikka masala, naan bread, samosas, and mango lassi.
- **Korean BBQ:** Bulgogi, kimchi, bibimbap, and japchae.
- **Surf and Turf Soiree:** Steak and lobster, mashed potatoes, grilled asparagus, and Caesar salad.
- **Thai Night:** Pad Thai, green curry, spring rolls, and mango sticky rice.
- **Hawaiian Poke Party:** A variety of poke bowls with fresh fish, rice, and assorted toppings.
- **Jamaican Jerk Jam:** Jerk chicken, festival bread, rice and peas, and rum punch.
- **New Orleans Night:** Po'boys, crawfish étouffée, beignets, and hurricanes.
- **Californian Cuisine:** Fish tacos, avocado salad, grilled vegetables, and key lime pie.
- **Global Potluck:** Each family member chooses a dish from a different country or region to create a diverse and flavorful meal with international flair.

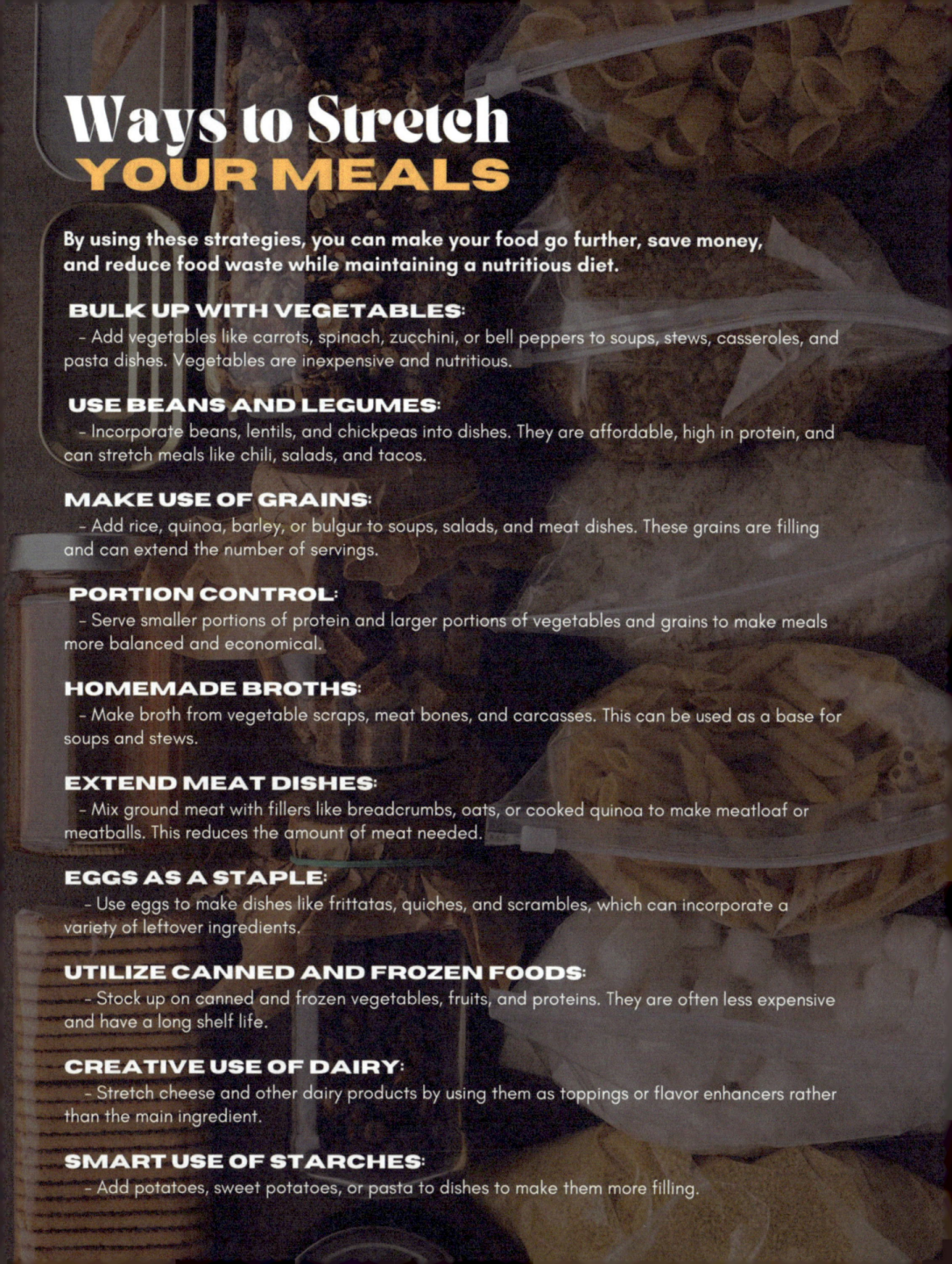

Ways to Stretch YOUR MEALS

By using these strategies, you can make your food go further, save money, and reduce food waste while maintaining a nutritious diet.

BULK UP WITH VEGETABLES:

– Add vegetables like carrots, spinach, zucchini, or bell peppers to soups, stews, casseroles, and pasta dishes. Vegetables are inexpensive and nutritious.

USE BEANS AND LEGUMES:

– Incorporate beans, lentils, and chickpeas into dishes. They are affordable, high in protein, and can stretch meals like chili, salads, and tacos.

MAKE USE OF GRAINS:

– Add rice, quinoa, barley, or bulgur to soups, salads, and meat dishes. These grains are filling and can extend the number of servings.

PORTION CONTROL:

– Serve smaller portions of protein and larger portions of vegetables and grains to make meals more balanced and economical.

HOMEMADE BROTHS:

– Make broth from vegetable scraps, meat bones, and carcasses. This can be used as a base for soups and stews.

EXTEND MEAT DISHES:

– Mix ground meat with fillers like breadcrumbs, oats, or cooked quinoa to make meatloaf or meatballs. This reduces the amount of meat needed.

EGGS AS A STAPLE:

– Use eggs to make dishes like frittatas, quiches, and scrambles, which can incorporate a variety of leftover ingredients.

UTILIZE CANNED AND FROZEN FOODS:

– Stock up on canned and frozen vegetables, fruits, and proteins. They are often less expensive and have a long shelf life.

CREATIVE USE OF DAIRY:

– Stretch cheese and other dairy products by using them as toppings or flavor enhancers rather than the main ingredient.

SMART USE OF STARCHES:

– Add potatoes, sweet potatoes, or pasta to dishes to make them more filling.

Busy Days

MEAL IDEAS

SHEET PAN CHICKEN AND VEGETABLES:
- Toss chicken breasts or thighs with olive oil, salt, pepper, and mixed vegetables (like carrots, potatoes, and broccoli) on a sheet pan. Bake at 400°F for 25-30 minutes.

ONE-POT PASTA:
- Combine pasta, a jar of marinara sauce, water or broth, and any vegetables or proteins (like sausage or chicken) in a pot. Cook until the pasta is done, stirring occasionally.

SUSHI BOWLS:
- Layer sushi rice in a bowl and top with diced cucumber, avocado, shredded carrots, and your choice of protein (like cooked shrimp or tofu). Drizzle with soy sauce and a bit of sriracha mayo.

TACO SALAD:
- Mix ground beef or turkey with taco seasoning, then serve over a bed of lettuce with beans, corn, cheese, salsa, and avocado.

BREAKFAST FOR DINNER:
- Make scrambled eggs, toast, and a side of fruit or quick-cooking bacon for a fast and easy meal.

QUESADILLAS:
- Fill tortillas with cheese and any other desired fillings (like beans, chicken, or vegetables), then cook in a skillet until the cheese is melted and the tortillas are crispy.

SLOW COOKER PULLED PORK:
- Cook pork shoulder with BBQ sauce in a slow cooker for 6-8 hours on low. Serve on buns with coleslaw.

PITA PIZZAS:
- Use pita bread as a base, spread with marinara sauce, and top with cheese and your favorite toppings. Bake at 400°F for 10-12 minutes.

CHICKEN CAESAR WRAPS:
- Fill tortillas with cooked chicken strips, romaine lettuce, Caesar dressing, and parmesan cheese for a quick and satisfying wrap.

INSTANT POT CHILI:
- Combine ground beef, beans, tomatoes, and chili seasoning in an Instant Pot and cook on high pressure for 20-25 minutes. Serve with cornbread or over rice.

ITALIAN SUB SANDWICHES:
- Layer slices of deli meats (such as salami, ham, and pepperoni) with provolone cheese, lettuce, tomato, onion, and Italian dressing on a sub roll.

SPAGHETTI AGLIO E OLIO:
- Cook spaghetti and toss with sautéed garlic, red pepper flakes, olive oil, and parsley. Top with grated Parmesan cheese.

BBQ CHICKEN FLATBREAD:
- Spread BBQ sauce on flatbread, top with shredded cooked chicken, red onions, and mozzarella cheese. Bake at 400°F for 8-10 minute.

CHICKPEA AND SPINACH CURRY:
- Simmer canned chickpeas and spinach in a curry sauce made with coconut milk and your favorite curry paste. Serve over rice or with naan bread.

STUFFED ZUCCHINI BOATS:
- Hollow out zucchini halves and fill with a mixture of cooked quinoa, marinara sauce, and ground turkey or sausage. Top with cheese and bake until zucchini is tender.

Alternative INGREDENTS

GLUTEN FREE

Tortillas (for tacos)	Romaine Lettuce
Buns	Portobello Mushrooms
Sandwich Bread	Coconut Wraps
Bread Crumbs	Ground Almond Meal
Spaghetti Noodles	Zucchini Noodles
Soy Sauce	Tamari or Coconut Aminos
Butter	Coconut Oil
Cornstarch	Arrowroot
Croutons	Nuts
Crackers	Rice Cakes
Couscous	Pulsed Cauliflower
Flour for baking	1/2 c rice flour + 1/4 c tapioca flour + 1/4 c potato starch

DAIRY FREE

Milk	Almond, Oat, Hemp, or Soy Milk
Butter	Coconut Oil
Yogurt	Coconut Yogurt
Buttermilk	Dairy Free Milk + Lemon Juice
Whip Cream	Coconut Cream
Cheese Sauce	Cashews + Nutritional Yeast
Parmesan Topping	Nutritional Yeast
Condensed Milk	Dairy Free Milk + Sugar + Dash of Salt
Coffee Cream	Coconut Cream
Sour Cream	Plain Greek Yogurt
Eggs For Baking	1 Tbsp Flaxseed + 3 Tbsp water= 1 Egg
Whip Cream	1 Canned Full Fat Coconut Cream + Sweetener (**Refrigerator overnight**)

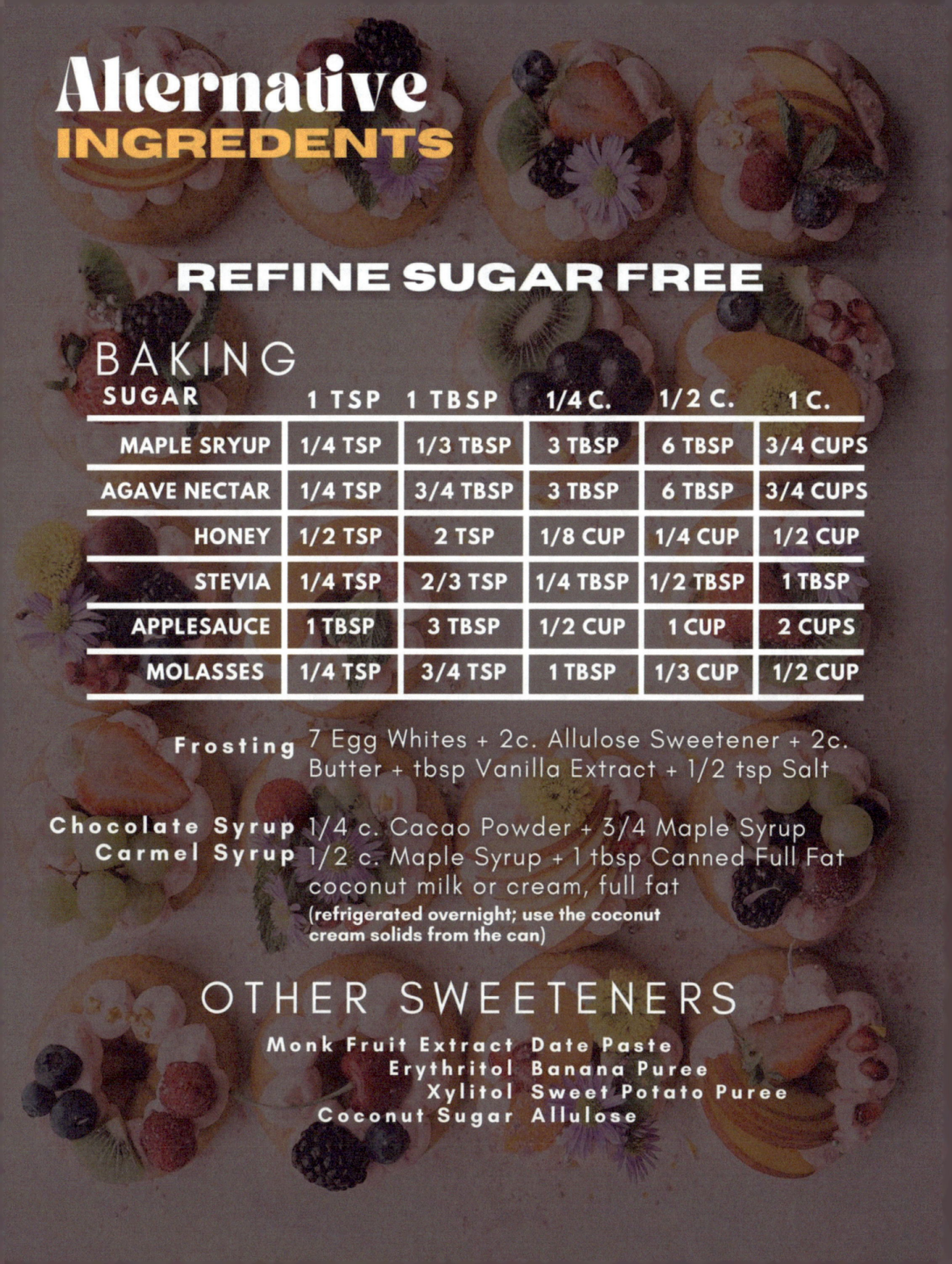

Alternative INGREDENTS

REFINE SUGAR FREE

BAKING

SUGAR	1 TSP	1 TBSP	1/4 C.	1/2 C.	1 C.
MAPLE SRYUP	1/4 TSP	1/3 TBSP	3 TBSP	6 TBSP	3/4 CUPS
AGAVE NECTAR	1/4 TSP	3/4 TBSP	3 TBSP	6 TBSP	3/4 CUPS
HONEY	1/2 TSP	2 TSP	1/8 CUP	1/4 CUP	1/2 CUP
STEVIA	1/4 TSP	2/3 TSP	1/4 TBSP	1/2 TBSP	1 TBSP
APPLESAUCE	1 TBSP	3 TBSP	1/2 CUP	1 CUP	2 CUPS
MOLASSES	1/4 TSP	3/4 TSP	1 TBSP	1/3 CUP	1/2 CUP

Frosting 7 Egg Whites + 2c. Allulose Sweetener + 2c. Butter + tbsp Vanilla Extract + 1/2 tsp Salt

Chocolate Syrup 1/4 c. Cacao Powder + 3/4 Maple Syrup
Carmel Syrup 1/2 c. Maple Syrup + 1 tbsp Canned Full Fat coconut milk or cream, full fat
(refrigerated overnight; use the coconut cream solids from the can)

OTHER SWEETENERS

Monk Fruit Extract Date Paste
Erythritol Banana Puree
Xylitol Sweet Potato Puree
Coconut Sugar Allulose

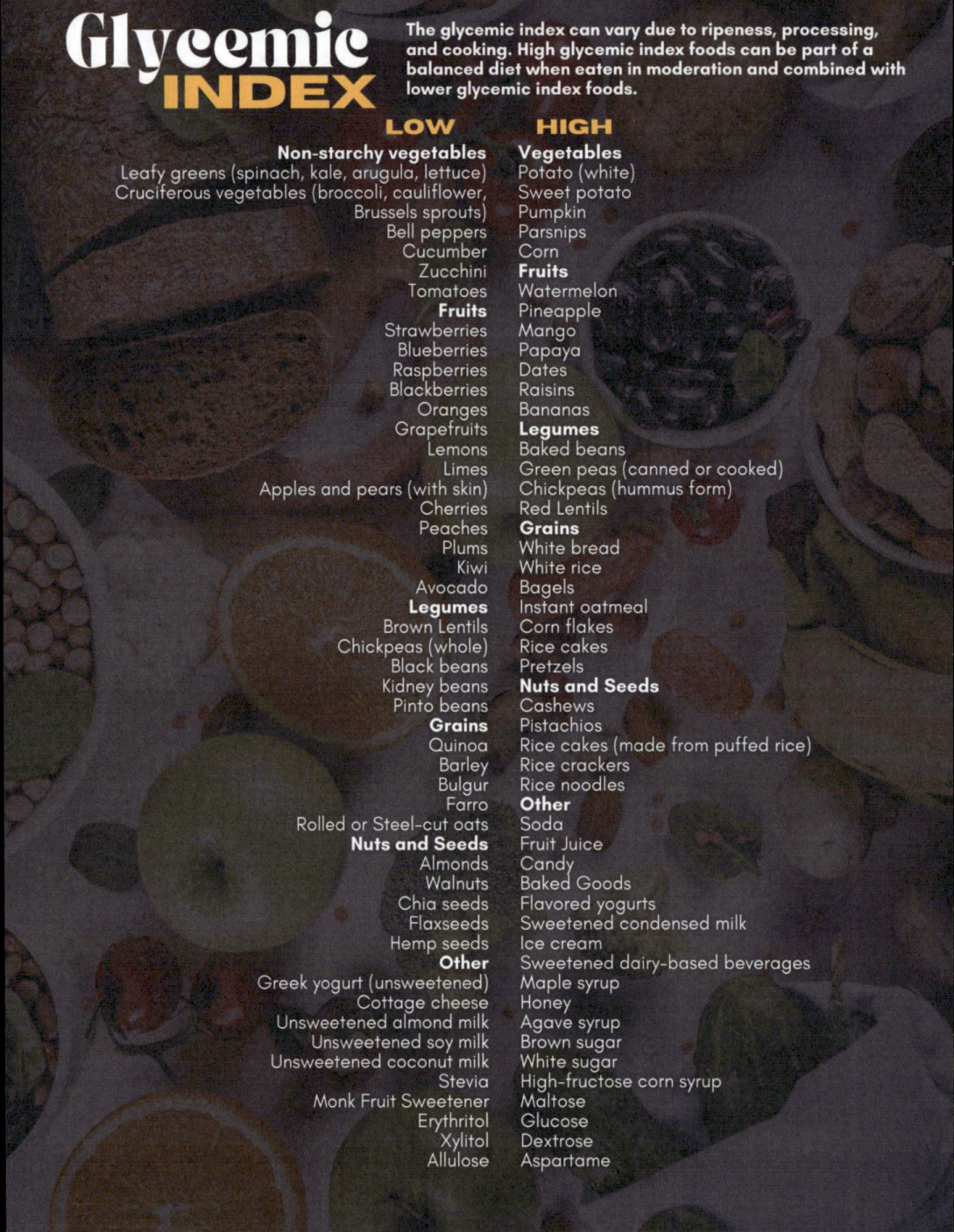

Fiber Facts for Family
BENEFITS

Fiber is often overlooked but plays a crucial role in maintaining steady energy levels for both children and moms. Understanding the importance of fiber can make a significant difference in keeping up with daily demands and ensuring overall health and well-being.

IMPROVES FOCUS
- Fiber helps maintain steady blood sugar levels, which can improve focus and concentration.

PREVENTS ENERGY SPIKES
- By slowing down sugar absorption, fiber prevents energy spikes and crashes that can affect behavior and attention.

SUPPORTS GUT HEALTH
- A healthy gut can positively impact brain function and mood, and fiber promotes a healthy gut microbiome.

REGULATES DIGESTION
- Fiber helps keep digestion regular, which can improve overall comfort and well-being, helping children feel their best.

BOOSTS BRAIN HEALTH
- Some fiber-rich foods, like fruits and vegetables, are also high in vitamins and minerals that are important for brain health.

PROMOTES STABLE MOOD
- Stable blood sugar levels can help maintain a more stable mood.

ENHANCES SKIN HEALTH
- Fiber can help flush out toxins from the body, which can lead to clearer skin and reduce the occurrence of skin issues like acne, even in children.

HELPS IN CLEANING THE BODY
- Fiber aids in the body's natural detoxification process by binding to waste products and toxins in the intestines and promoting their elimination, which can help reduce the toxic load on a child's developing body.

IMPROVES SLEEP QUALITY
- A healthy digestive system and stable blood sugar levels can contribute to better sleep.

SNACK ON HYDRATING FOODS
- Watermelon, cantaloupe, and grapes are fiber-rich fruits with high water content,which helps keep you and your family hydrated and feeling good.

SUPPORTS DENTAL HEALTH
- Chewing fiber-rich foods, such as raw fruits and vegetables, stimulates saliva production, which helps neutralize acids and cleanse the mouth, promoting better dental health and reducing the risk of cavities.

Now you see why fiber is the real MVP for you and your family's meals. But remember, more fiber calls for more H_2O! Dive into our Macro-nutrients page for plenty of fiber rich foods to include in your meal planning.

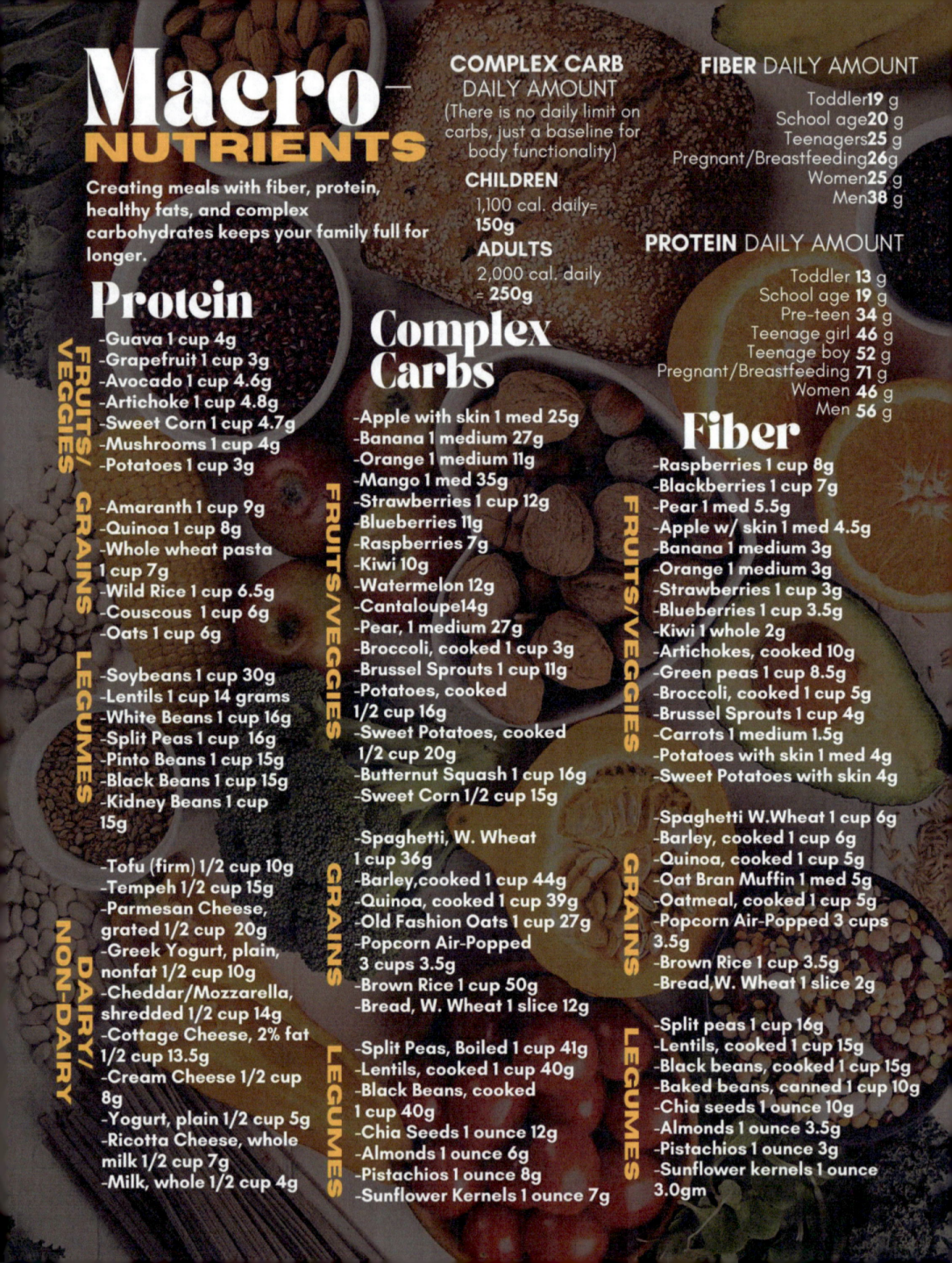

For the first week, this planner will be your sous-chef, guiding you through the essential techniques and strategies of our unique planning system. Just like in a top-tier kitchen, mastering these basics is crucial. This period is your chance to experiment, refine, and perfect your approach, molding these methods to suit your own lifestyle. Embrace the challenge, adapt the system, and let's see how you can elevate your productivity to a Michelin-star level. Ready, set, plan!

This section will teach you how to batch plan meals for a more streamlined cooking process.

Section TWO

- Month Overview Guide
- Month Overviews
- Batch Planner Guide
- Batch Planners
- Meal Planning Reflection
- Inventory Checklist Guide
- Inventory Checklists

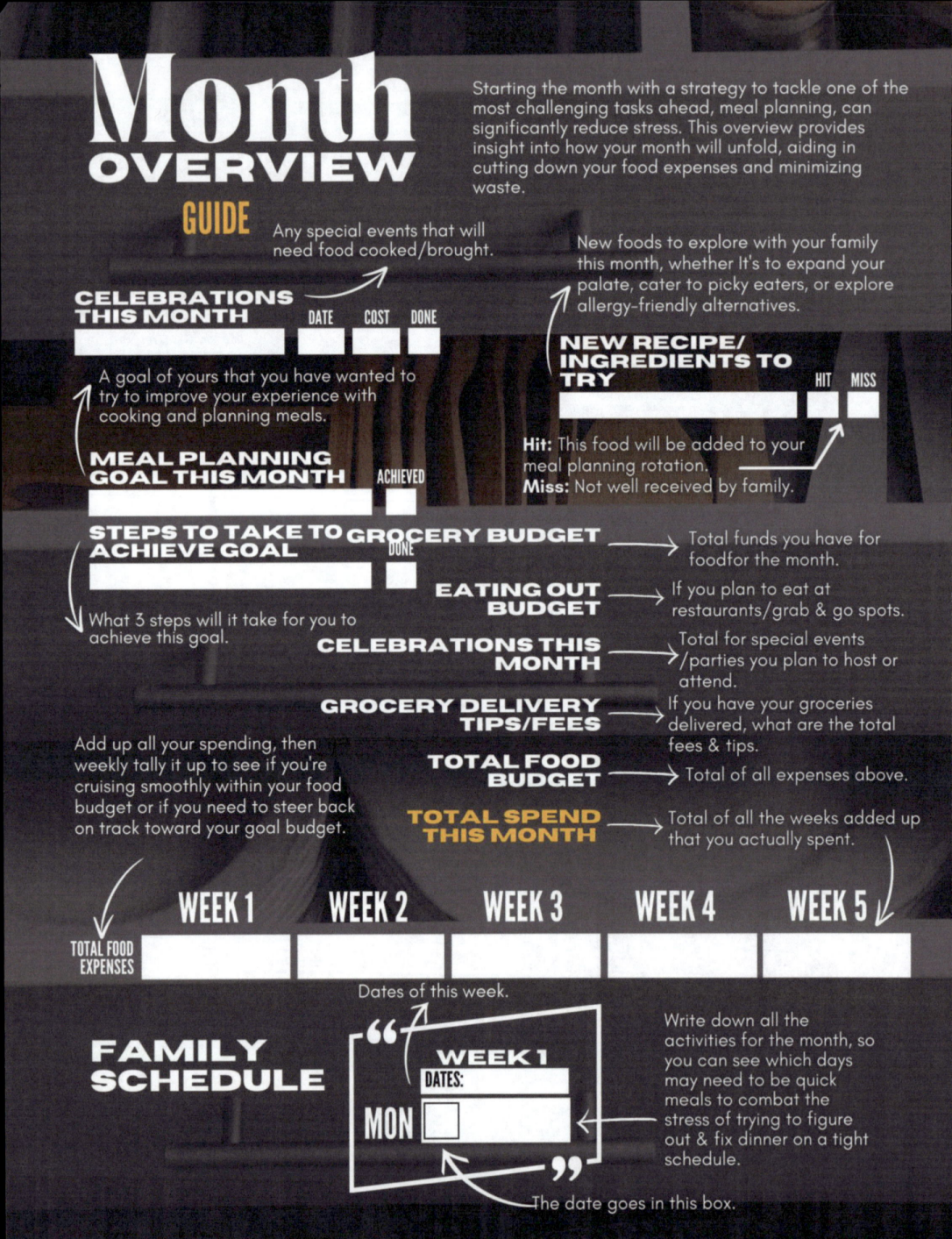

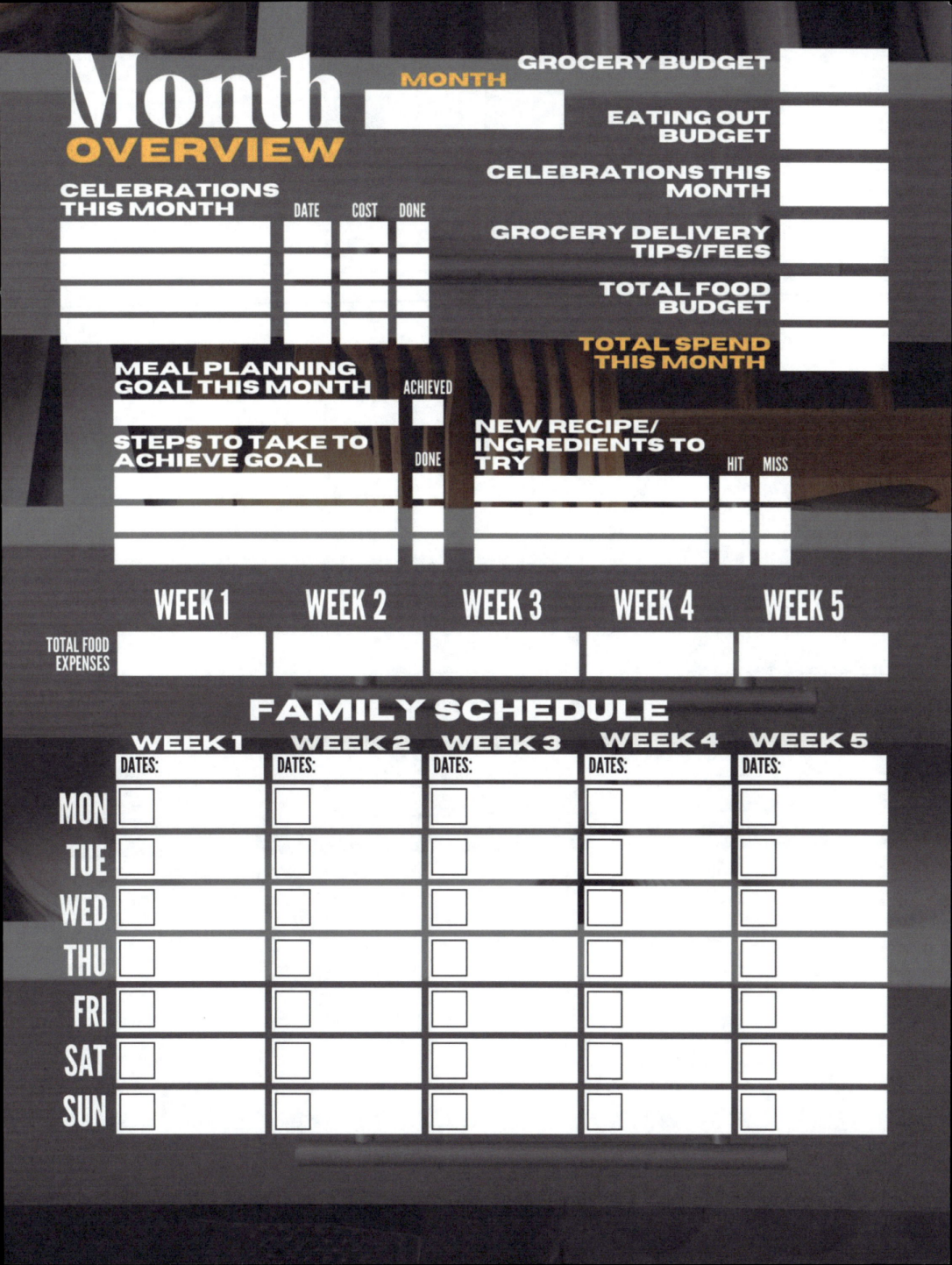

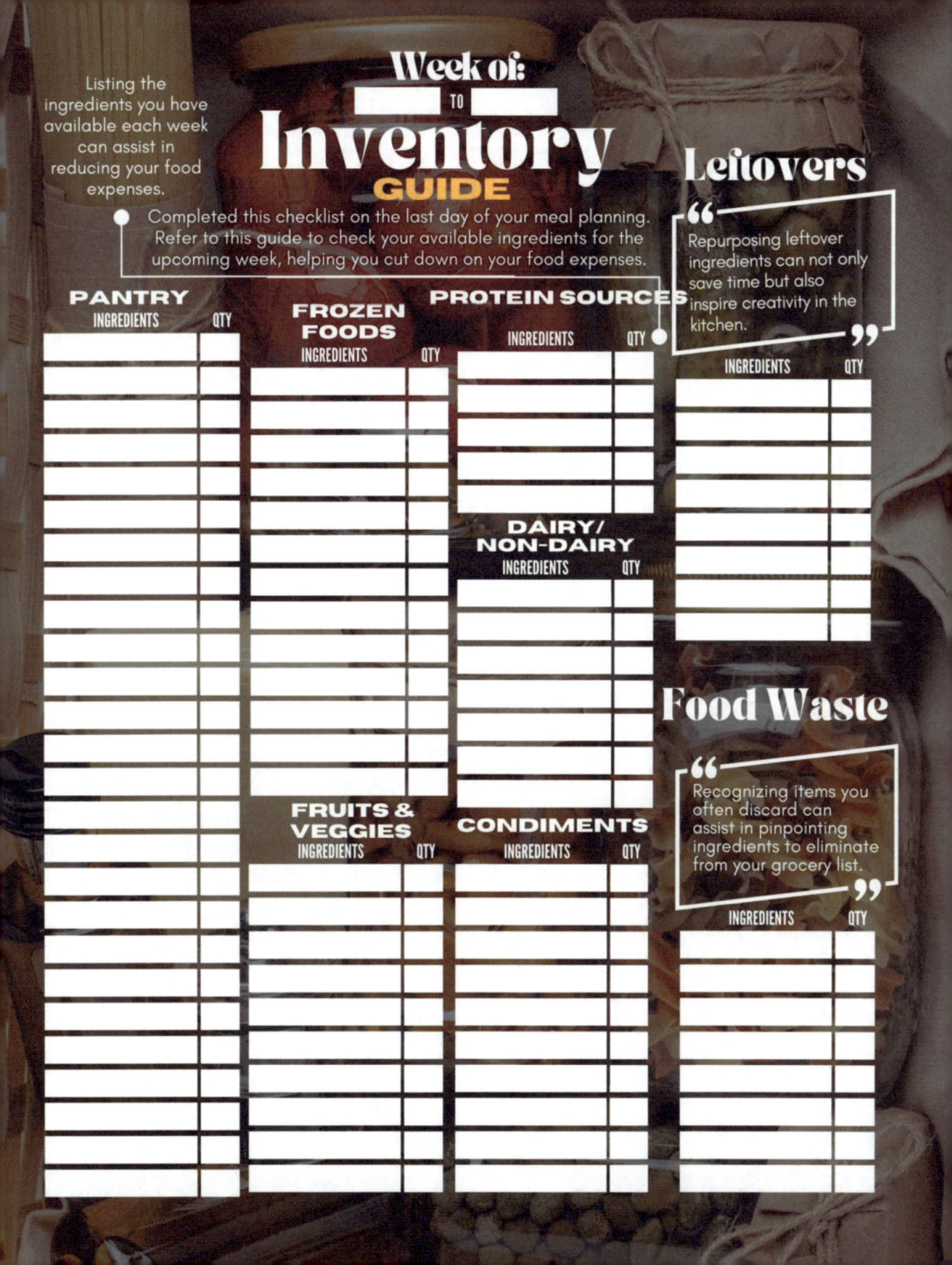

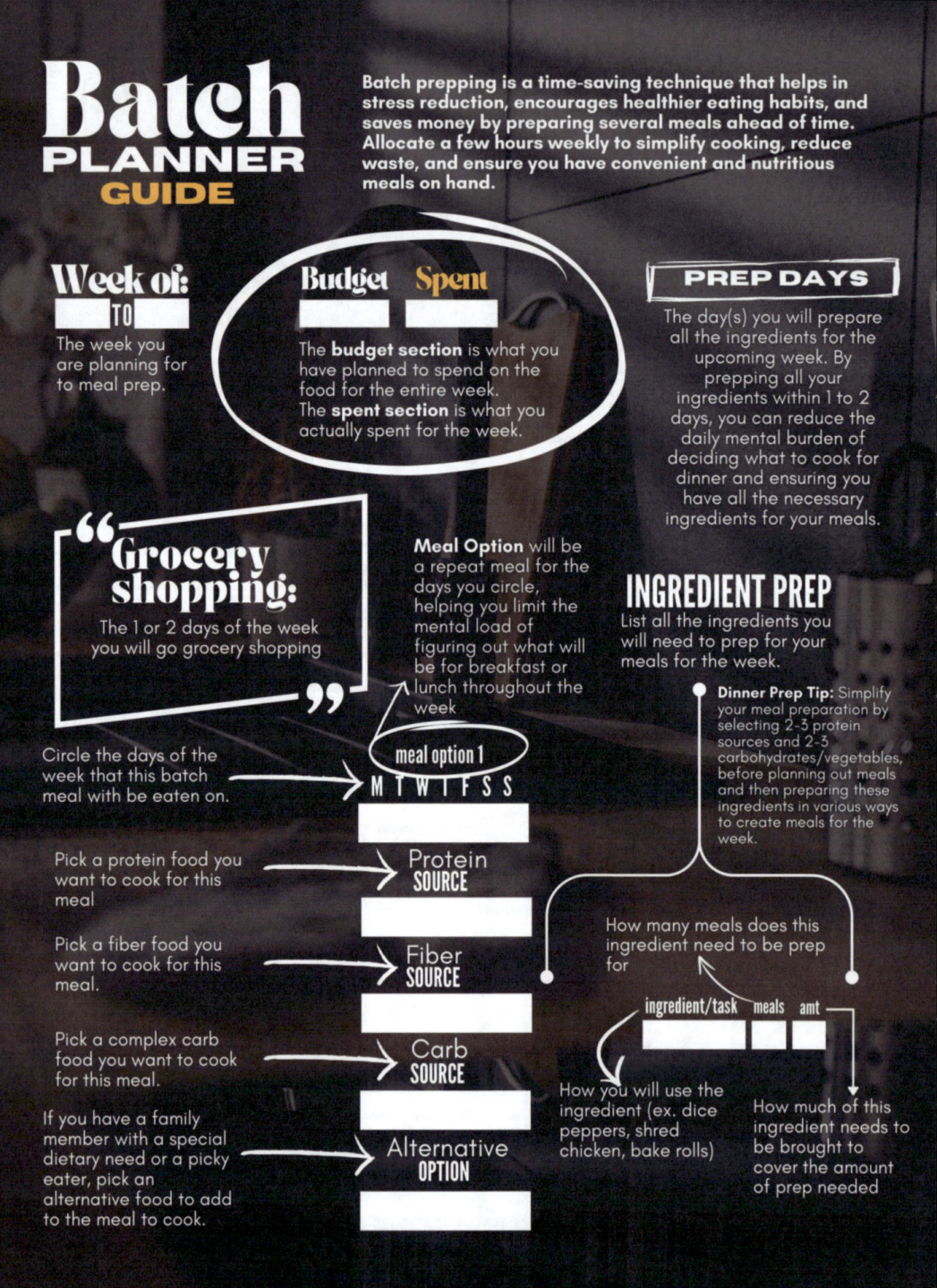

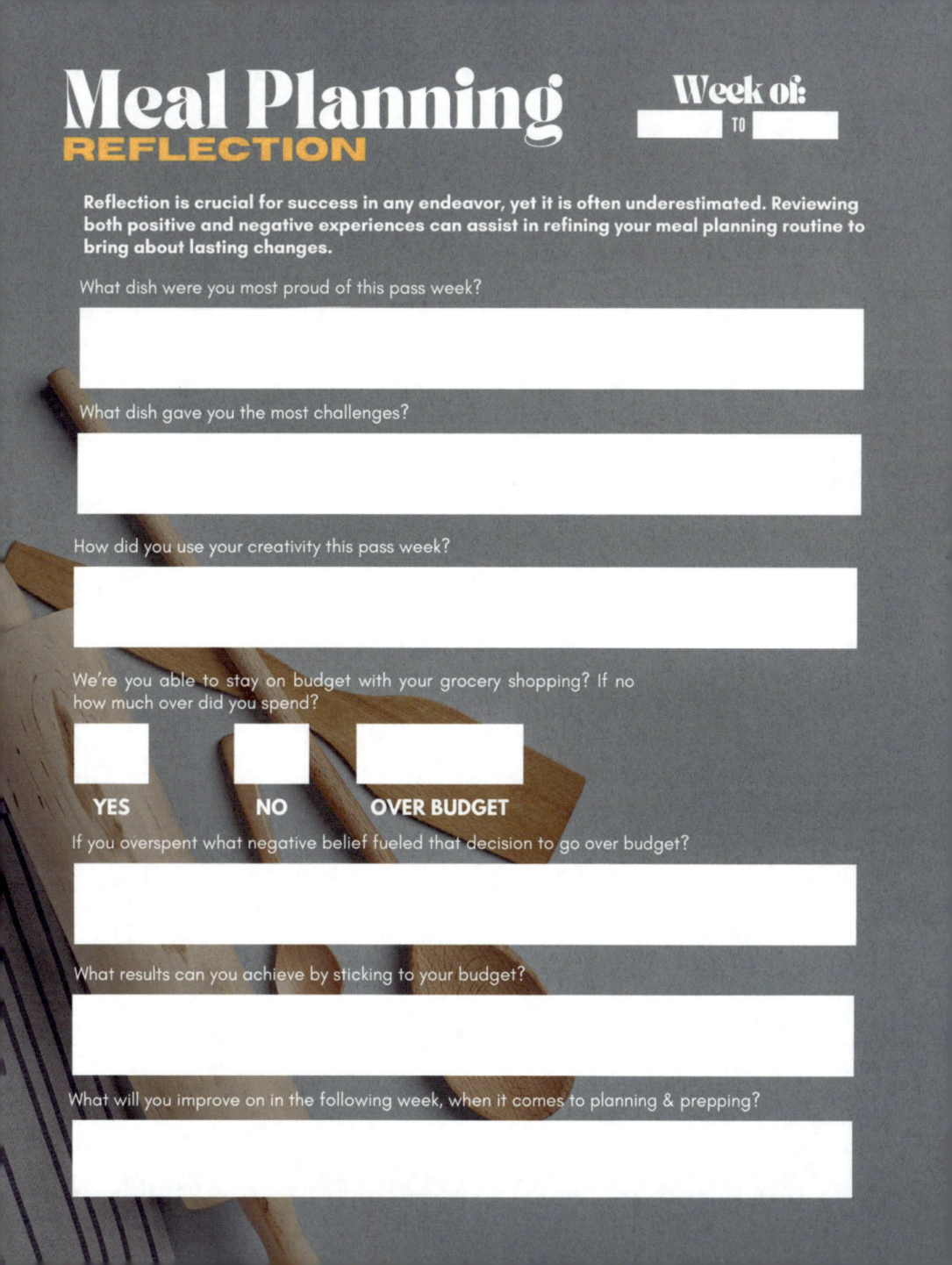

Meal Planning
REFLECTION

Week of:
_____ TO _____

Reflection is crucial for success in any endeavor, yet it is often underestimated. Reviewing both positive and negative experiences can assist in refining your meal planning routine to bring about lasting changes.

What dish were you most proud of this pass week?

What dish gave you the most challenges?

How did you use your creativity this pass week?

We're you able to stay on budget with your grocery shopping? If no how much over did you spend?

YES   **NO**   **OVER BUDGET**

If you overspent what negative belief fueled that decision to go over budget?

What results can you achieve by sticking to your budget?

What will you improve on in the following week, when it comes to planning & prepping?

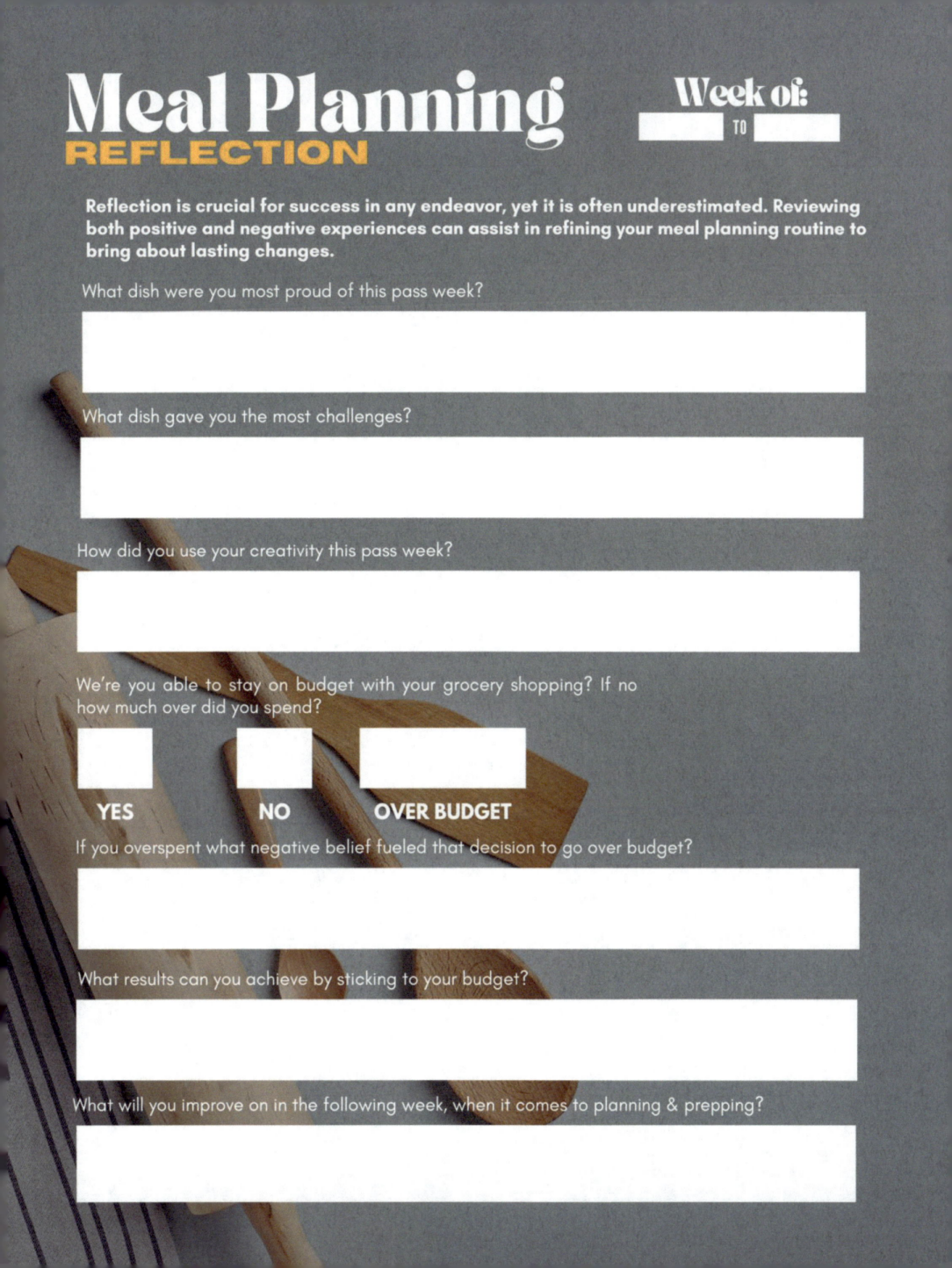

Meal Planning
REFLECTION

Week of:
_____ to _____

Reflection is crucial for success in any endeavor, yet it is often underestimated. Reviewing both positive and negative experiences can assist in refining your meal planning routine to bring about lasting changes.

What dish were you most proud of this pass week?

_____

What dish gave you the most challenges?

_____

How did you use your creativity this pass week?

_____

We're you able to stay on budget with your grocery shopping? If no how much over did you spend?

☐ **YES** ☐ **NO** ☐ **OVER BUDGET**

If you overspent what negative belief fueled that decision to go over budget?

_____

What results can you achieve by sticking to your budget?

_____

What will you improve on in the following week, when it comes to planning & prepping?

_____

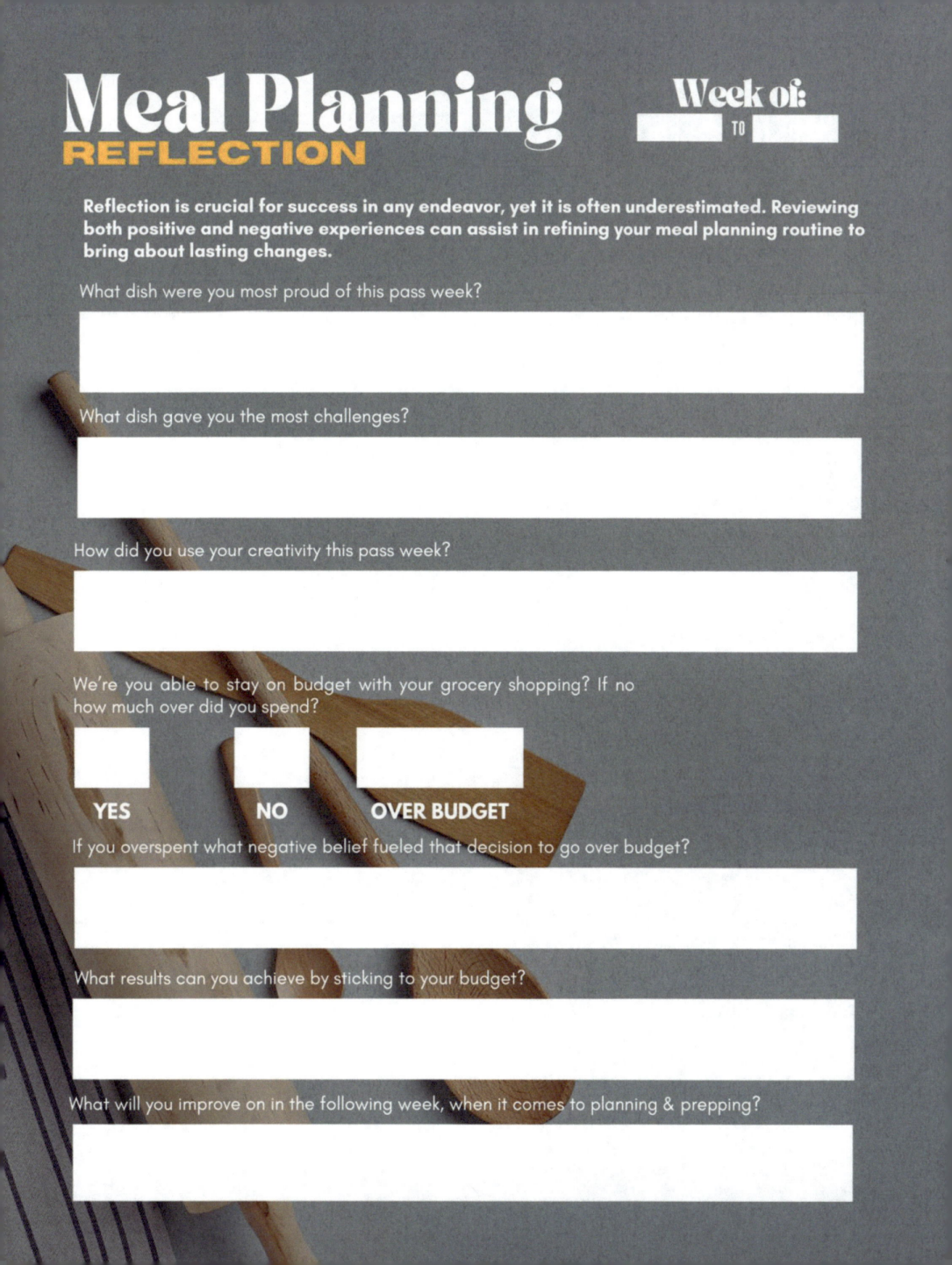

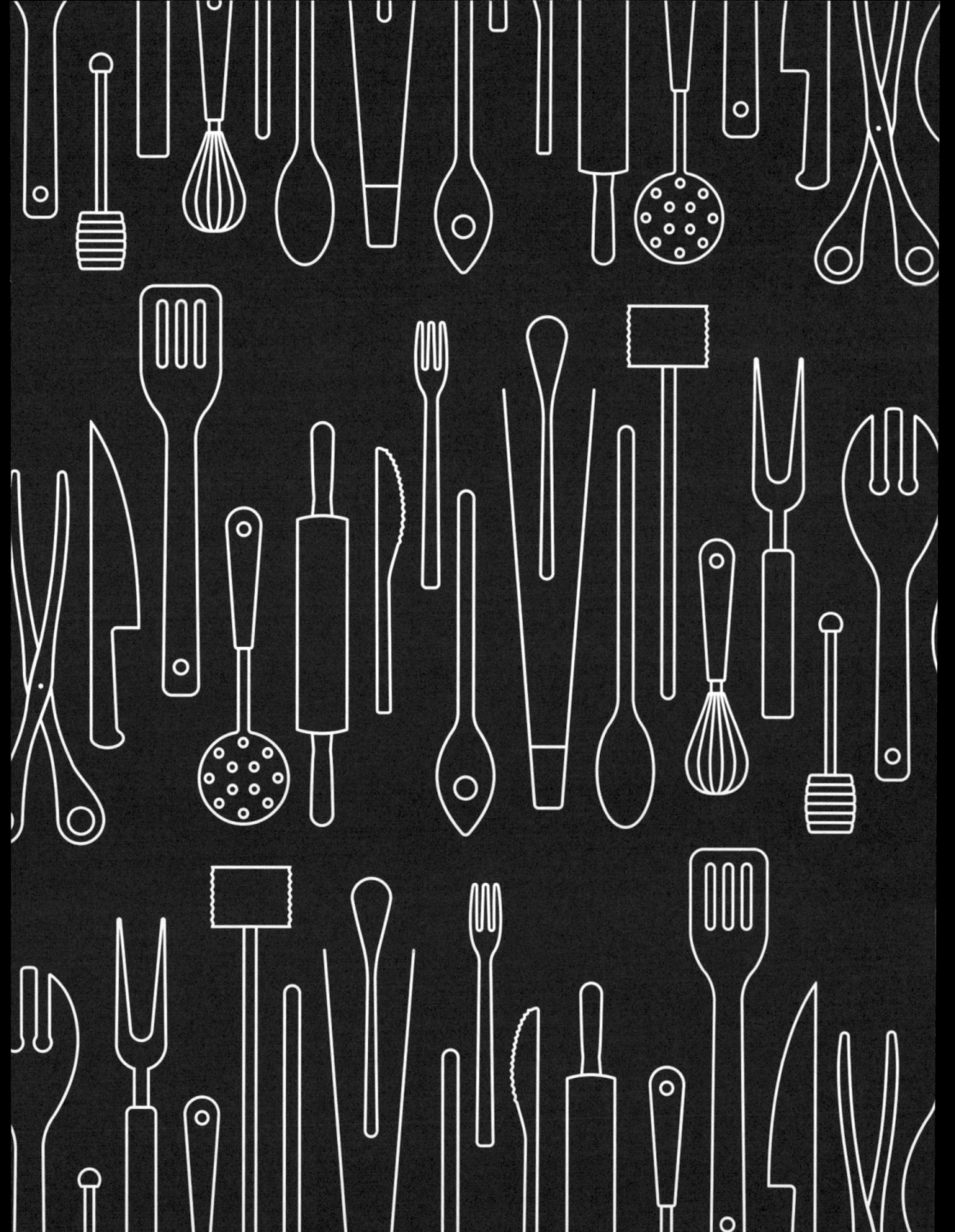

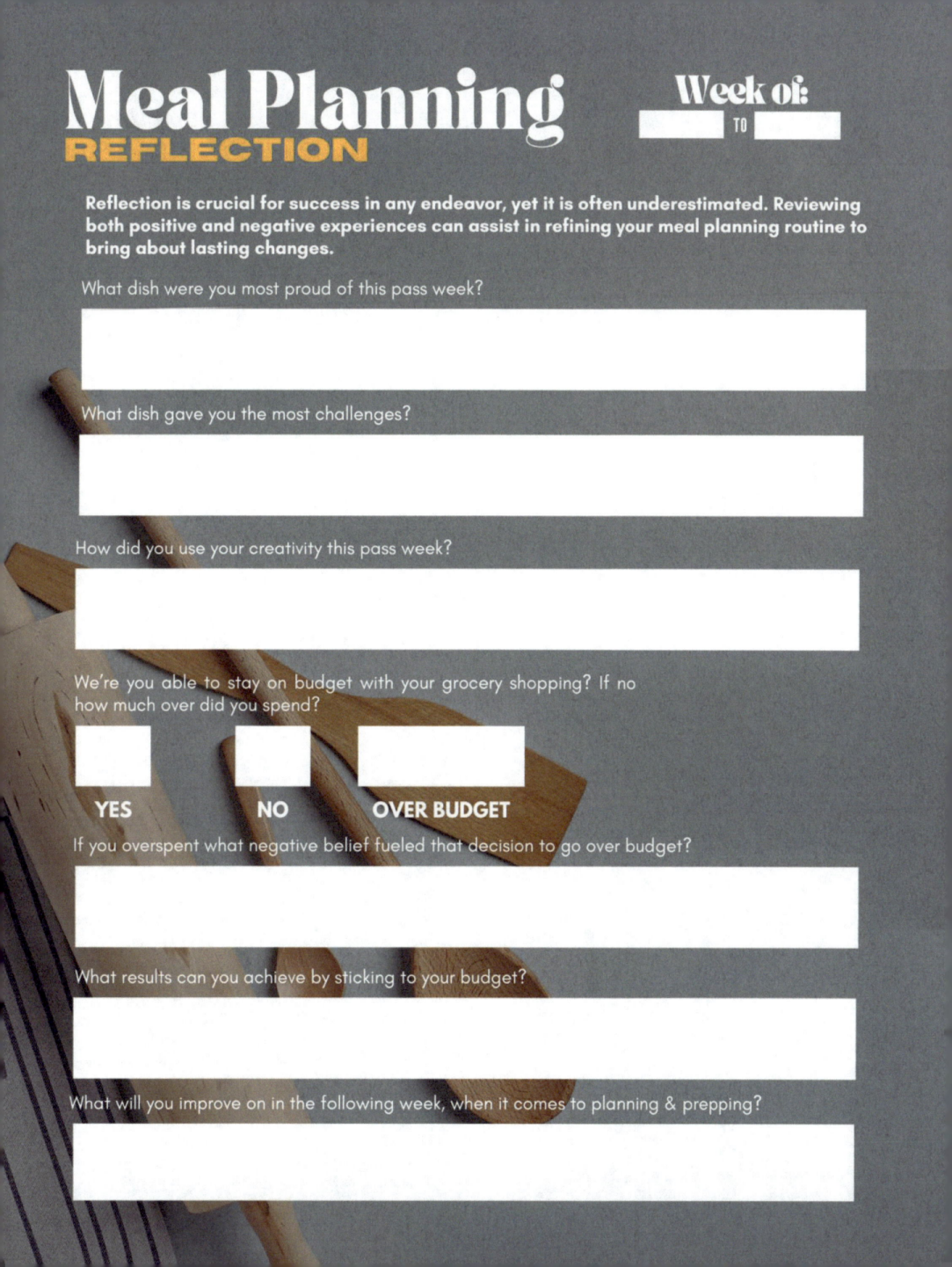

Meal Planning
REFLECTION

Week of:
_____ TO _____

Reflection is crucial for success in any endeavor, yet it is often underestimated. Reviewing both positive and negative experiences can assist in refining your meal planning routine to bring about lasting changes.

What dish were you most proud of this pass week?

_____

What dish gave you the most challenges?

_____

How did you use your creativity this pass week?

_____

We're you able to stay on budget with your grocery shopping? If no how much over did you spend?

☐ **YES** ☐ **NO** ☐ **OVER BUDGET**

If you overspent what negative belief fueled that decision to go over budget?

_____

What results can you achieve by sticking to your budget?

_____

What will you improve on in the following week, when it comes to planning & prepping?

_____

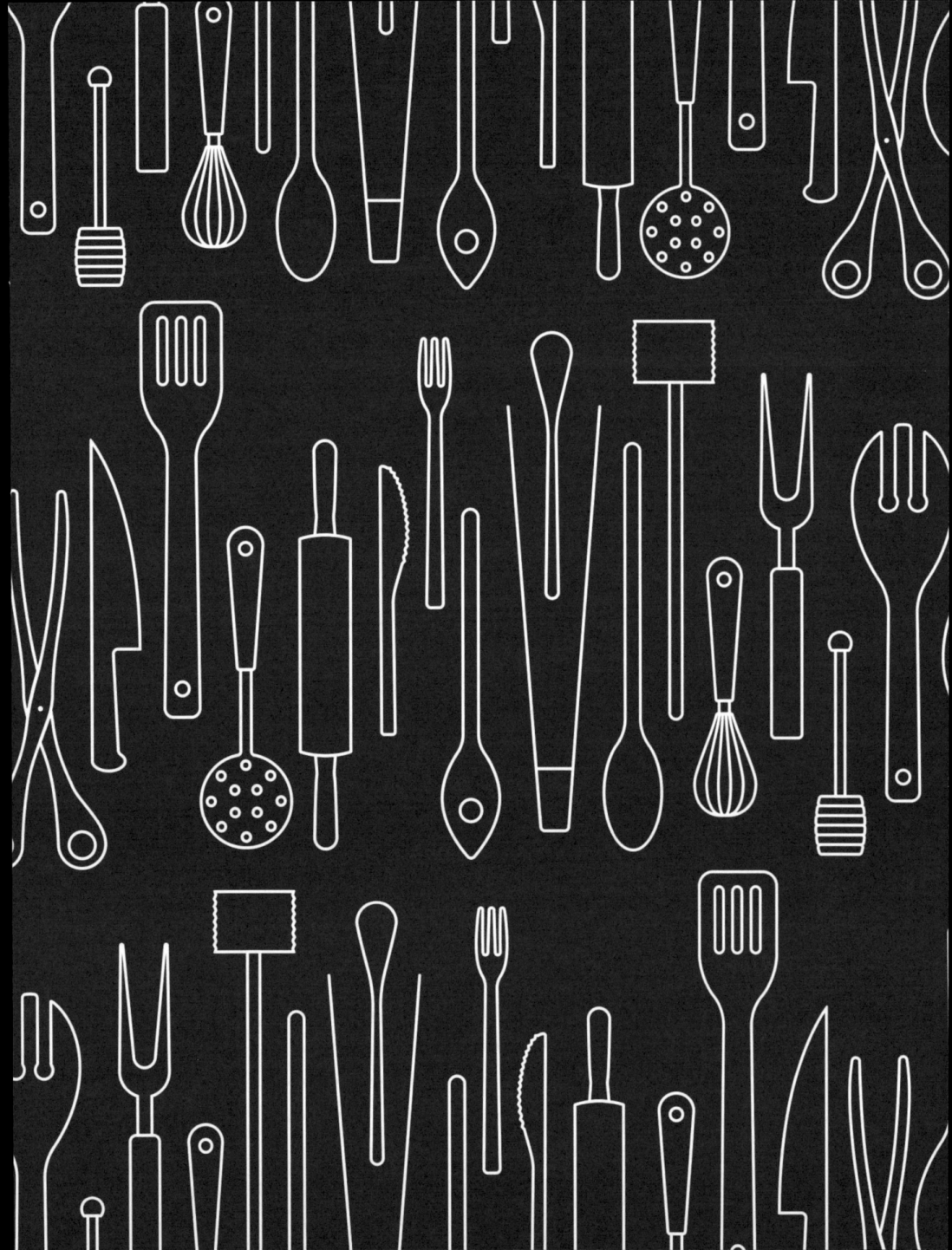

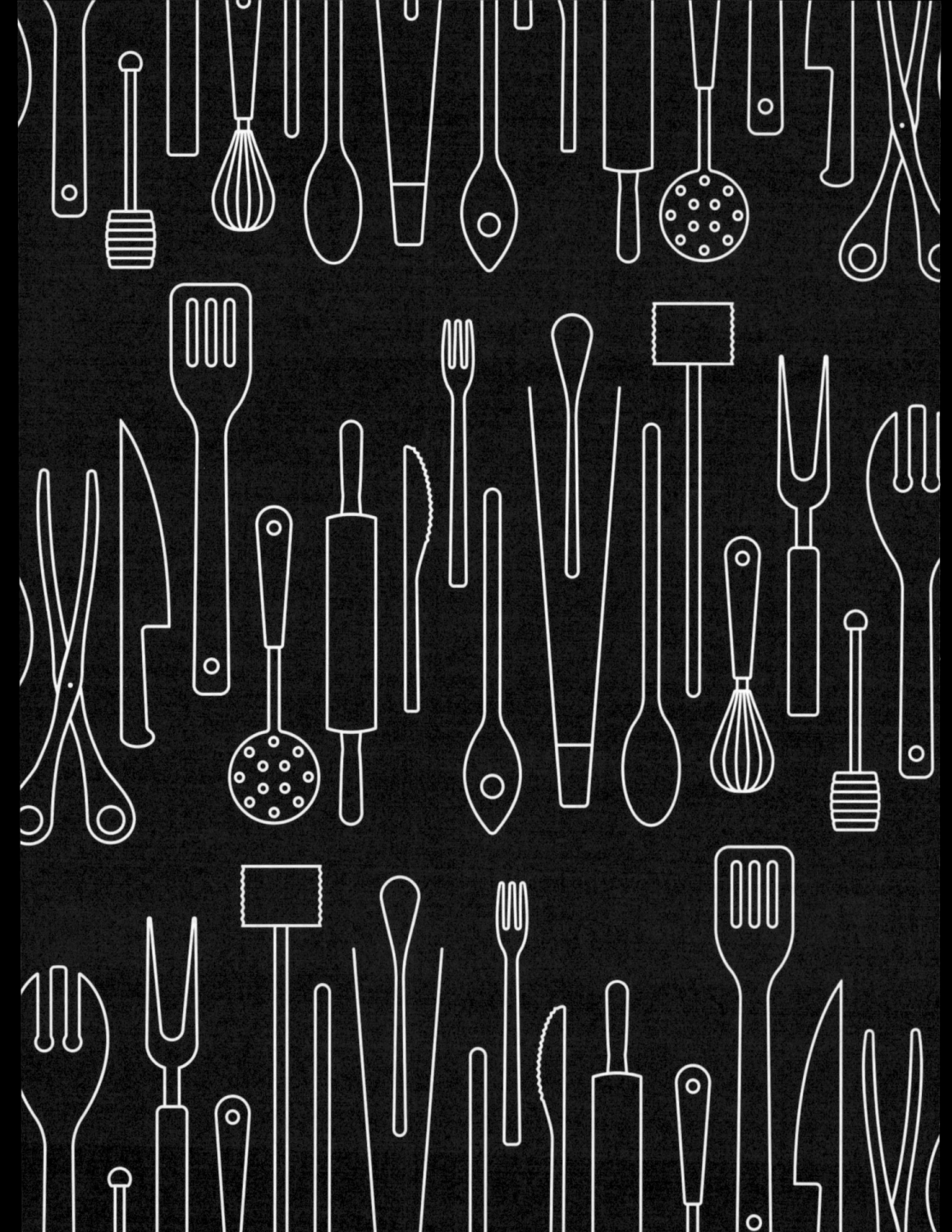

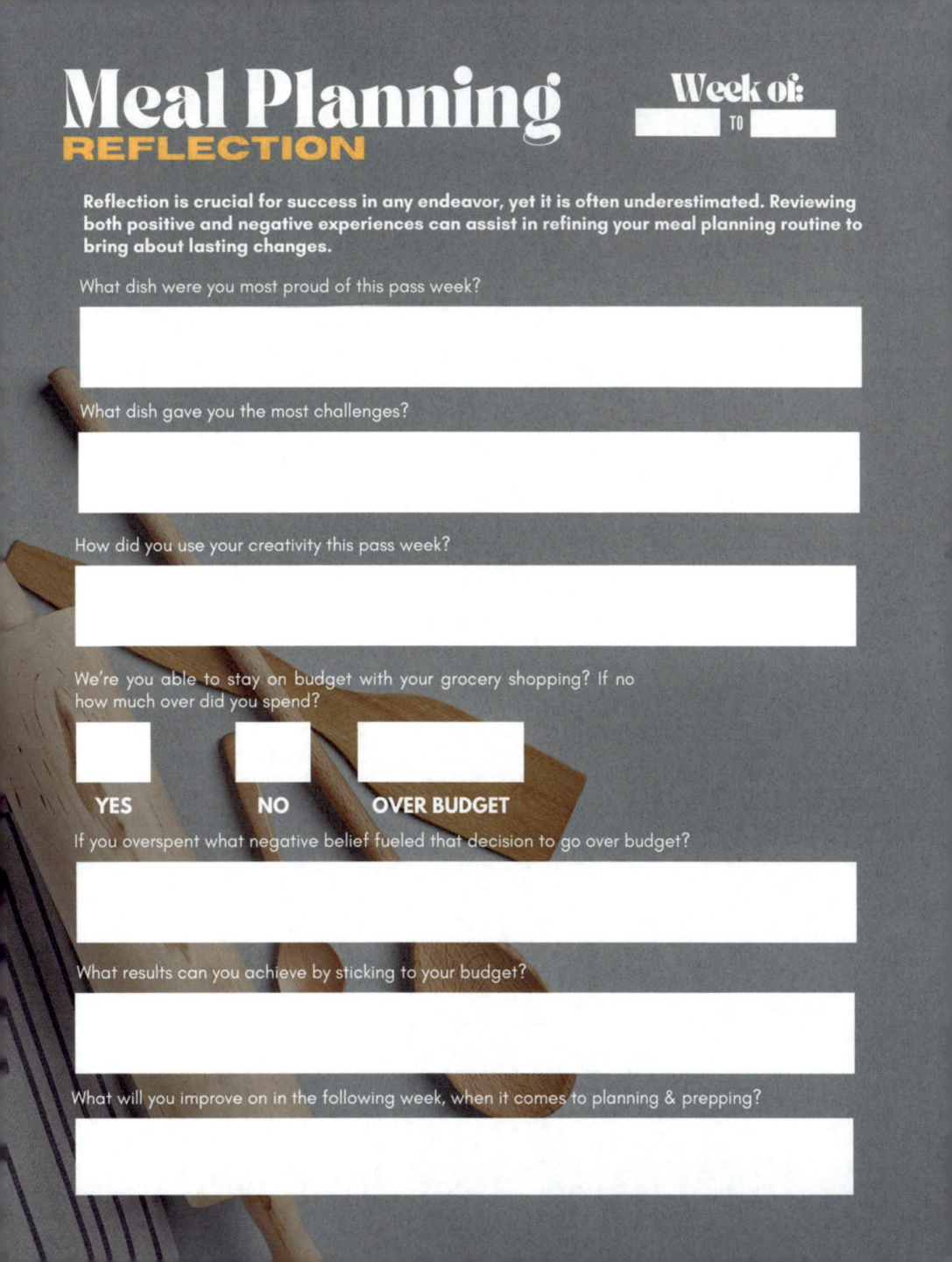

Meal Planning
REFLECTION

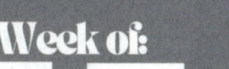

Reflection is crucial for success in any endeavor, yet it is often underestimated. Reviewing both positive and negative experiences can assist in refining your meal planning routine to bring about lasting changes.

What dish were you most proud of this pass week?

What dish gave you the most challenges?

How did you use your creativity this pass week?

We're you able to stay on budget with your grocery shopping? If no how much over did you spend?

YES | **NO** | **OVER BUDGET**

If you overspent what negative belief fueled that decision to go over budget?

What results can you achieve by sticking to your budget?

What will you improve on in the following week, when it comes to planning & prepping?

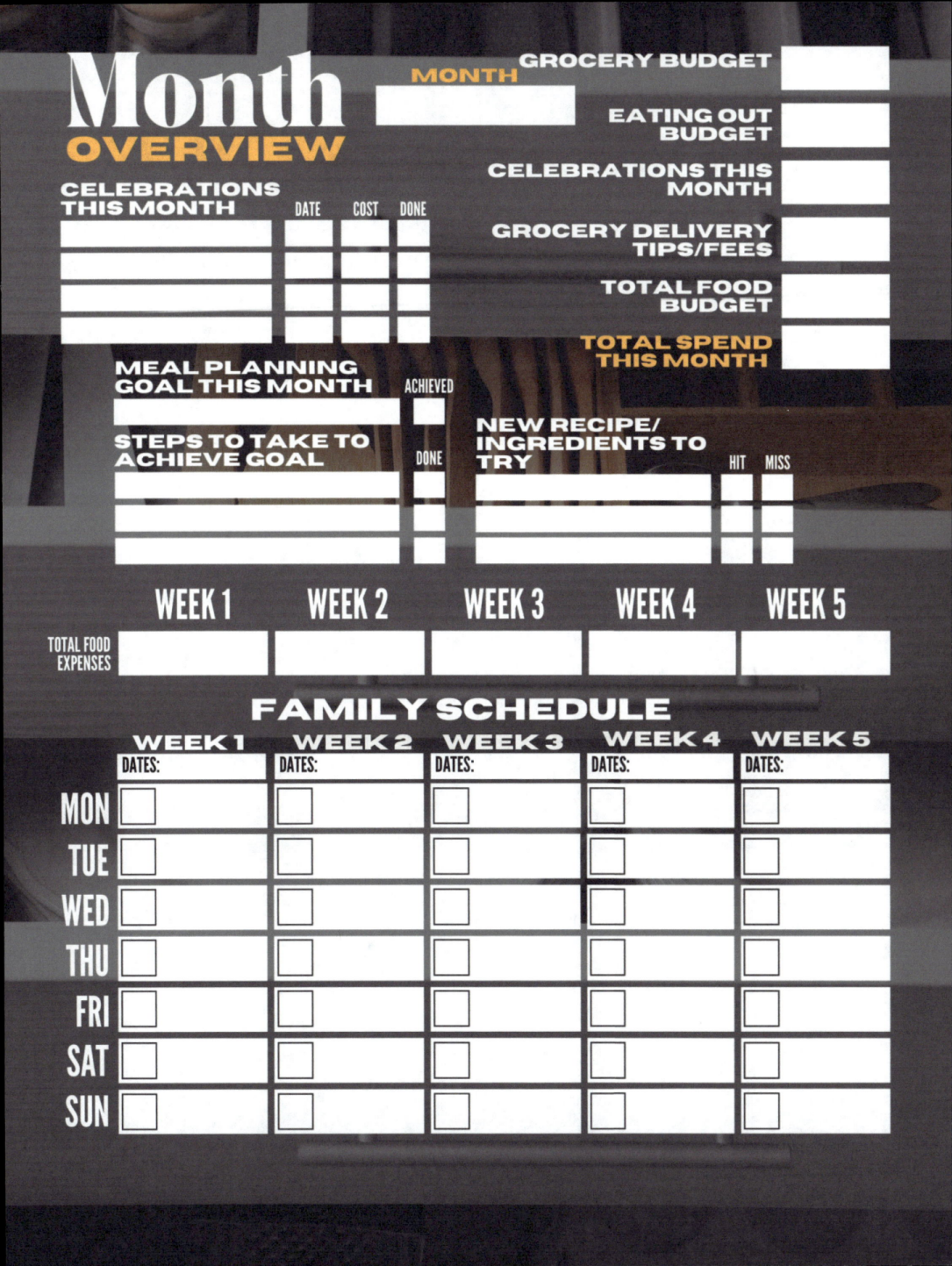

Meal Planning

REFLECTION

Week of:
_____ TO _____

Reflection is crucial for success in any endeavor, yet it is often underestimated. Reviewing both positive and negative experiences can assist in refining your meal planning routine to bring about lasting changes.

What dish were you most proud of this pass week?

_____

What dish gave you the most challenges?

_____

How did you use your creativity this pass week?

_____

We're you able to stay on budget with your grocery shopping? If no how much over did you spend?

☐ **YES** ☐ **NO** ☐ **OVER BUDGET**

If you overspent what negative belief fueled that decision to go over budget?

_____

What results can you achieve by sticking to your budget?

_____

What will you improve on in the following week, when it comes to planning & prepping?

_____

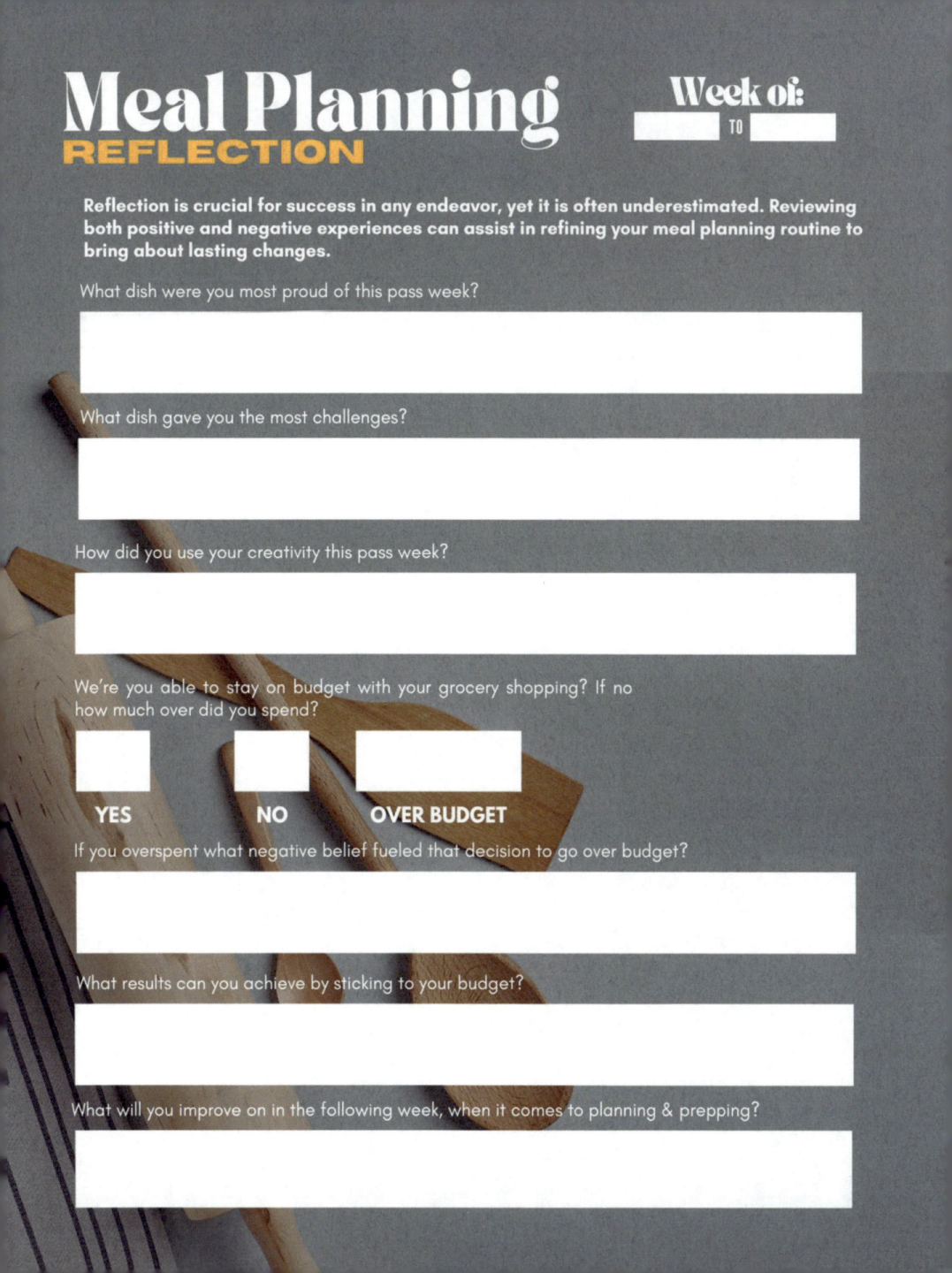

Meal Planning
REFLECTION

Reflection is crucial for success in any endeavor, yet it is often underestimated. Reviewing both positive and negative experiences can assist in refining your meal planning routine to bring about lasting changes.

What dish were you most proud of this pass week?

What dish gave you the most challenges?

How did you use your creativity this pass week?

We're you able to stay on budget with your grocery shopping? If no how much over did you spend?

YES   **NO**   **OVER BUDGET**

If you overspent what negative belief fueled that decision to go over budget?

What results can you achieve by sticking to your budget?

What will you improve on in the following week, when it comes to planning & prepping?

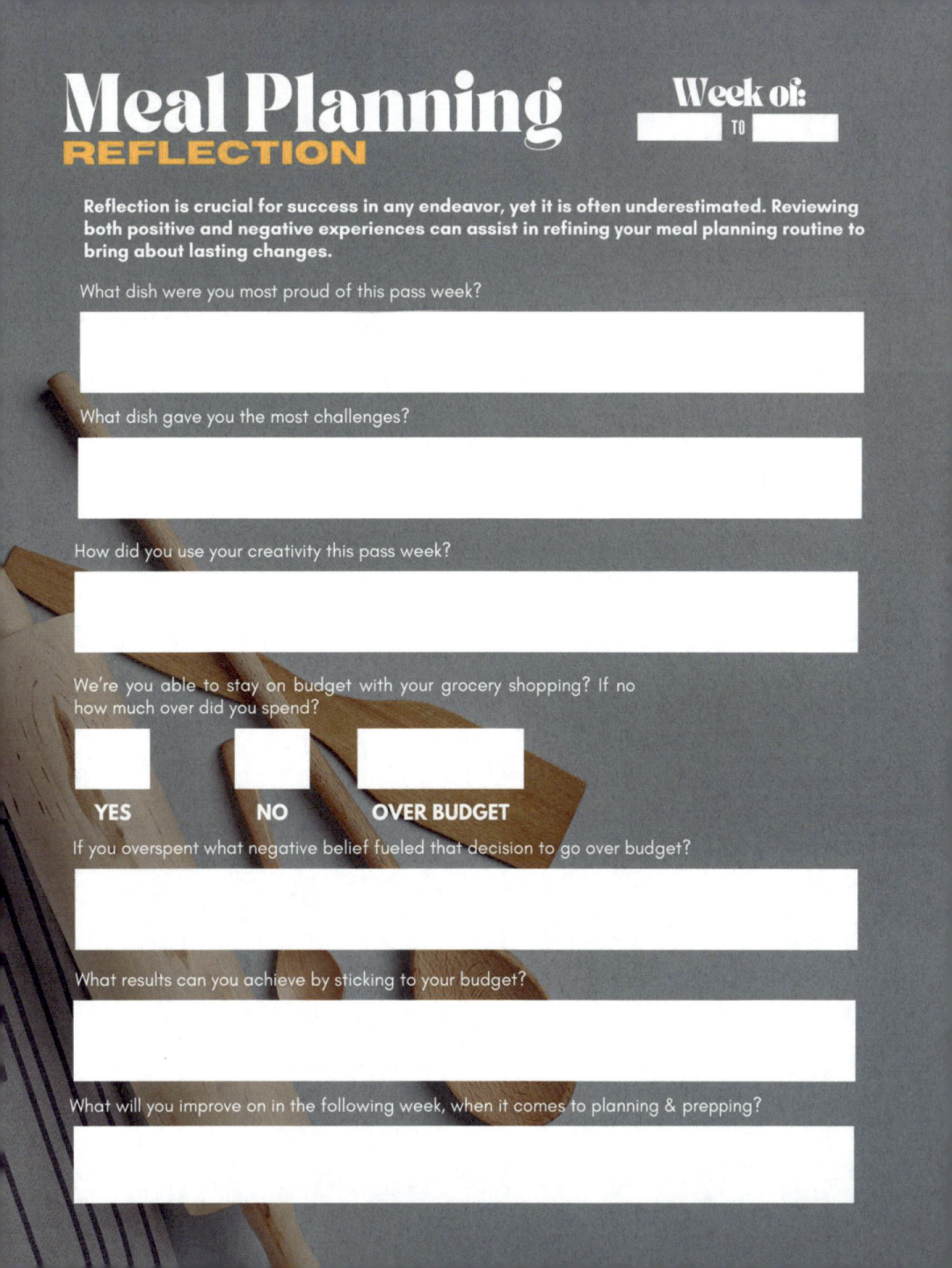

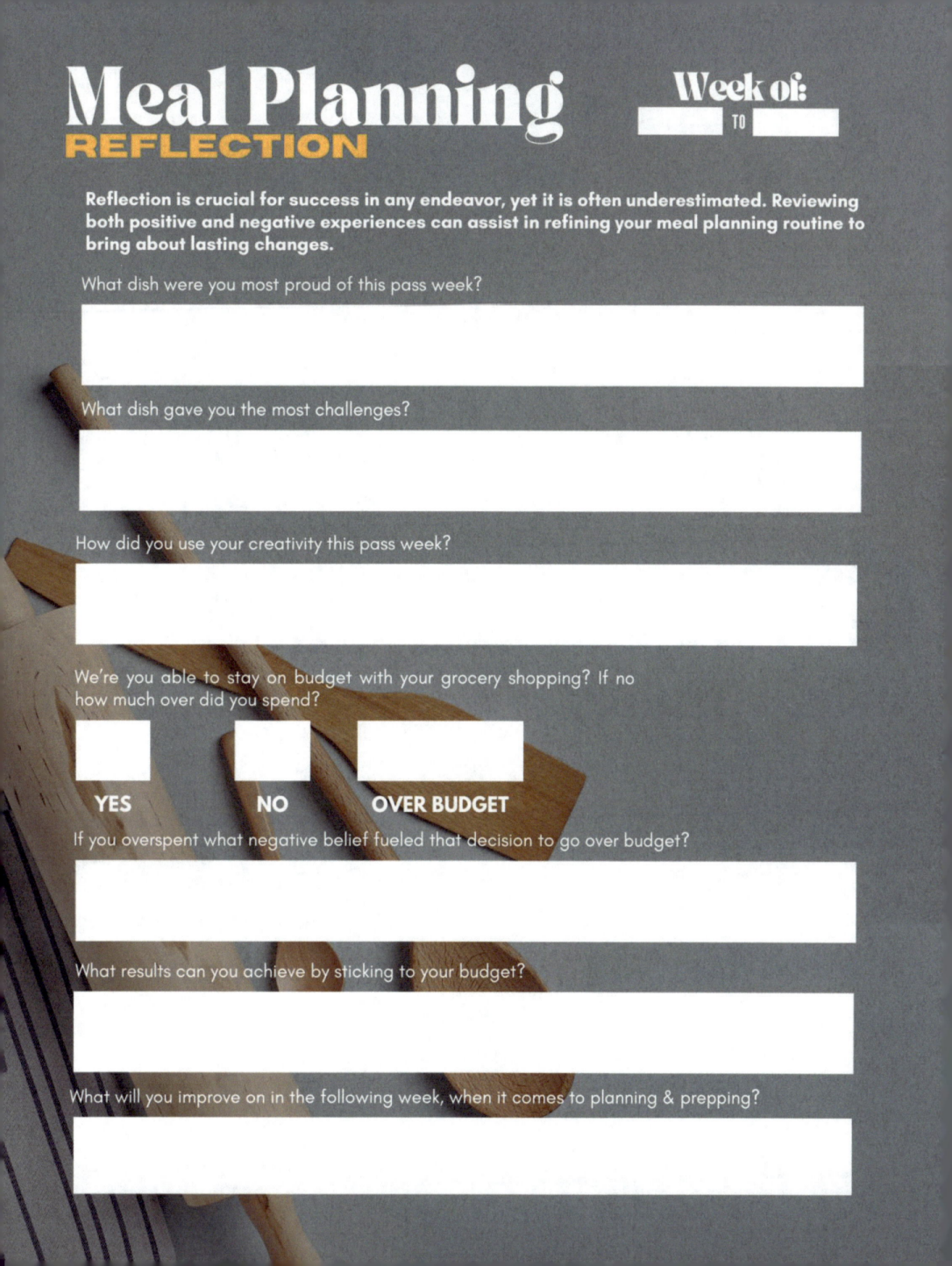

Meal Planning
REFLECTION

Week of:
_____ to _____

Reflection is crucial for success in any endeavor, yet it is often underestimated. Reviewing both positive and negative experiences can assist in refining your meal planning routine to bring about lasting changes.

What dish were you most proud of this pass week?

_____

What dish gave you the most challenges?

_____

How did you use your creativity this pass week?

_____

We're you able to stay on budget with your grocery shopping? If no how much over did you spend?

☐ **YES** ☐ **NO** ☐ **OVER BUDGET**

If you overspent what negative belief fueled that decision to go over budget?

_____

What results can you achieve by sticking to your budget?

_____

What will you improve on in the following week, when it comes to planning & prepping?

_____

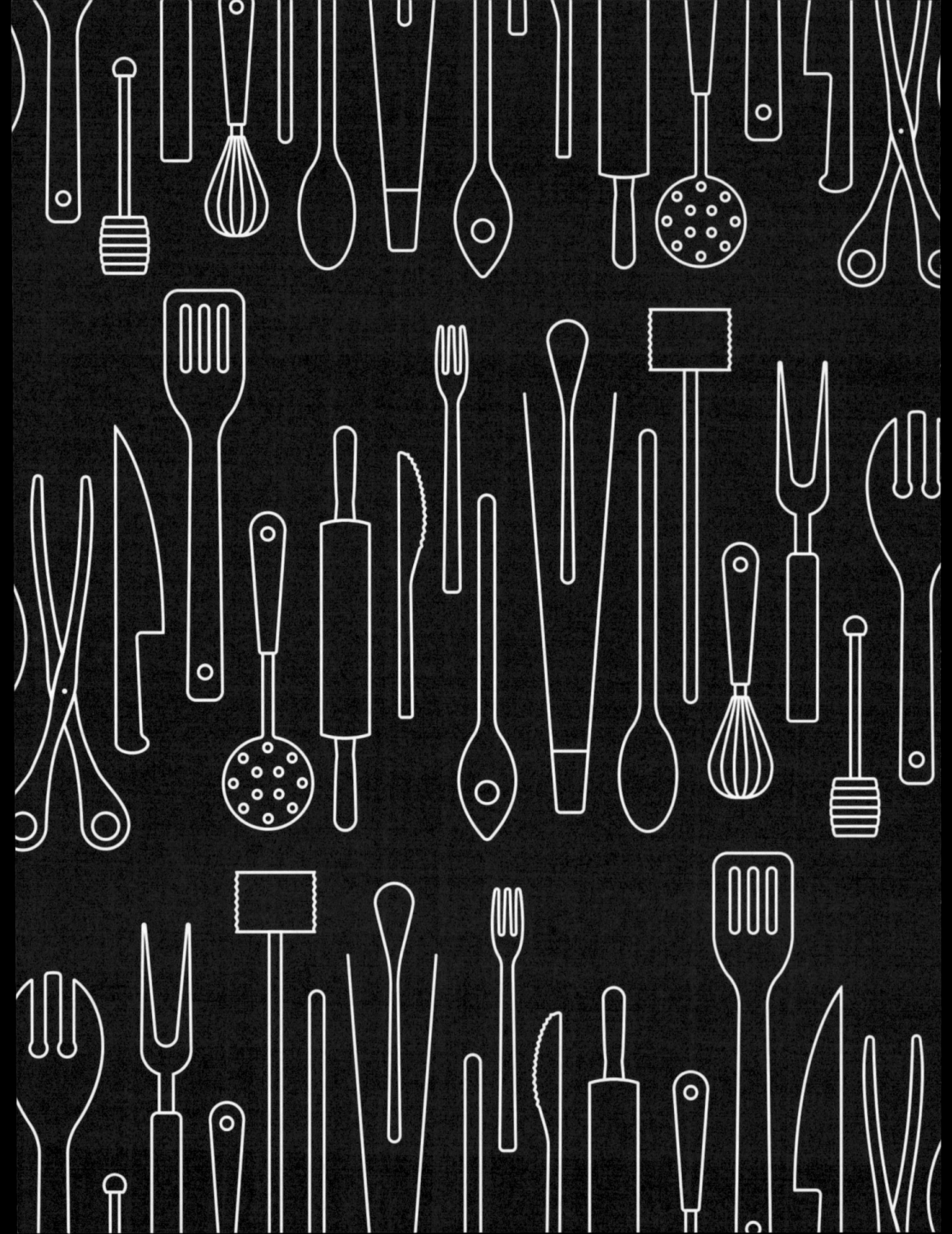

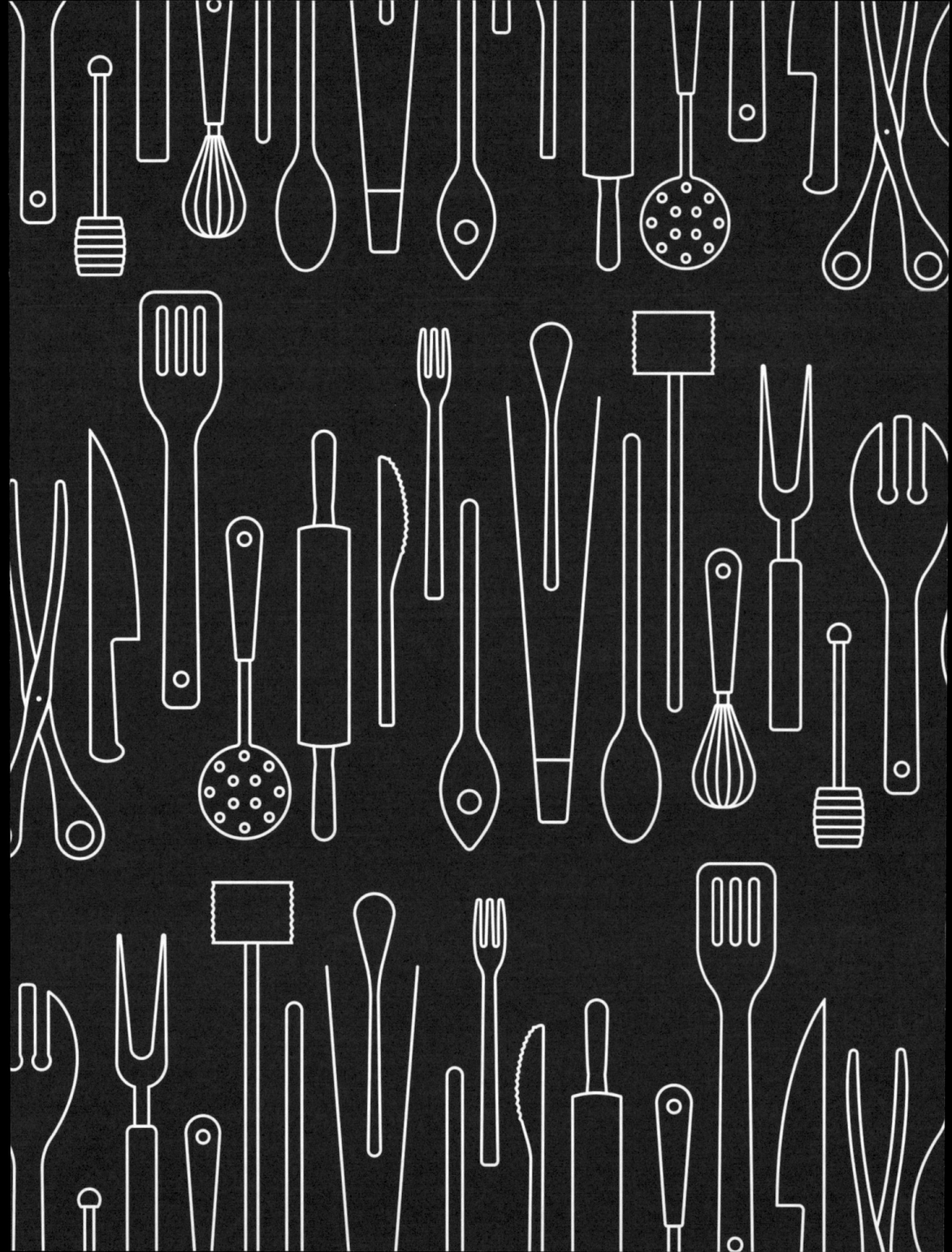

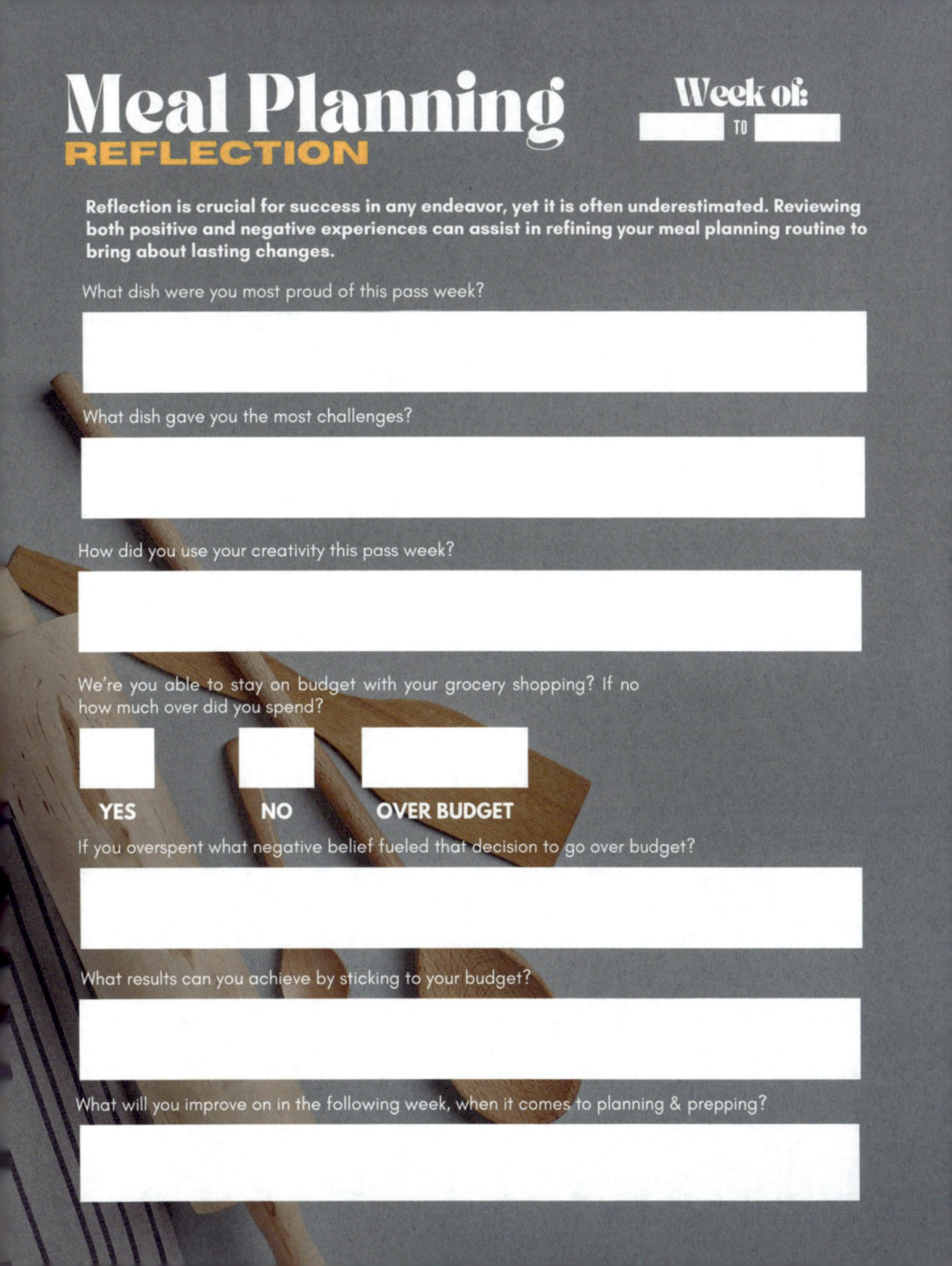

Meal Planning
REFLECTION

Week of:
_____ TO _____

Reflection is crucial for success in any endeavor, yet it is often underestimated. Reviewing both positive and negative experiences can assist in refining your meal planning routine to bring about lasting changes.

What dish were you most proud of this pass week?

What dish gave you the most challenges?

How did you use your creativity this pass week?

We're you able to stay on budget with your grocery shopping? If no how much over did you spend?

YES   **NO**   **OVER BUDGET**

If you overspent what negative belief fueled that decision to go over budget?

What results can you achieve by sticking to your budget?

What will you improve on in the following week, when it comes to planning & prepping?

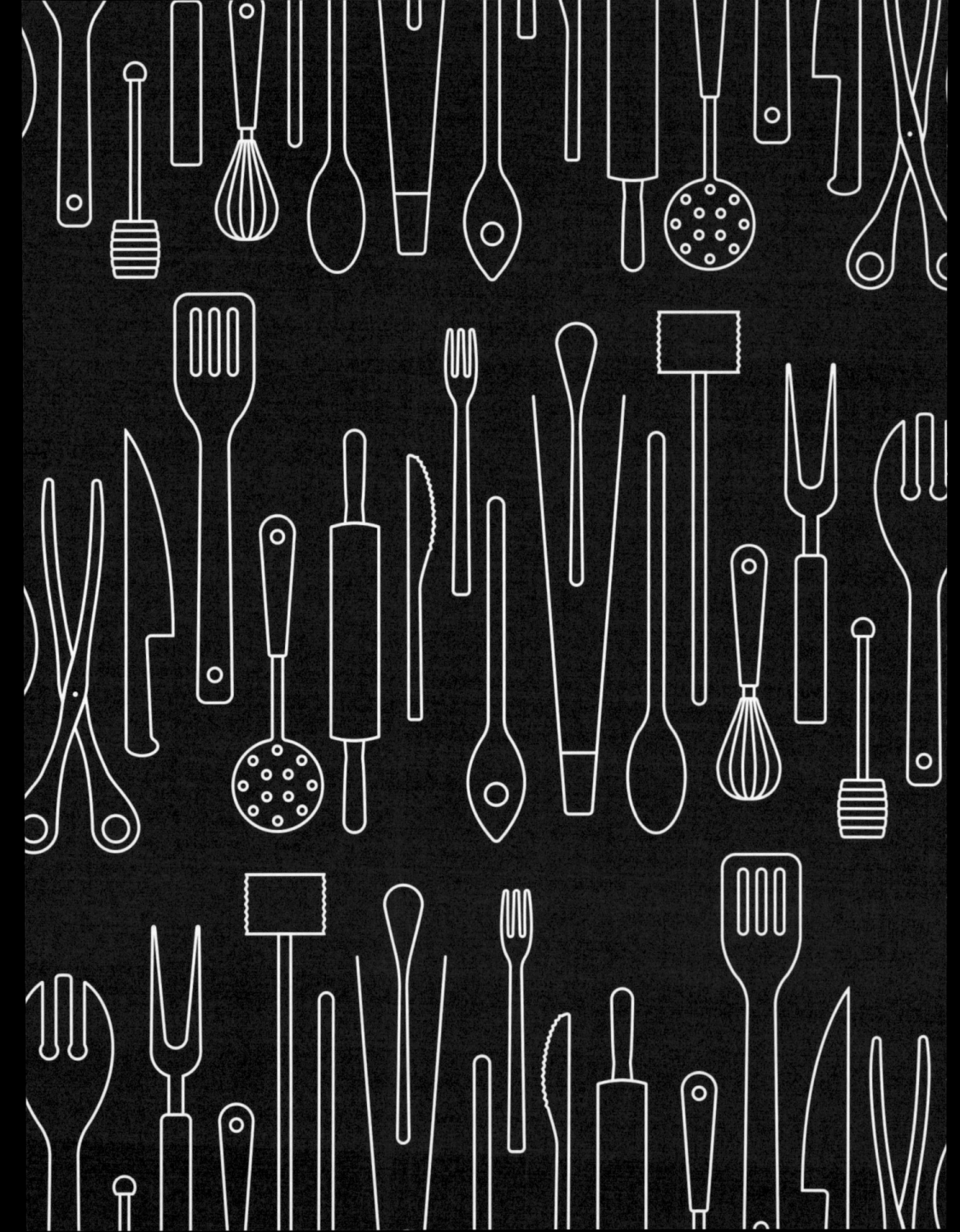

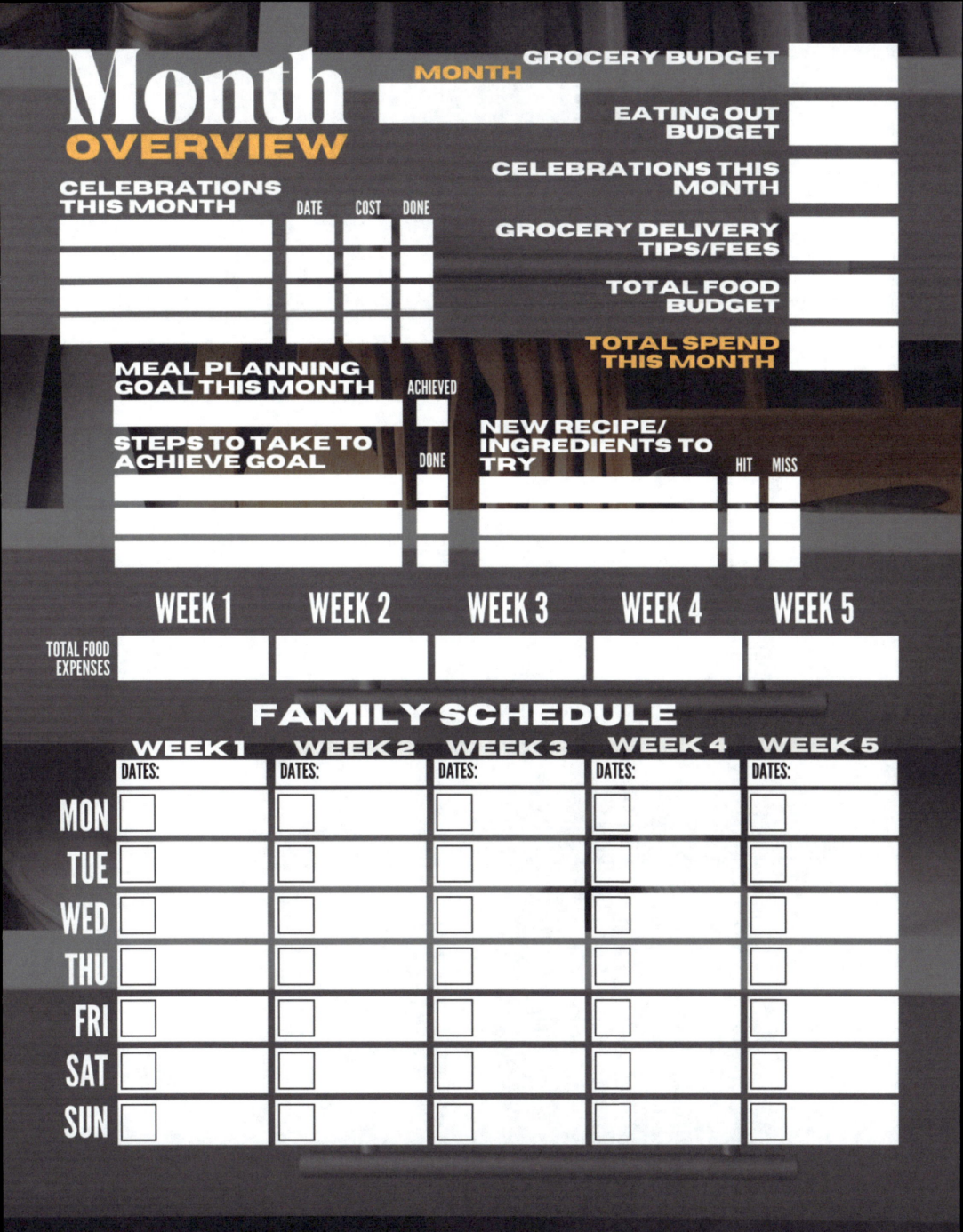

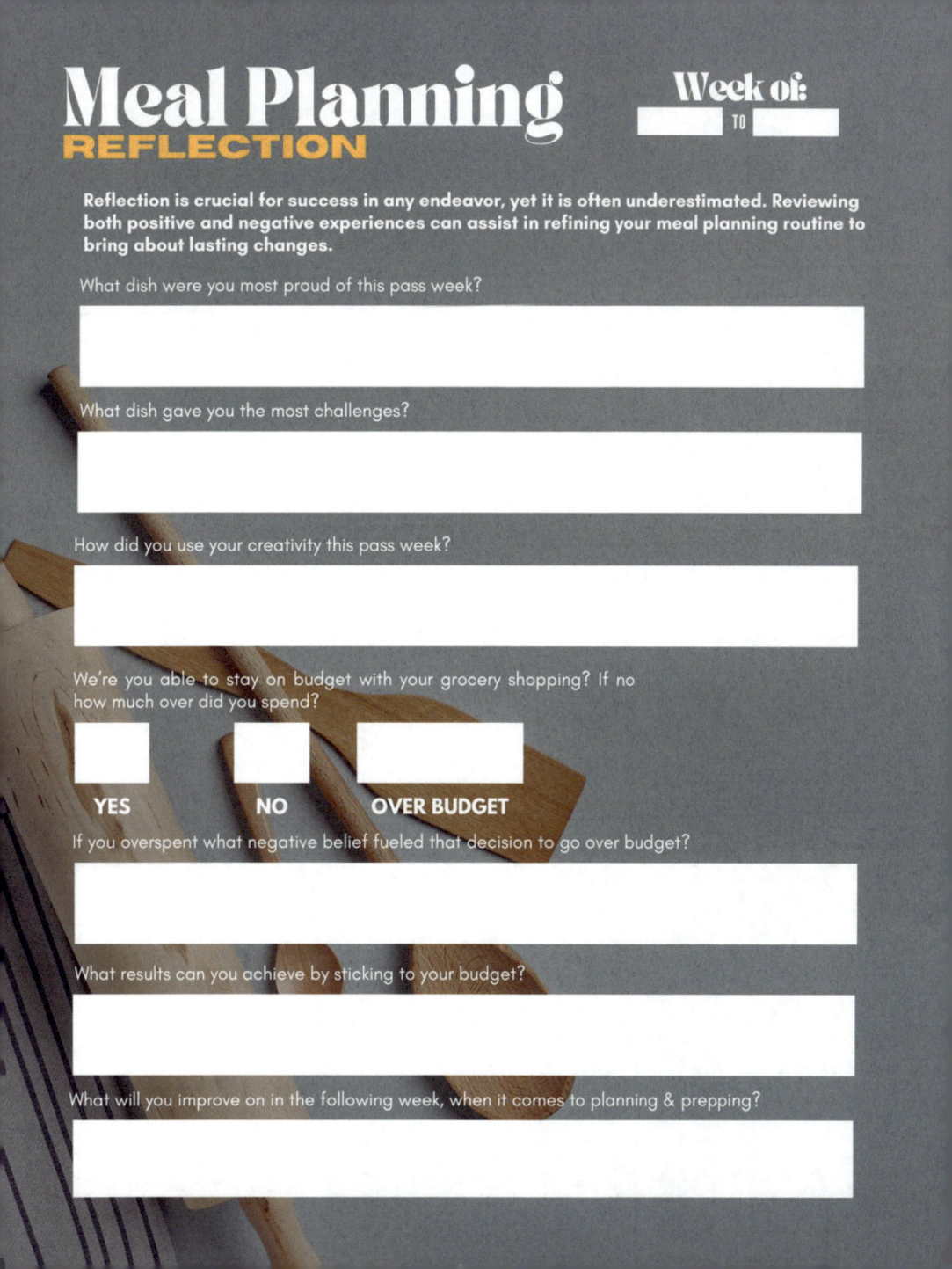

Meal Planning
REFLECTION

Week of:
_____ TO _____

Reflection is crucial for success in any endeavor, yet it is often underestimated. Reviewing both positive and negative experiences can assist in refining your meal planning routine to bring about lasting changes.

What dish were you most proud of this pass week?

_____

What dish gave you the most challenges?

_____

How did you use your creativity this pass week?

_____

We're you able to stay on budget with your grocery shopping? If no how much over did you spend?

YES   **NO**   **OVER BUDGET**

If you overspent what negative belief fueled that decision to go over budget?

_____

What results can you achieve by sticking to your budget?

_____

What will you improve on in the following week, when it comes to planning & prepping?

_____

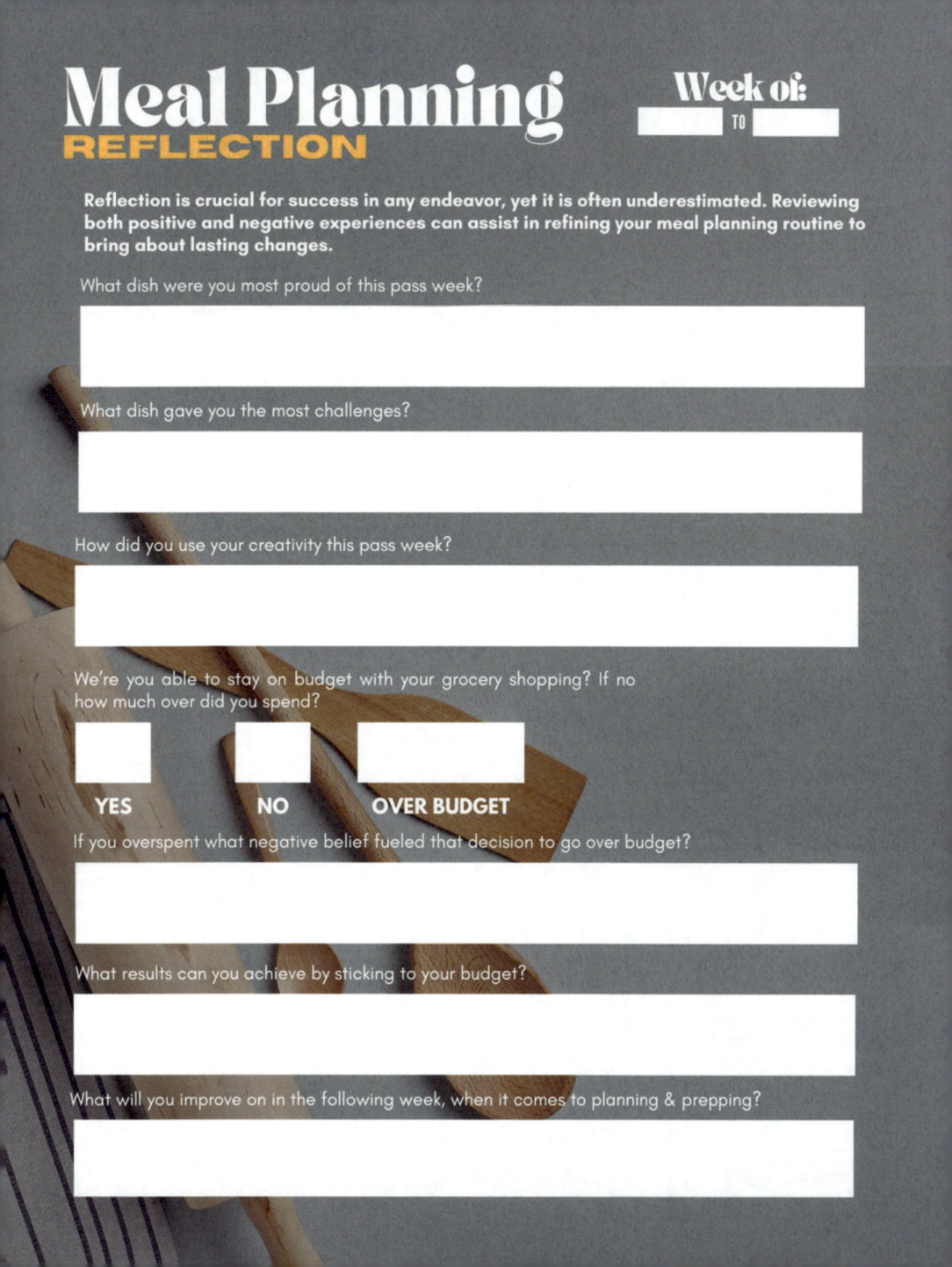

Meal Planning
REFLECTION

Week of:
_____ TO _____

Reflection is crucial for success in any endeavor, yet it is often underestimated. Reviewing both positive and negative experiences can assist in refining your meal planning routine to bring about lasting changes.

What dish were you most proud of this pass week?

_____

What dish gave you the most challenges?

_____

How did you use your creativity this pass week?

_____

We're you able to stay on budget with your grocery shopping? If no how much over did you spend?

☐ **YES** ☐ **NO** ☐ **OVER BUDGET**

If you overspent what negative belief fueled that decision to go over budget?

_____

What results can you achieve by sticking to your budget?

_____

What will you improve on in the following week, when it comes to planning & prepping?

_____

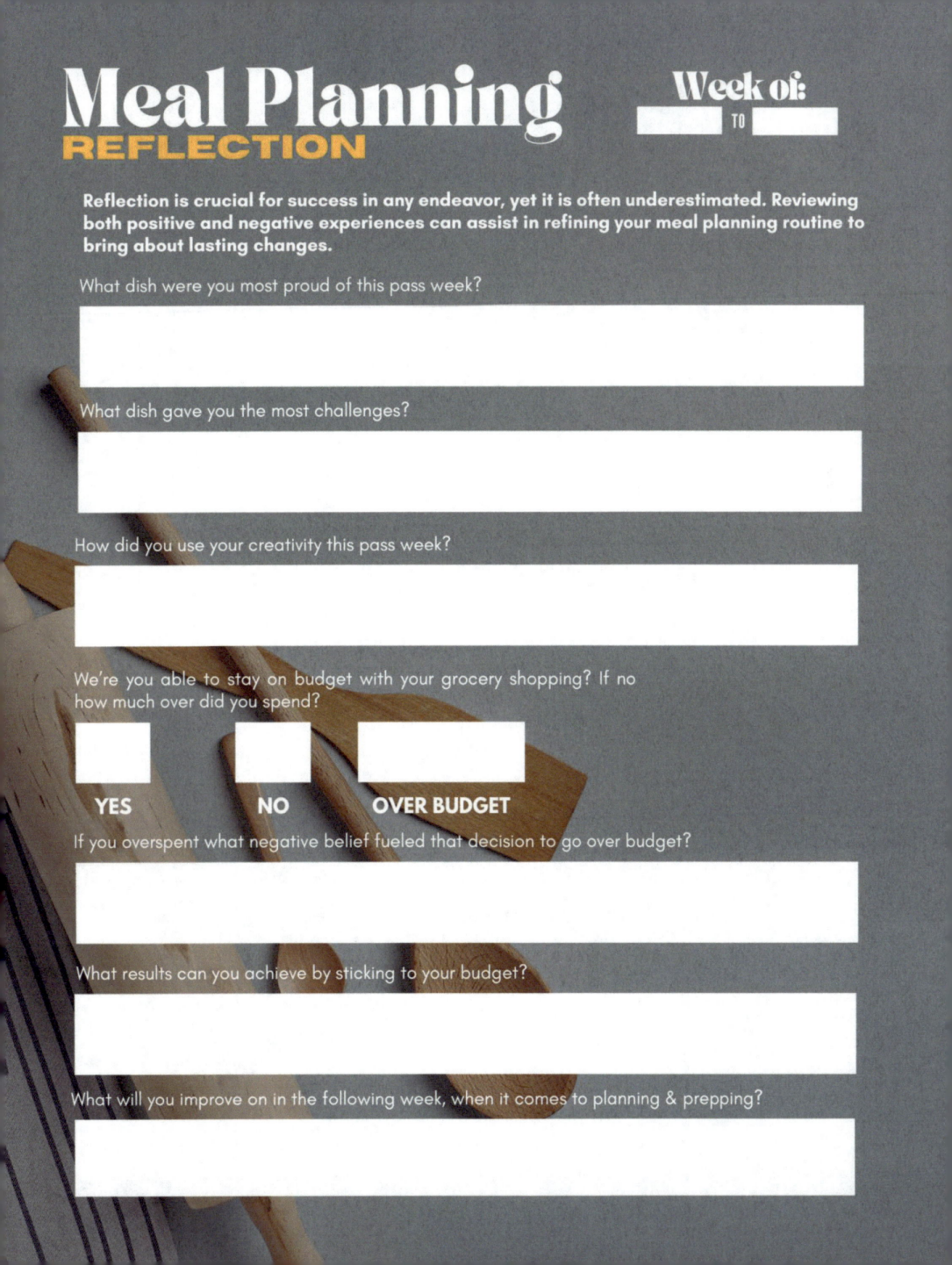

Meal Planning
REFLECTION

Week of:
_____ TO _____

Reflection is crucial for success in any endeavor, yet it is often underestimated. Reviewing both positive and negative experiences can assist in refining your meal planning routine to bring about lasting changes.

What dish were you most proud of this pass week?

_____

What dish gave you the most challenges?

_____

How did you use your creativity this pass week?

_____

We're you able to stay on budget with your grocery shopping? If no how much over did you spend?

☐ **YES** ☐ **NO** ☐ **OVER BUDGET**

If you overspent what negative belief fueled that decision to go over budget?

_____

What results can you achieve by sticking to your budget?

_____

What will you improve on in the following week, when it comes to planning & prepping?

_____

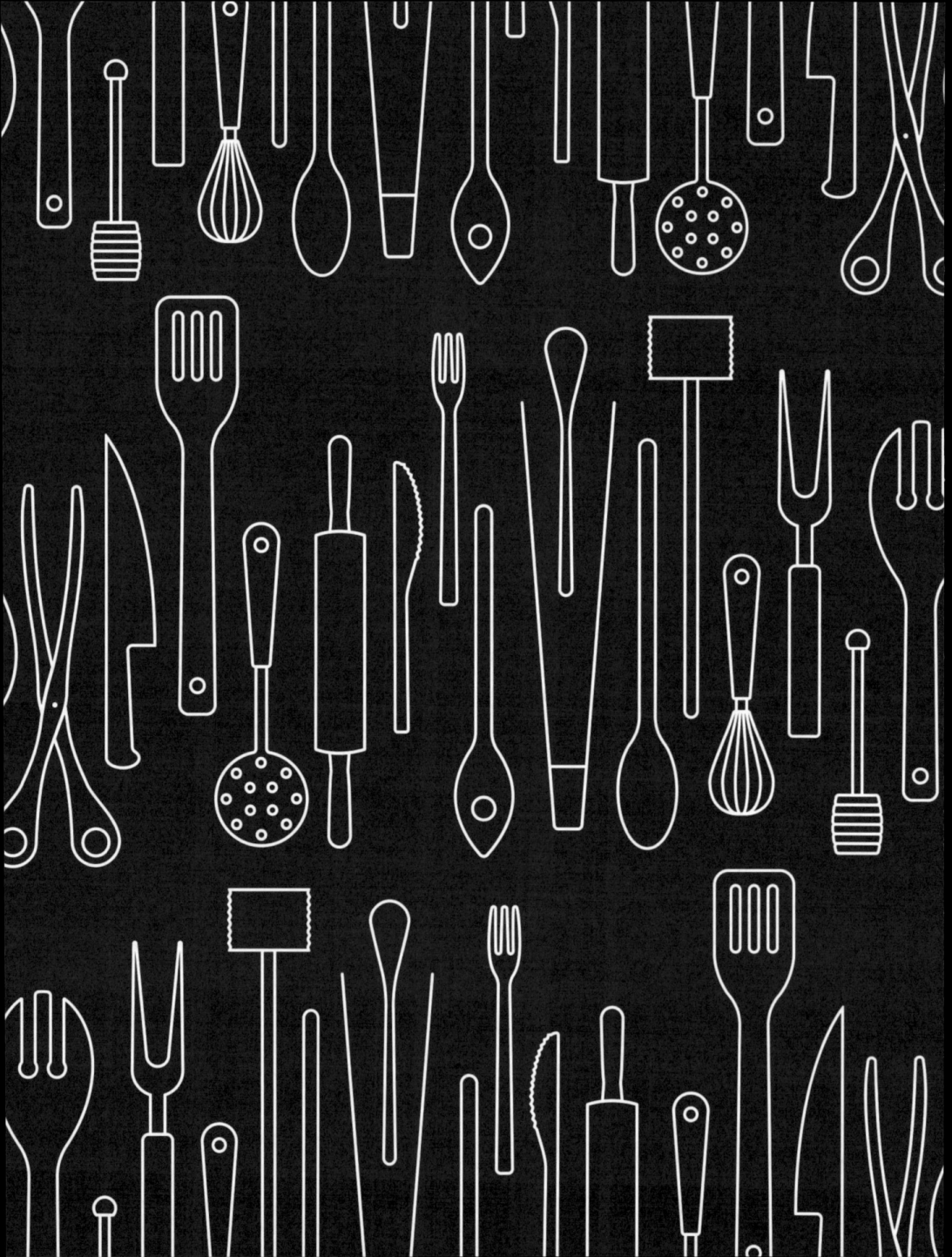

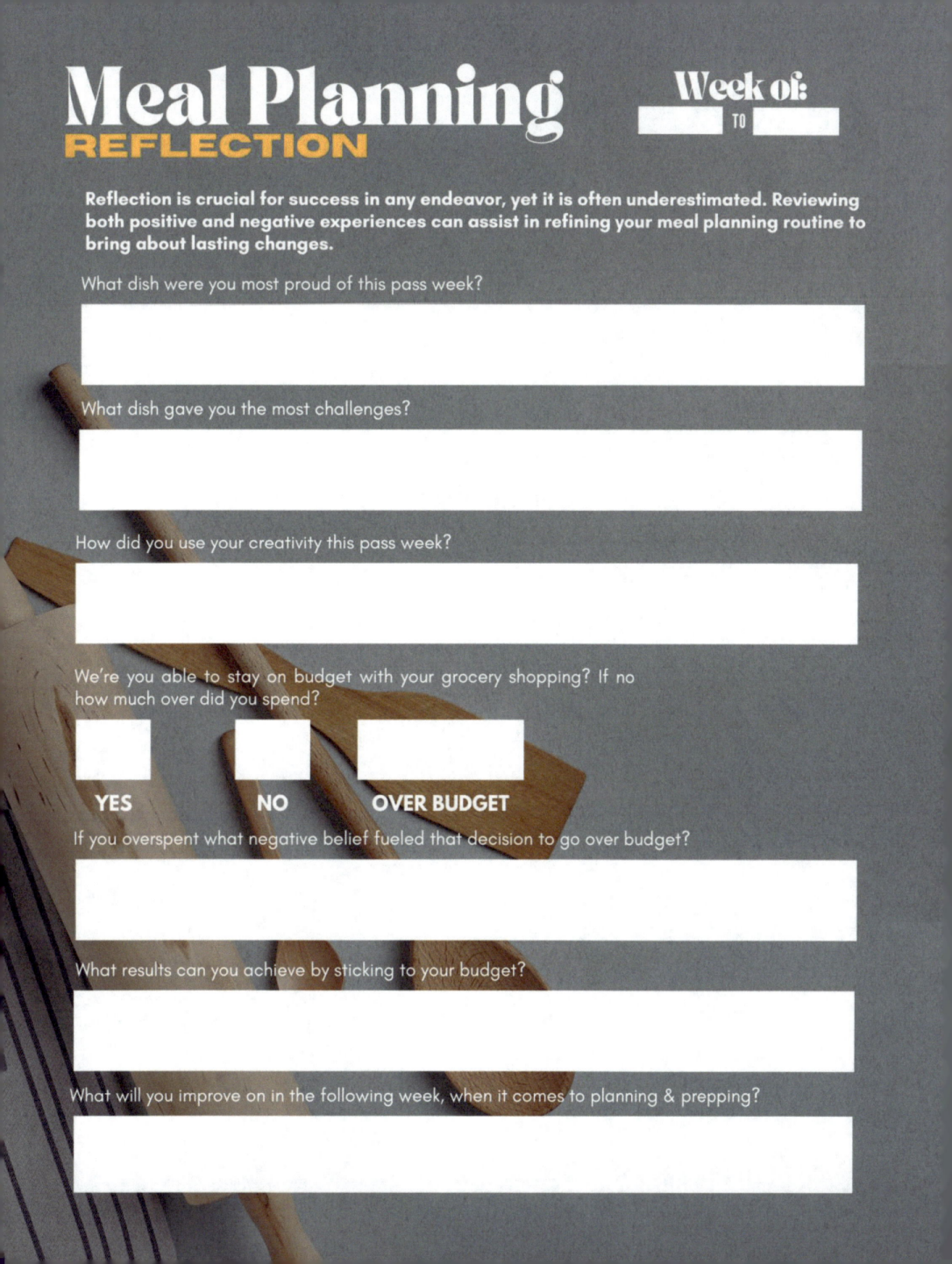

Meal Planning
REFLECTION

Week of:
_____ TO _____

Reflection is crucial for success in any endeavor, yet it is often underestimated. Reviewing both positive and negative experiences can assist in refining your meal planning routine to bring about lasting changes.

What dish were you most proud of this pass week?

_____

What dish gave you the most challenges?

_____

How did you use your creativity this pass week?

_____

We're you able to stay on budget with your grocery shopping? If no how much over did you spend?

☐ **YES** ☐ **NO** ☐ **OVER BUDGET**

If you overspent what negative belief fueled that decision to go over budget?

_____

What results can you achieve by sticking to your budget?

_____

What will you improve on in the following week, when it comes to planning & prepping?

_____

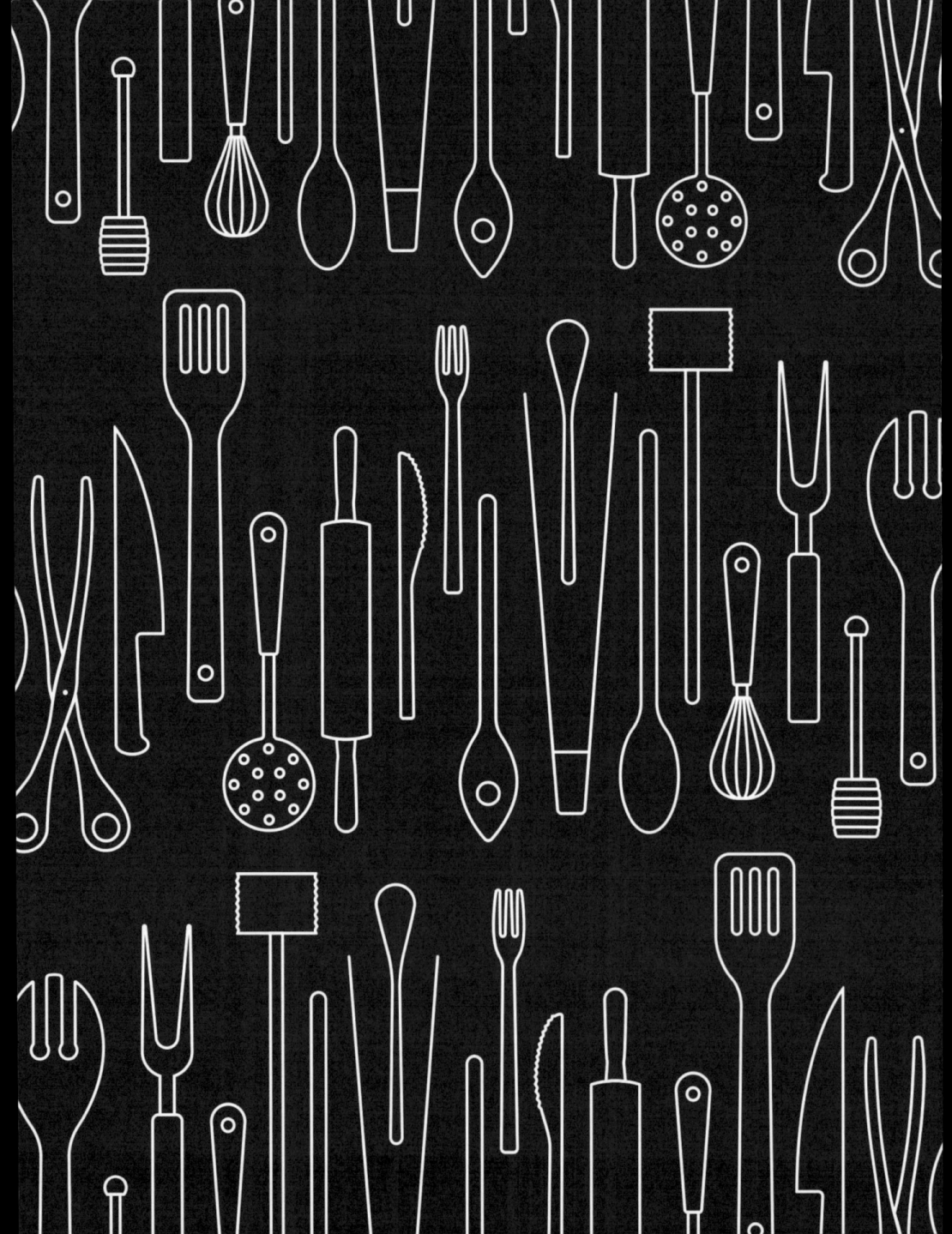

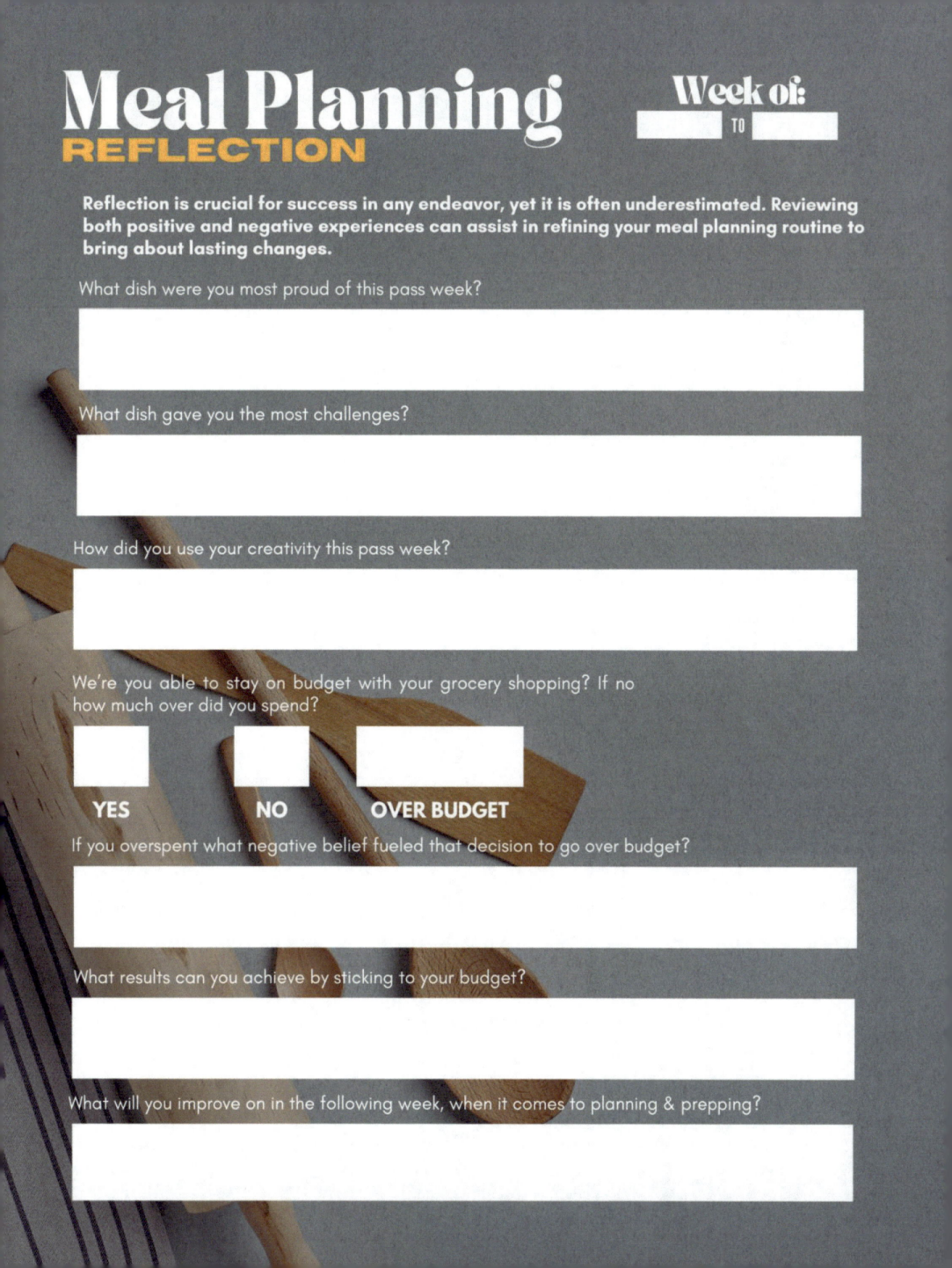

Meal Planning
REFLECTION

Week of:
_____ TO _____

Reflection is crucial for success in any endeavor, yet it is often underestimated. Reviewing both positive and negative experiences can assist in refining your meal planning routine to bring about lasting changes.

What dish were you most proud of this pass week?

What dish gave you the most challenges?

How did you use your creativity this pass week?

We're you able to stay on budget with your grocery shopping? If no how much over did you spend?

YES | **NO** | **OVER BUDGET**

If you overspent what negative belief fueled that decision to go over budget?

What results can you achieve by sticking to your budget?

What will you improve on in the following week, when it comes to planning & prepping?

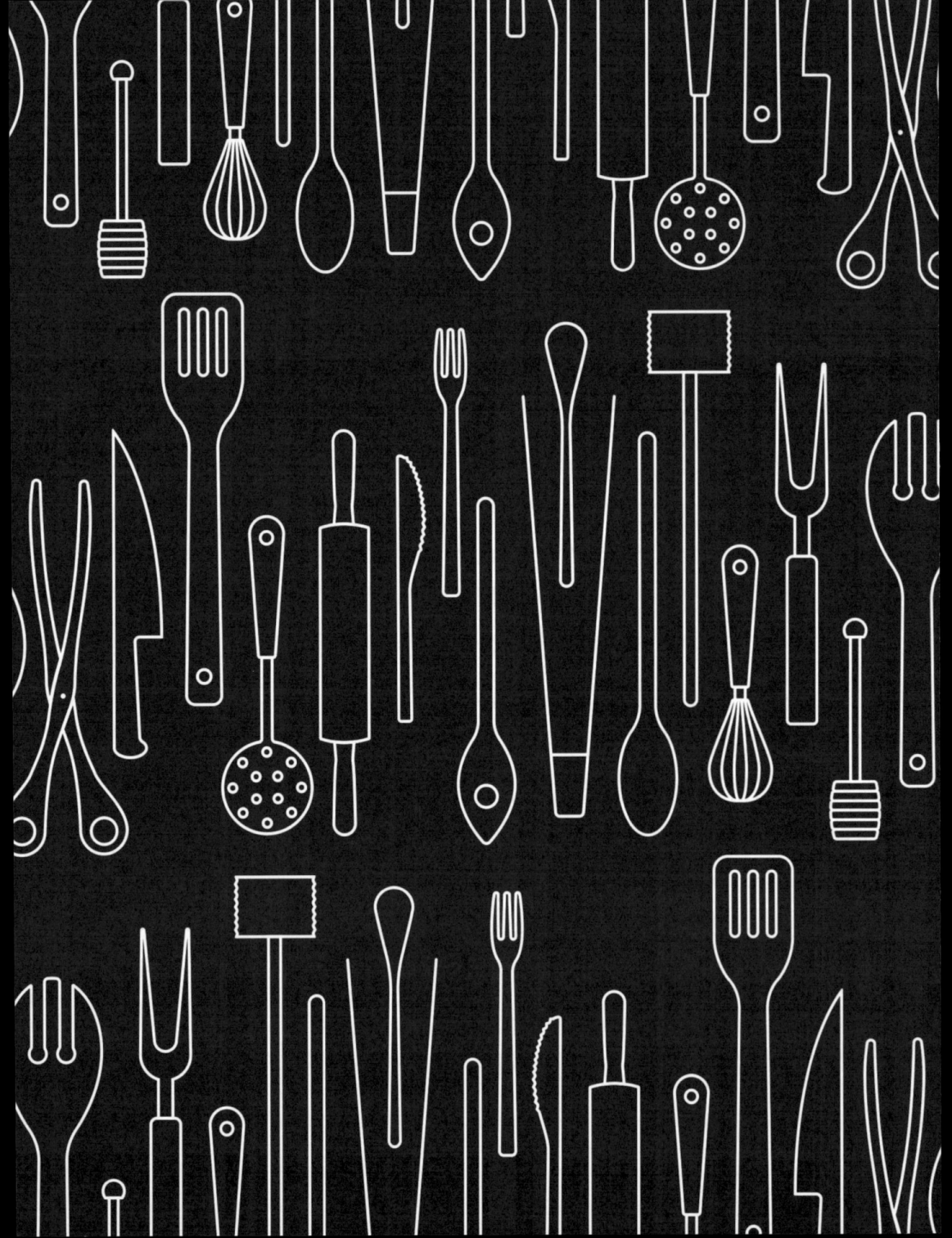

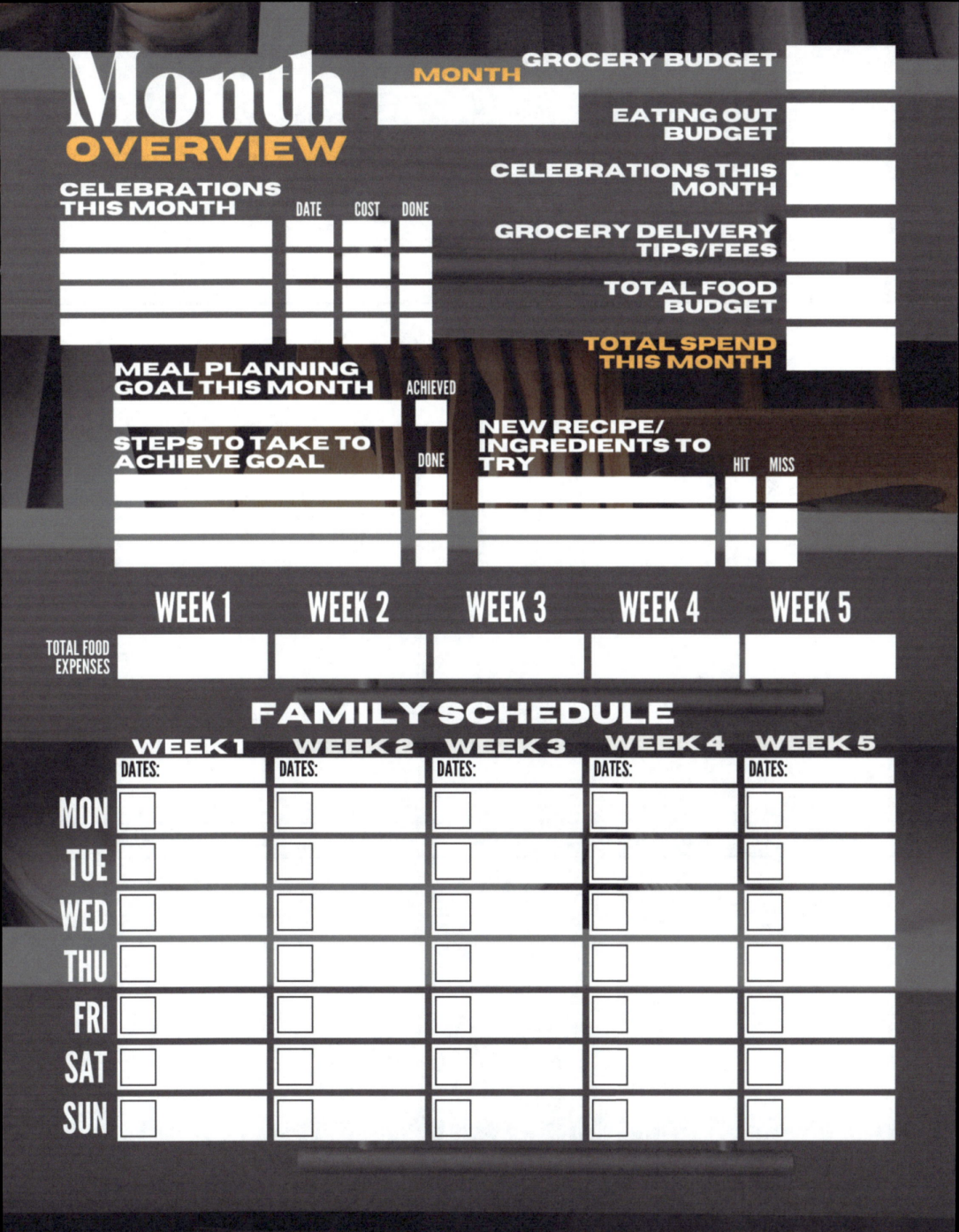

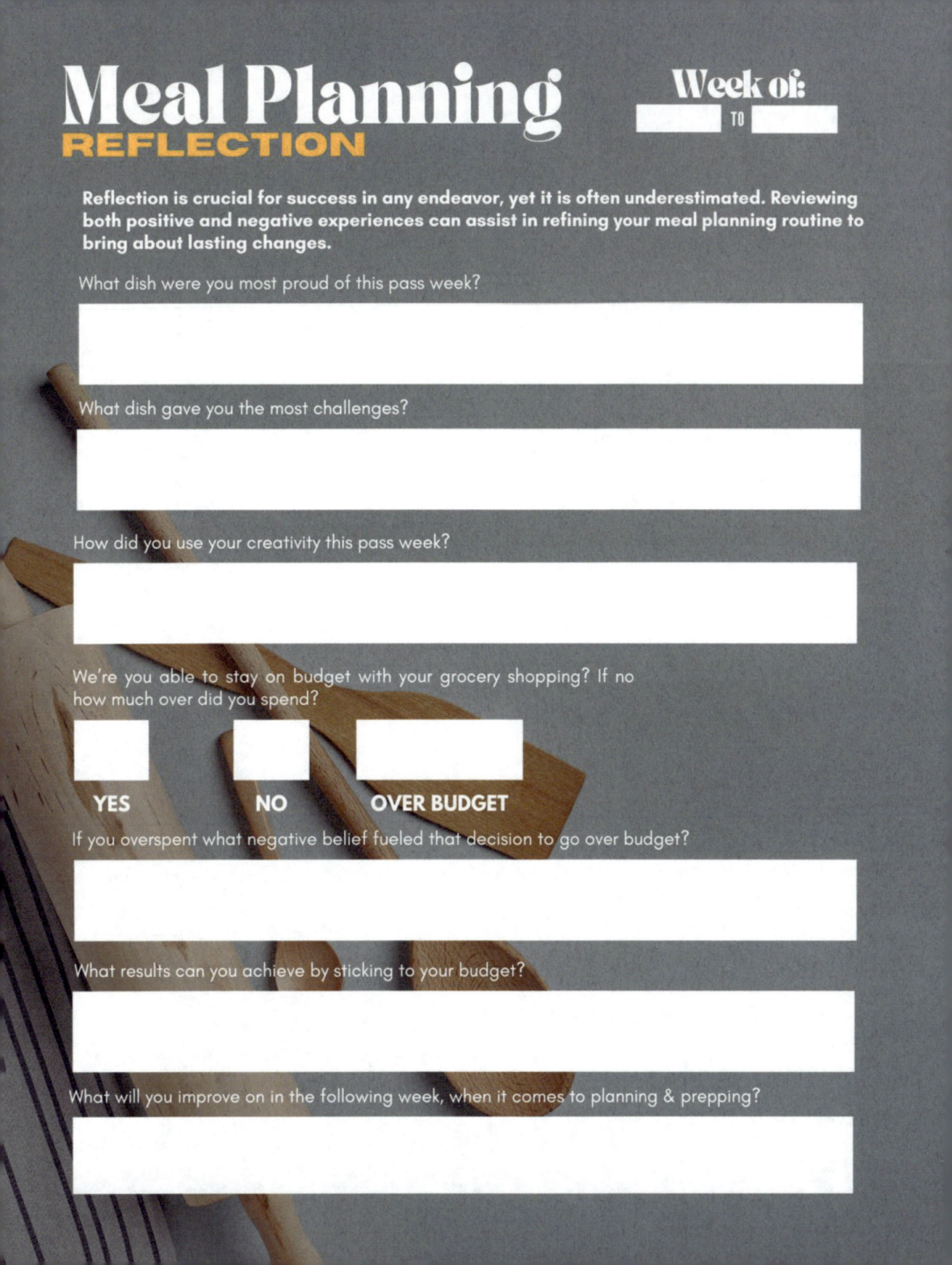

Meal Planning
REFLECTION

Week of:
_____ to _____

Reflection is crucial for success in any endeavor, yet it is often underestimated. Reviewing both positive and negative experiences can assist in refining your meal planning routine to bring about lasting changes.

What dish were you most proud of this pass week?

_____

What dish gave you the most challenges?

_____

How did you use your creativity this pass week?

_____

We're you able to stay on budget with your grocery shopping? If no how much over did you spend?

☐ **YES** ☐ **NO** ☐ **OVER BUDGET**

If you overspent what negative belief fueled that decision to go over budget?

_____

What results can you achieve by sticking to your budget?

_____

What will you improve on in the following week, when it comes to planning & prepping?

_____

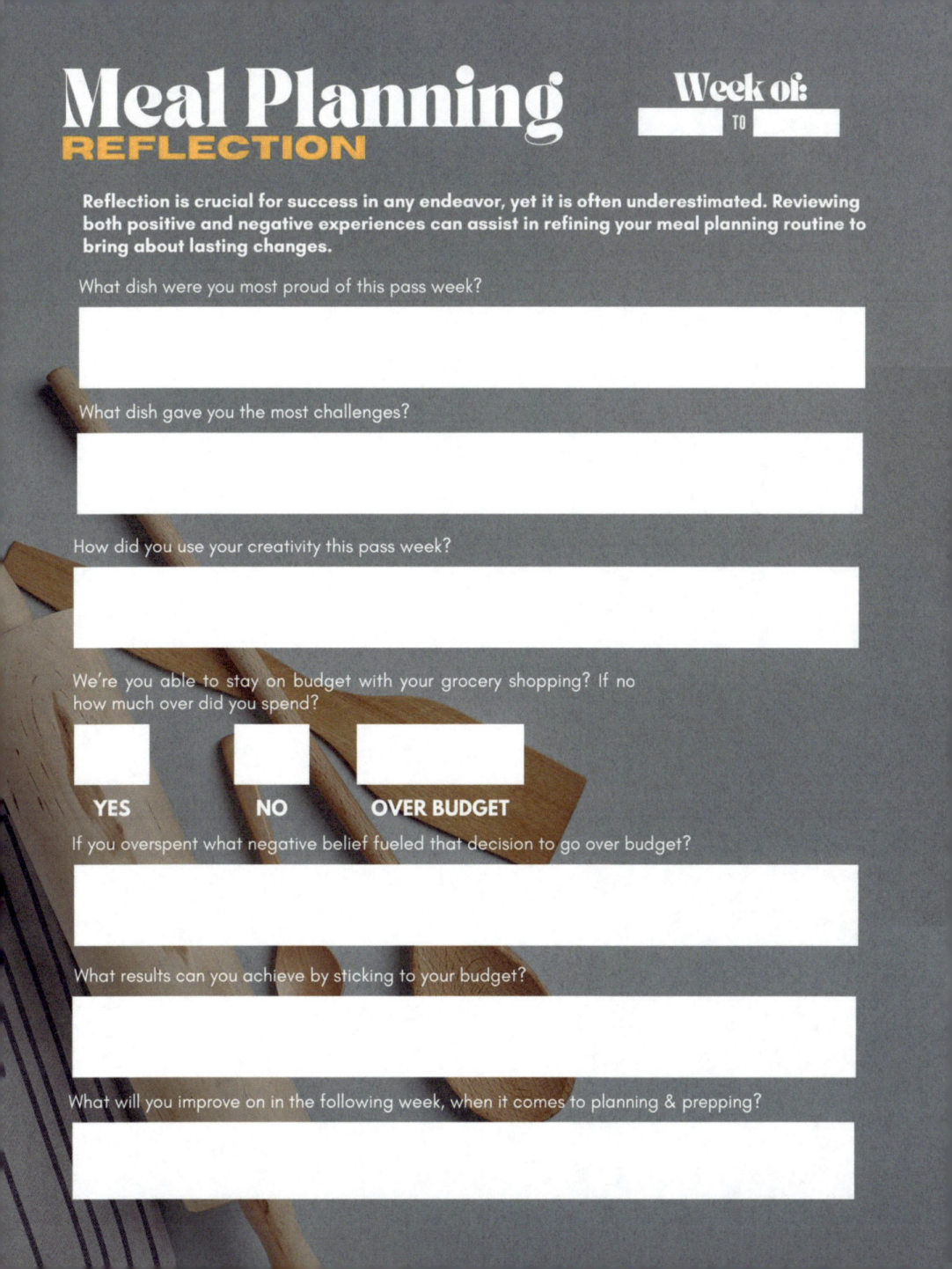

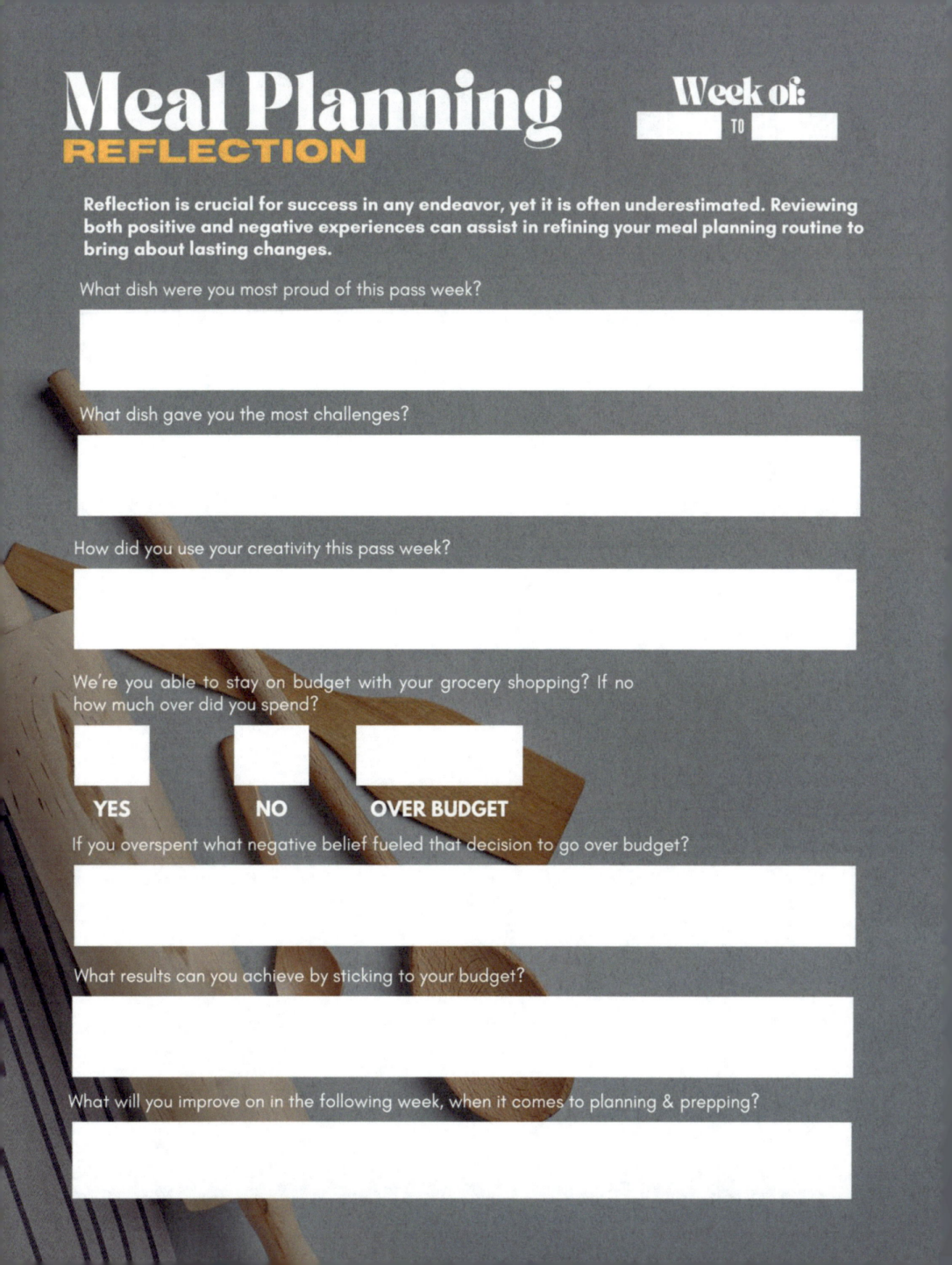

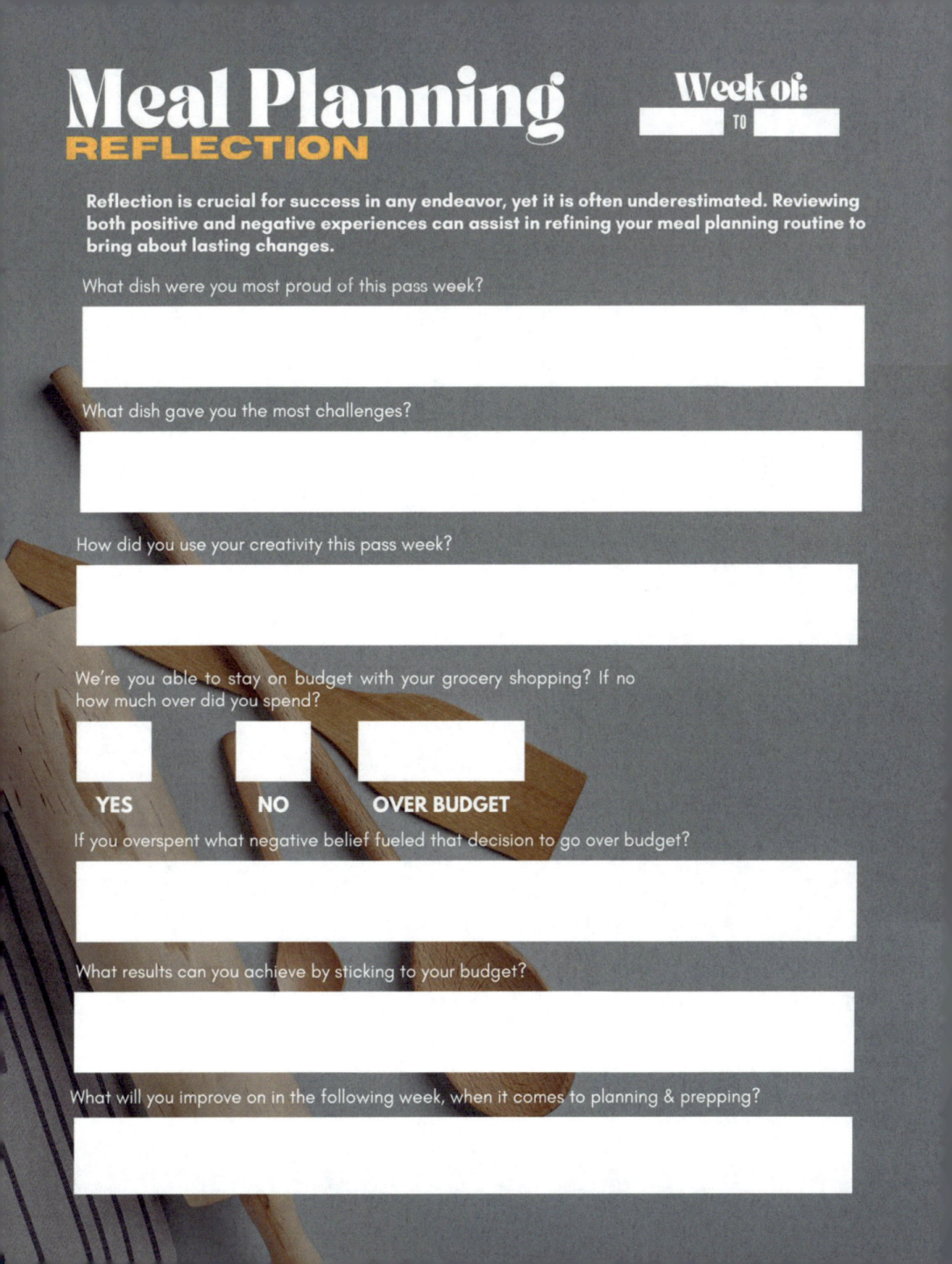

Meal Planning
REFLECTION

Week of:
_____ TO _____

Reflection is crucial for success in any endeavor, yet it is often underestimated. Reviewing both positive and negative experiences can assist in refining your meal planning routine to bring about lasting changes.

What dish were you most proud of this pass week?

_____

What dish gave you the most challenges?

_____

How did you use your creativity this pass week?

_____

We're you able to stay on budget with your grocery shopping? If no how much over did you spend?

☐ **YES** ☐ **NO** ☐ **OVER BUDGET**

If you overspent what negative belief fueled that decision to go over budget?

_____

What results can you achieve by sticking to your budget?

_____

What will you improve on in the following week, when it comes to planning & prepping?

_____

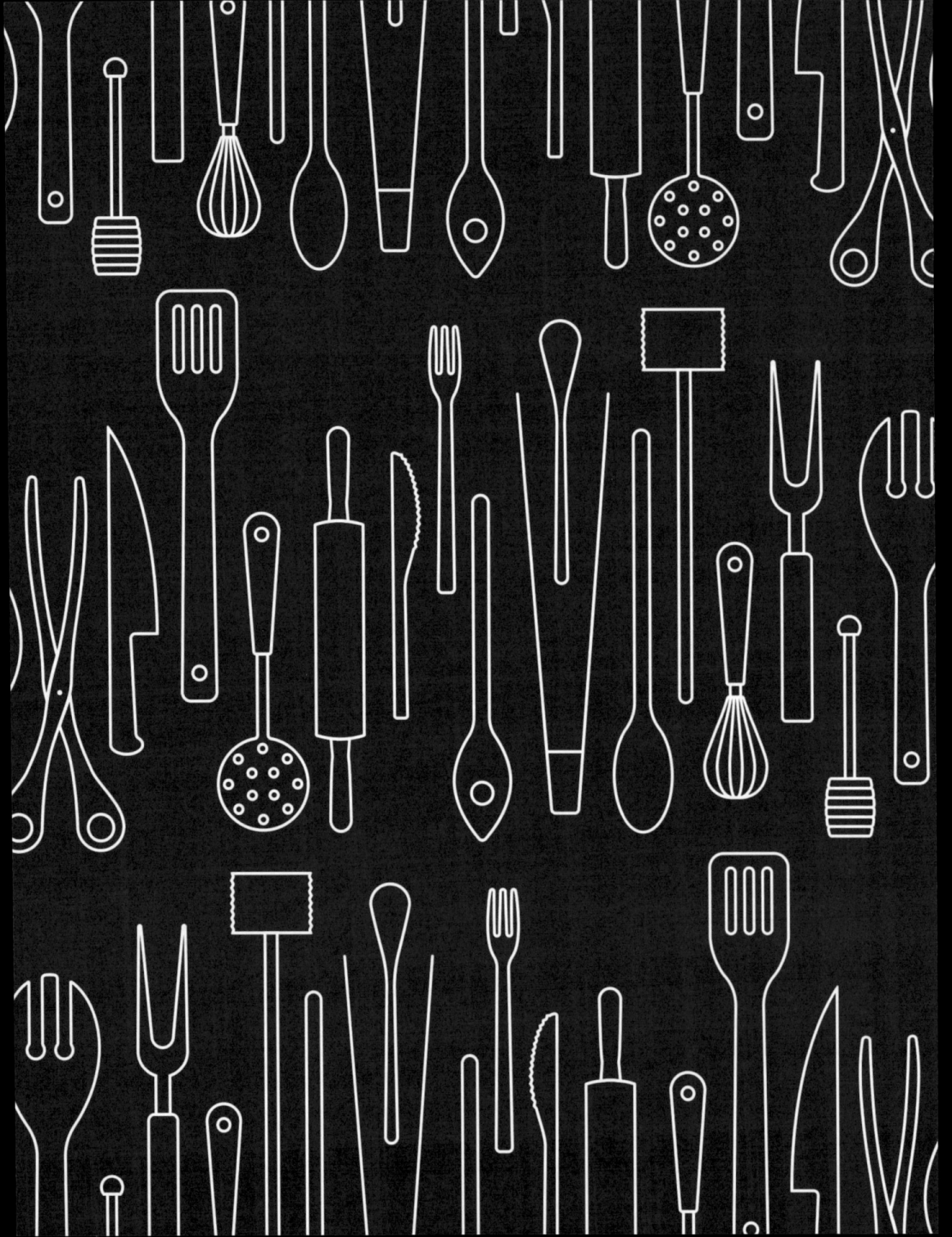

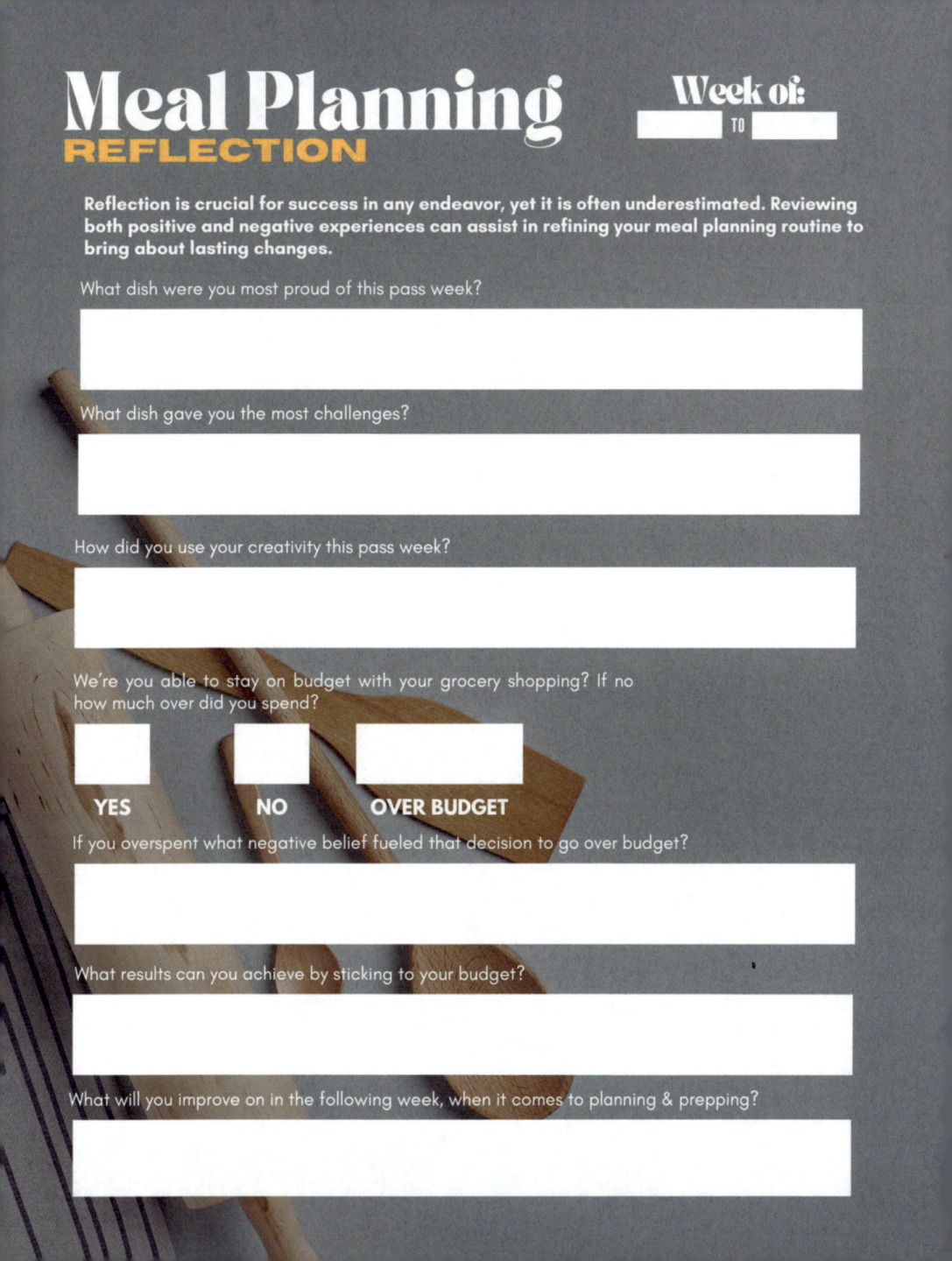

Meal Planning REFLECTION

Week of:
_____ TO _____

Reflection is crucial for success in any endeavor, yet it is often underestimated. Reviewing both positive and negative experiences can assist in refining your meal planning routine to bring about lasting changes.

What dish were you most proud of this pass week?

What dish gave you the most challenges?

How did you use your creativity this pass week?

We're you able to stay on budget with your grocery shopping? If no how much over did you spend?

YES | **NO** | **OVER BUDGET**

If you overspent what negative belief fueled that decision to go over budget?

What results can you achieve by sticking to your budget?

What will you improve on in the following week, when it comes to planning & prepping?

Section THREE

- Avoiding Store Tactics
- Produce Shopping Guide
- Produce In Season
- Storage Guide (Fruits)
- Storage Guide (Vegetables)
- Storage Guide (Proteins & Carbs)
- Shopping Lists
- Events & Parties Planners

This section is dedicated to developing confidence as a shopper.

Avoiding Store TACTICS

Strategic tips for grocery shopping that aim to assist you in steering clear of common store tactics used to promote spending:

PERIMETER SHOPPING:

Stay on the perimeter of the store where fresh food sections like dairy, meat, and bakery are usually located. These tend to be less processed and healthier.

AISLES:

Avoid wandering up and down every aisle. Only go down aisles where you need specific items from your list.

Middle aisles often contain processed and packaged foods that are more likely to be impulse buys.

END CAPS (END OF AISLES):

Be cautious of end caps as they often feature promotional items that are not necessarily on sale or needed.

EYE-LEVEL PRODUCTS:

Manufacturers pay for prime shelf placement. Look at higher or lower shelves for potentially better deals and prices.

BAKERY SECTION:

Fresh bread smell is used to entice buying. Stick to your list and avoid extras unless necessary.

DAIRY SECTION:

Dairy is usually at the back to make you walk through the store. Stick to your list and avoid picking up unnecessary items along the way.

MEAT SECTION:

Check for sales but only buy what you can use before the expiration date or can freeze.

CHECKOUT:

The checkout area is designed for impulse buys. Avoid grabbing candy, magazines, or other small items.

COMPARE UNIT PRICES:

Check the unit price labels to compare costs between different sizes and brands.

AVOID LARGE CARTS:

If you don't need much, use a basket or a smaller cart. Large carts can make you feel like you need to buy more to fill it.

STORE BRANDS:

Store brands are often cheaper and of similar quality to name brands.

COUPONS AND APPS:

Use coupons wisely. Don't buy something just because you have a coupon. Check store apps for digital coupons and discounts.

REVIEW RECEIPTS:

Check your receipt for any errors and ensure you were charged correctly, especially for sale items.

Produce
SHOPPING GUIDE

DIRTY DOZEN

The Environmental Working Group (EWG) has created a list that ranks fruits and vegetables according to their pesticide residue levels. It is advisable to purchase organic versions of these products.

- Strawberries **(Most contaminated)**
- Spinach
- Kale, Collard, and Mustard Greens
- Peaches
- Pears
- Nectarines
- Apples
- Grapes
- Bell and Hot Peppers
- Cherries
- Blueberries
- Green Beans

PLU (PRICE LOOK-UP) CODES

Understanding these codes enables you to make informed decisions about the produce you buy, aligning with your preferences for organic, conventional, or GMO foods.

CONVENTIONALLY GROWN PRODUCE

- These items have a 4-digit code that starts with a 3 or 4.
- Example: A conventionally grown apple might have a PLU code like 4131 or 4011.

ORGANIC PRODUCE

- These items have a 5-digit code that starts with a 9.
- Example: An organic apple might have a PLU code like 94131 or 94011.

GENETICALLY MODIFIED PRODUCE (GMO)

- These items have a 5-digit code that starts with an 8.
- Example: A genetically modified apple might have a PLU code like 84131 or 84011.
- Note: This system for identifying GMOs is not commonly used in retail settings, and GMO produce is often not labeled as such.

KEY POINTS

- Look for the 9: For organic produce, always look for a 5-digit code beginning with 9.
- Beware of the 8: While less common in retail, a 5-digit code starting with 8 indicates genetically modified produce.
- Common 4-Digit Codes: Most conventional produce will have a simple 4-digit code.

Storage GUIDE FRUITS

APPLES
- Whole Lifespan: 4-6 weeks
- Cut Lifespan: 3-5 days

Storage:
- Whole: Store in the refrigerator crisper drawer.
- Cut: Store in an airtight container or plastic bag with a splash of lemon juice to prevent browning.

BANANAS
- Whole Lifespan: 2-7 days (at room temperature)
- Cut Lifespan: 1-2 days

Storage:
- Whole: Store at room temperature. Refrigerate when ripe to extend freshness.
- Cut: Store in an airtight container with a splash of lemon juice to prevent browning.

BERRIES (STRAWBERRIES, BLUEBERRIES, RASPBERRIES, BLACKBERRIES)
- Whole Lifespan: 3-7 days
- Cut Lifespan: 1-3 days

Storage:
- Whole: Store unwashed in a breathable container or the original packaging in the refrigerator.
- Cut: Store in an airtight container lined with a paper towel.

GRAPES
- Whole Lifespan: 1-2 weeks
- Cut Lifespan: 3-5 days

Storage:
- Whole: Store in a breathable bag or the original packaging in the refrigerator.
- Cut: Store in an airtight container.

CITRUS FRUITS (ORANGES, LEMONS, LIMES, GRAPEFRUITS)
- Whole Lifespan: 3-4 weeks
- Cut Lifespan: 3-4 days

Storage:
- Whole: Store in the refrigerator crisper drawer.
- Cut: Store in an airtight container or wrapped in plastic wrap.

PINEAPPLE
- Whole Lifespan: 1-2 weeks (at room temperature)
- Cut Lifespan: 3-5 days

Storage:
- Whole: Store at room temperature until ripe, then refrigerate.
- Cut: Store in an airtight container.

MELONS (WATERMELON, CANTALOUPE, HONEYDEW)
- Whole Lifespan: 1-2 weeks (at room temperature)
- Cut Lifespan: 3-5 days

Storage:
- Whole: Store at room temperature until ripe, then refrigerate.
- Cut: Store in an airtight container.

MANGOES
- Whole Lifespan: 1 week (at room temperature)
- Cut Lifespan: 3-5 days

Storage:
- Whole: Store at room temperature until ripe, then refrigerate.
- Cut: Store in an airtight container.

PEACHES, PLUMS, AND NECTARINES
- Whole Lifespan: 3-5 days (at room temperature)
- Cut Lifespan: 3-4 days

Storage:
- Whole: Store at room temperature until ripe, then refrigerate.
- Cut: Store in an airtight container.

KIWIS
- Whole Lifespan: 1-2 weeks
- Cut Lifespan: 3-4 days

Storage:
- Whole: Store in the refrigerator crisper drawer.
- Cut: Store in an airtight container.

CHERRIES
- Whole Lifespan: 5-7 days
- Cut Lifespan: 1-2 days

Storage:
- Whole: Store unwashed in an airtight container or the original packaging in the refrigerator.
- Cut: Store in an airtight container.

PEARS
- Whole Lifespan: 1-2 weeks (at room temperature)
- Cut Lifespan: 3-5 days

Storage:
- Whole: Store at room temperature until ripe, then refrigerate.
- Cut: Store in an airtight container with a splash of lemon juice to prevent browning.

Storage GUIDE VEGETABLES

Cooked Vegetables: Good for 3-4 days stored in an airtight container in the refrigerator.

CARROTS
- Whole Lifespan: Up to 3-4 weeks
- Cut Lifespan: 1-2 weeks
- **Storage:**
- Whole: Store in a plastic bag in the crisper drawer. Remove tops if they have them to prevent moisture loss.
- Cut: Store in a sealed container or plastic bag with a damp paper towel.

PEPPERS (GREEN, RED, YELLOW, ORANGE)
- Whole Lifespan: 1-2 weeks
- Cut Lifespan: 3-5 days
- **Storage:**
- Whole: Store in a plastic bag in the crisper drawer.
- Cut: Store in a sealed container or plastic bag.

BROCCOLI
- Whole Lifespan: 1-2 weeks
- Cut Lifespan: 2-3 days
- **Storage:**
- Whole: Store in a breathable bag or wrap in a damp paper towel and place in a plastic bag in the crisper drawer.
- Cut: Store in a sealed container or plastic bag.

CAULIFLOWER
- Whole Lifespan: 2-3 weeks
- Cut Lifespan: 1-2 weeks
- **Storage:**
- Whole: Store in a plastic bag or loosely wrapped in plastic in the crisper drawer.
- Cut: Store in a sealed container or plastic bag.

SPINACH/LETTUCE
- Whole Lifespan: 5-7 days
- Cut Lifespan: 3-5 days
- **Storage:**
- Store in a breathable bag or container with a paper towel to absorb excess moisture.

CUCUMBERS
- Whole Lifespan: 1 week
- Cut Lifespan: 1-2 days
- **Storage:**
- Whole: Store in the crisper drawer of the refrigerator.
- Cut: Store in a sealed container or plastic bag with a damp paper towel.

AVOCADO
- Cut Lifespan: 1-2 days
- **Storage:** Store in an airtight container in the refrigerator. To prevent browning, sprinkle with lemon or lime juice.

SQUASH (E.G, ZUCCHINI, YELLOW SQUASH)
- Whole Lifespan: 1-2 weeks
- Cut Lifespan: 3-4 days
- **Storage:**
- Whole: Store in a plastic bag in the crisper drawer.
- Cut: Store in a sealed container or plastic bag.

ONIONS
- Whole Lifespan: 1-2 months
- Cut Lifespan: 7-10 days
- **Storage:**
- Whole: Store in a cool, dry, well-ventilated place. Avoid storing in plastic bags as they can trap moisture and cause spoilage.
- Cut: Store in an airtight container or tightly wrapped in plastic wrap or aluminum foil in the refrigerator.

CELERY
- Whole Lifespan: 2-3 weeks
- Cut Lifespan: 1-2 weeks
- **Storage:**
- Whole: Wrap in aluminum foil and place in the crisper drawer.
- Cut: Store in a sealed container with water.

CABBAGE
- Whole Lifespan: 1-2 months
- Cut Lifespan: 1-2 weeks
- **Storage:**
- Whole: Store in a plastic bag in the crisper drawer.
- Cut: Store in a sealed container or plastic bag.

TOMATOES
- Whole Lifespan: 1 week (better at room temperature if not fully ripe)
- Cut Lifespan: 2-3 days
- **Storage:**
- Whole: Store at room temperature until ripe, then refrigerate if necessary.
- Cut: Store in a sealed container.

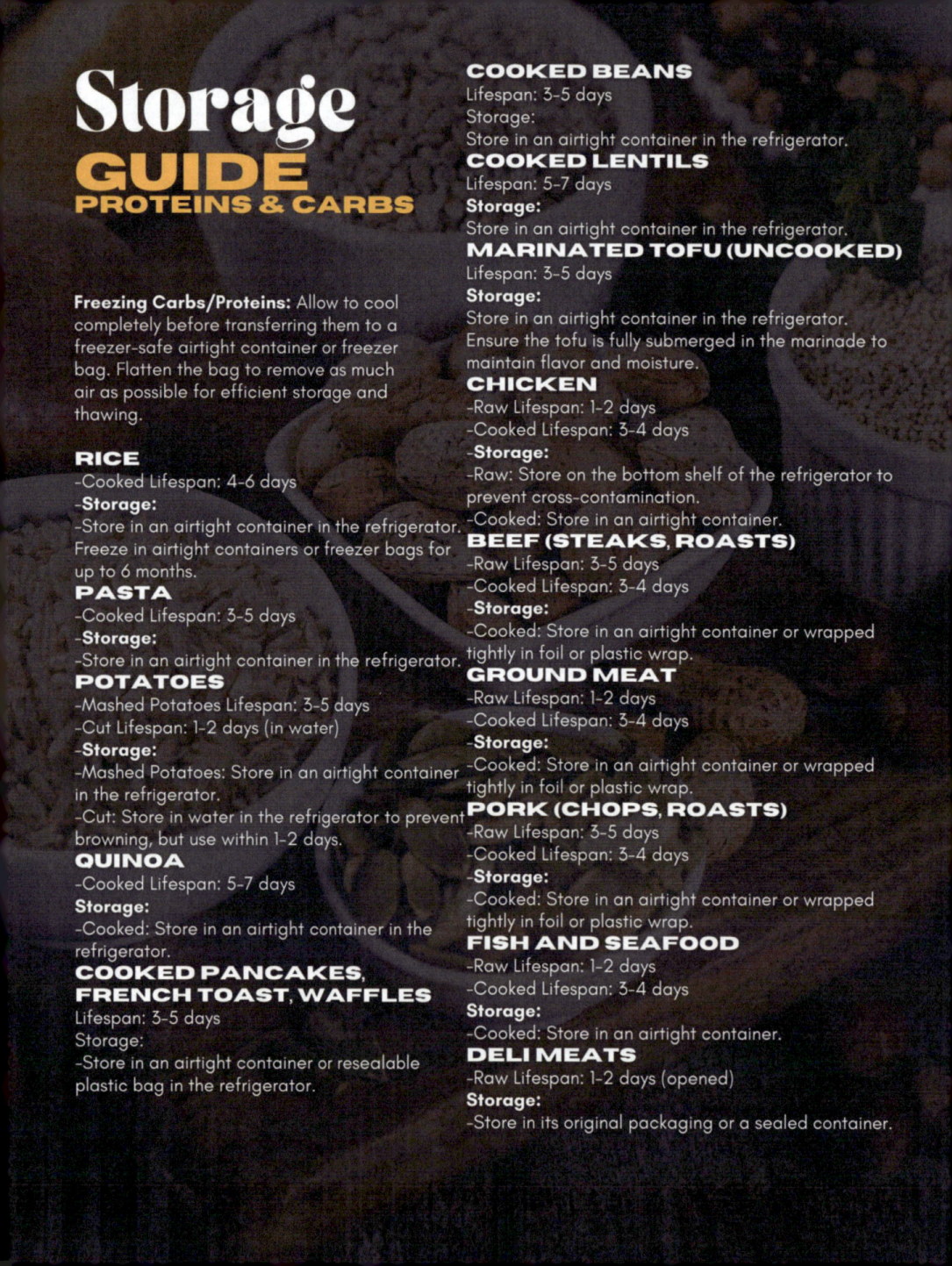

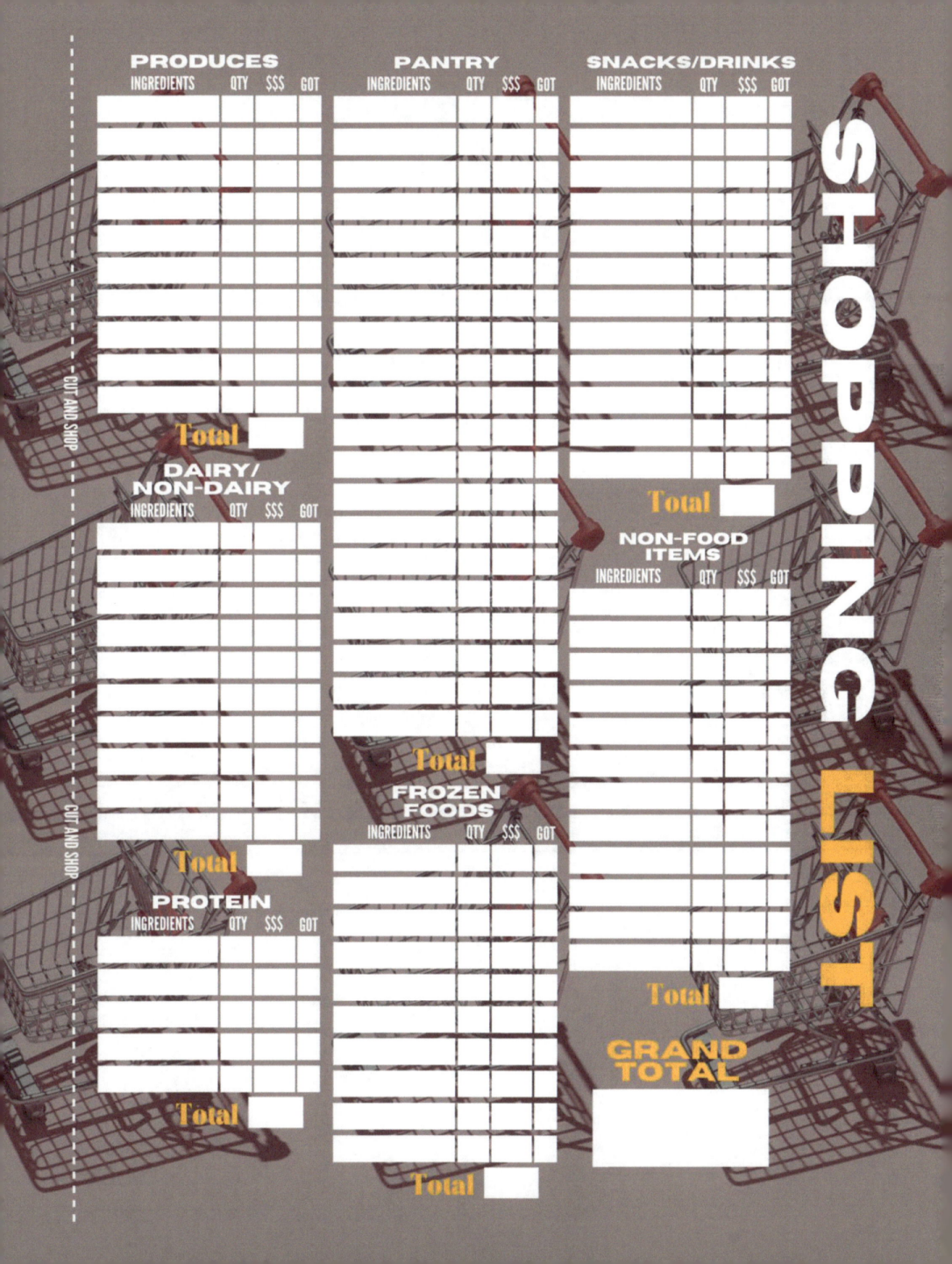

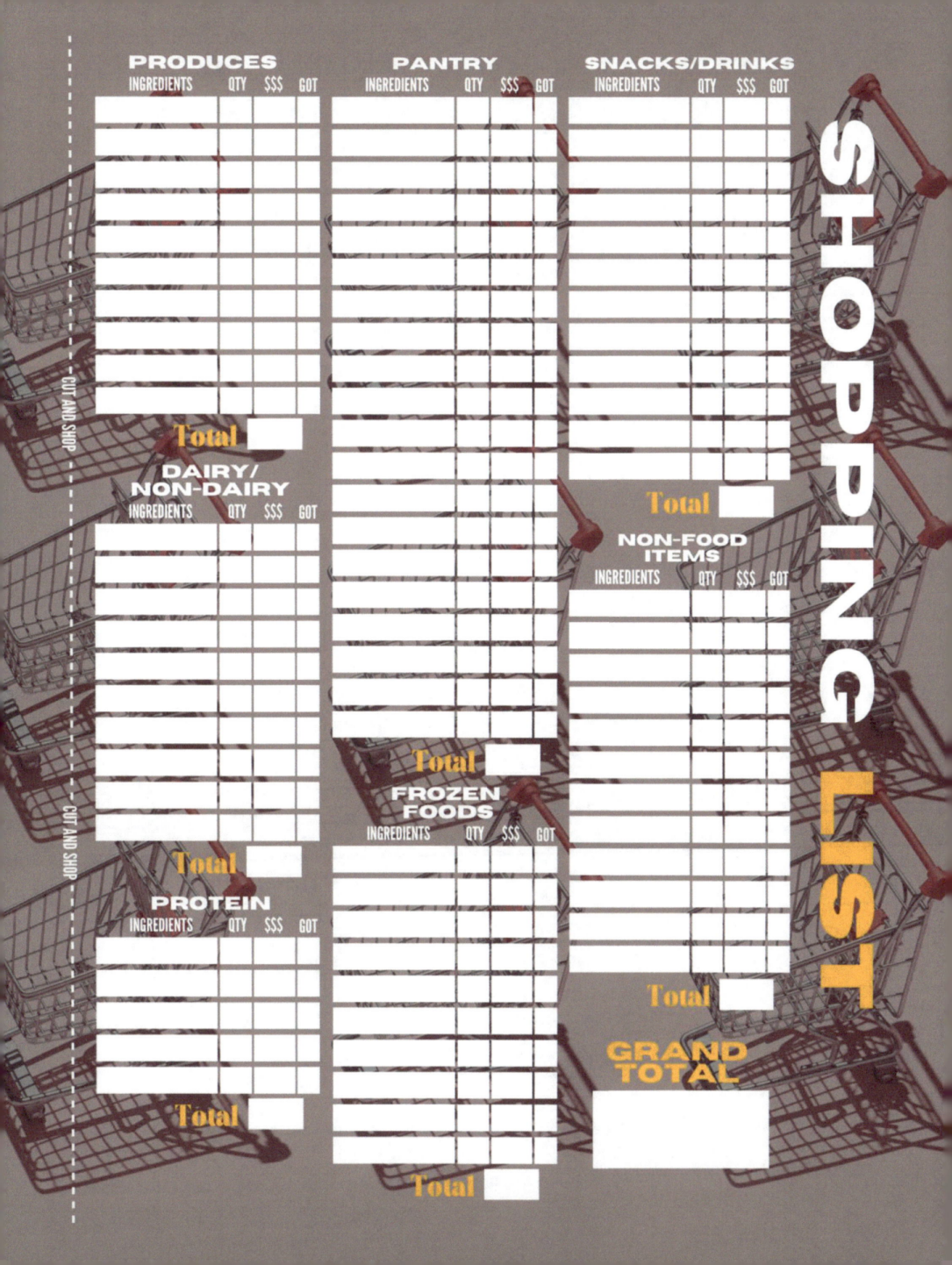

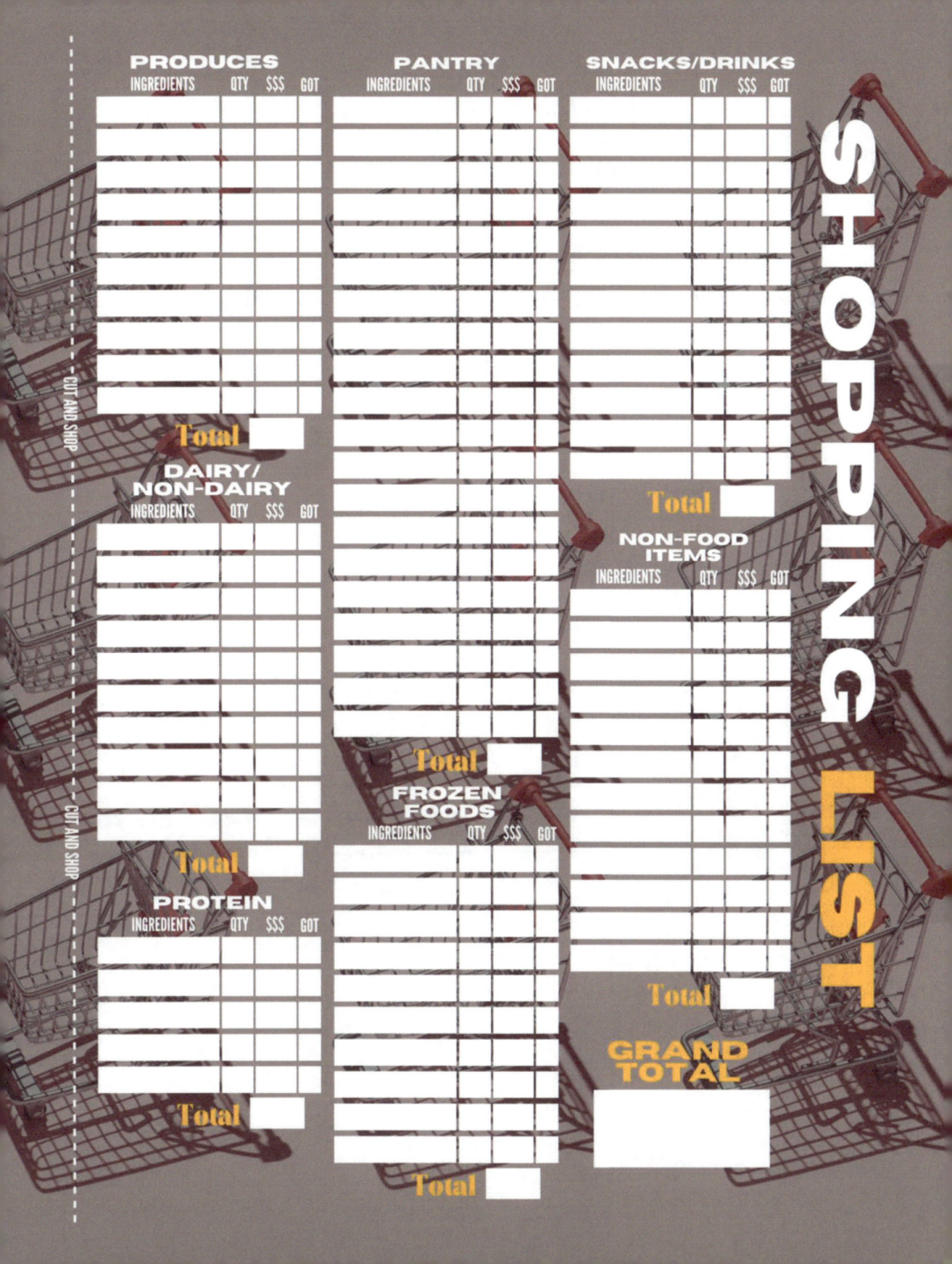

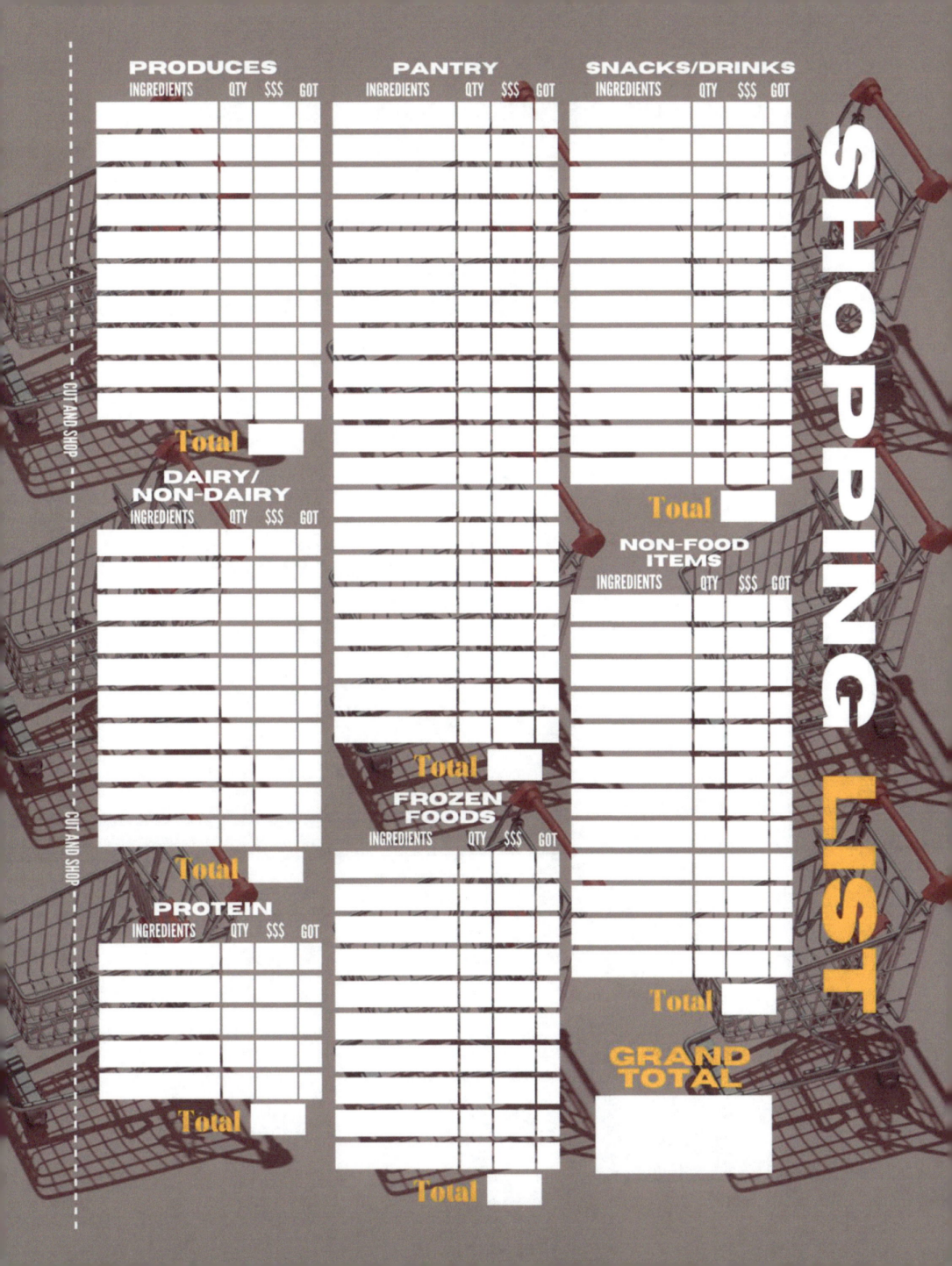

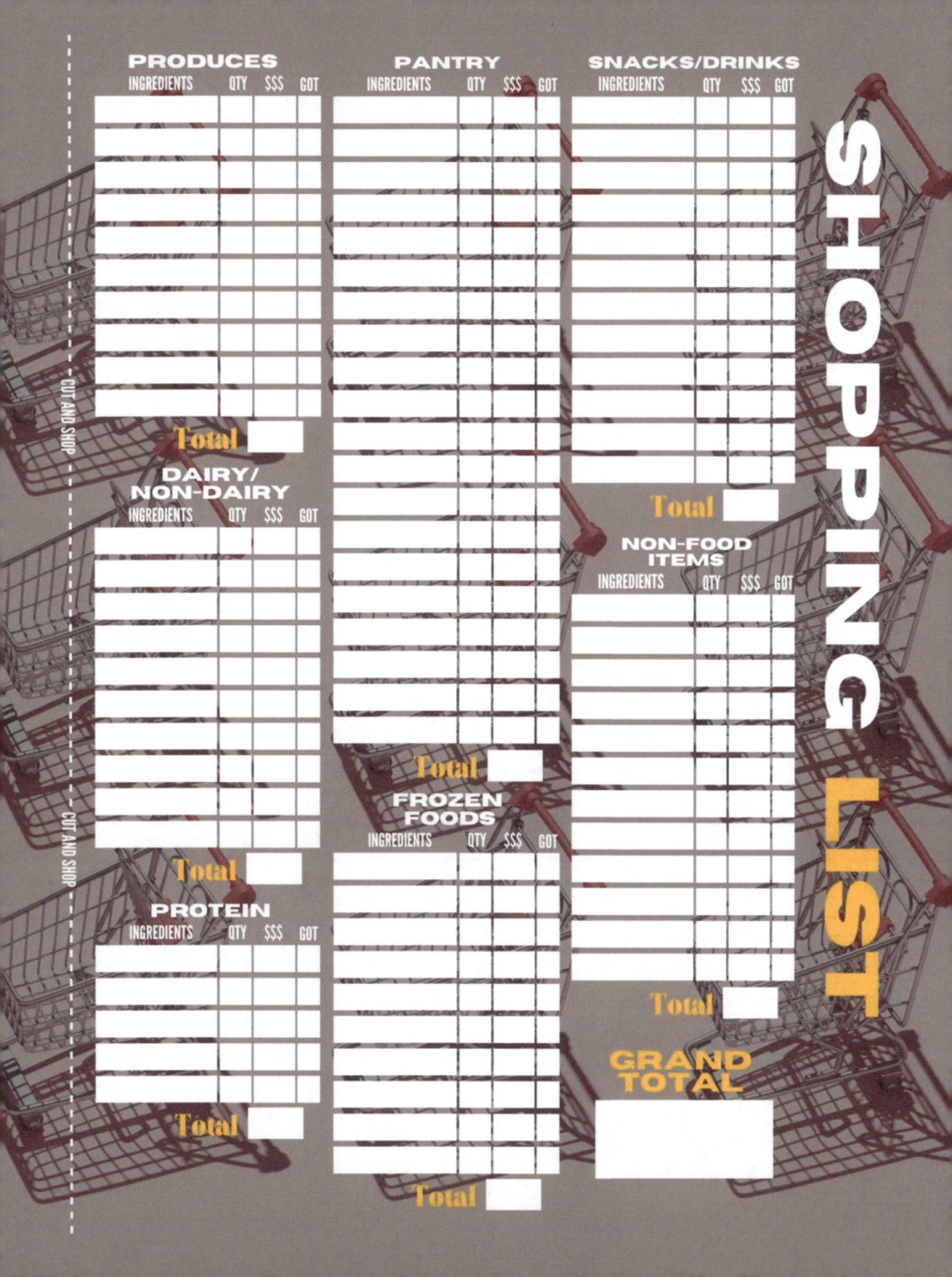

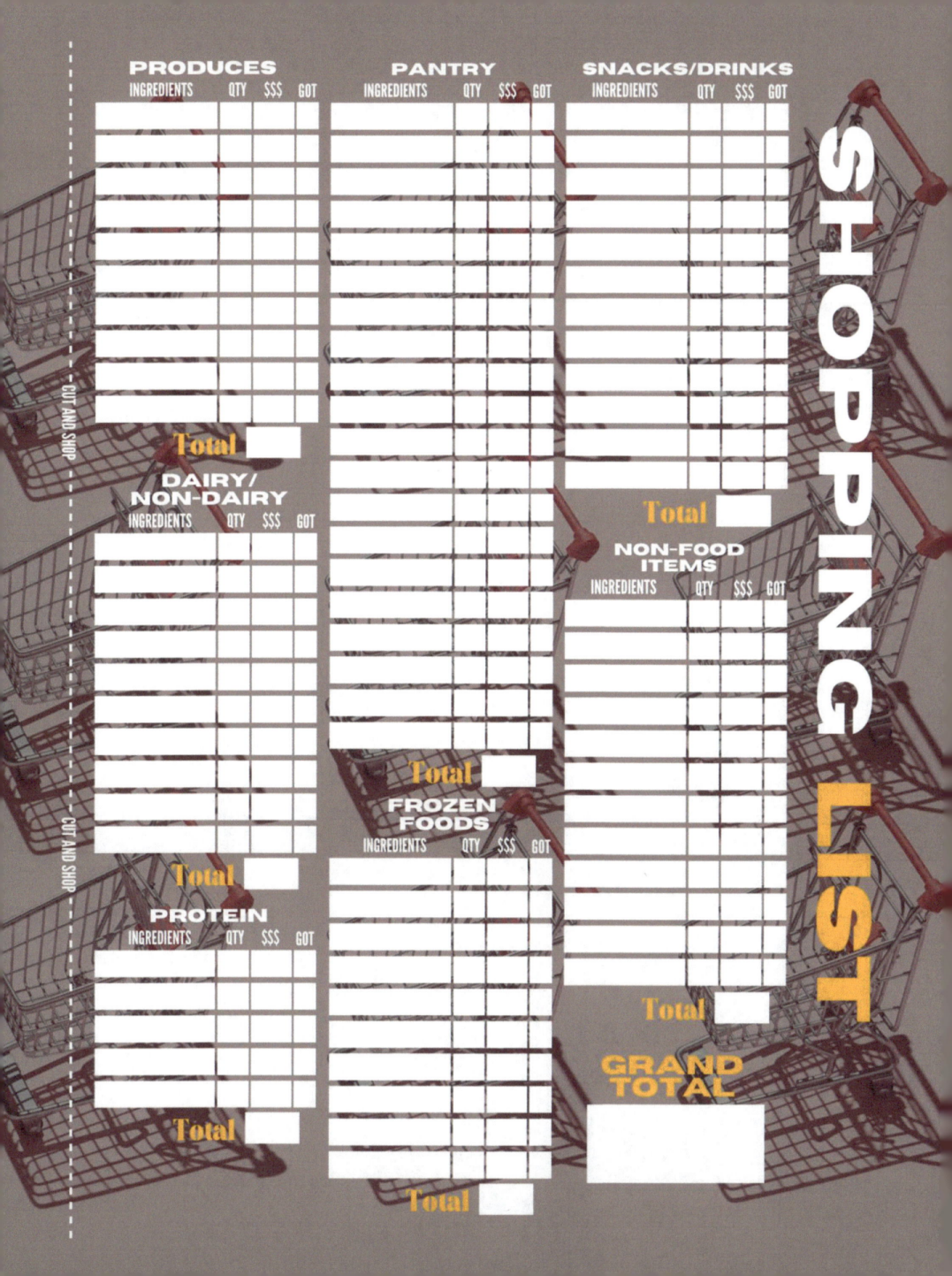

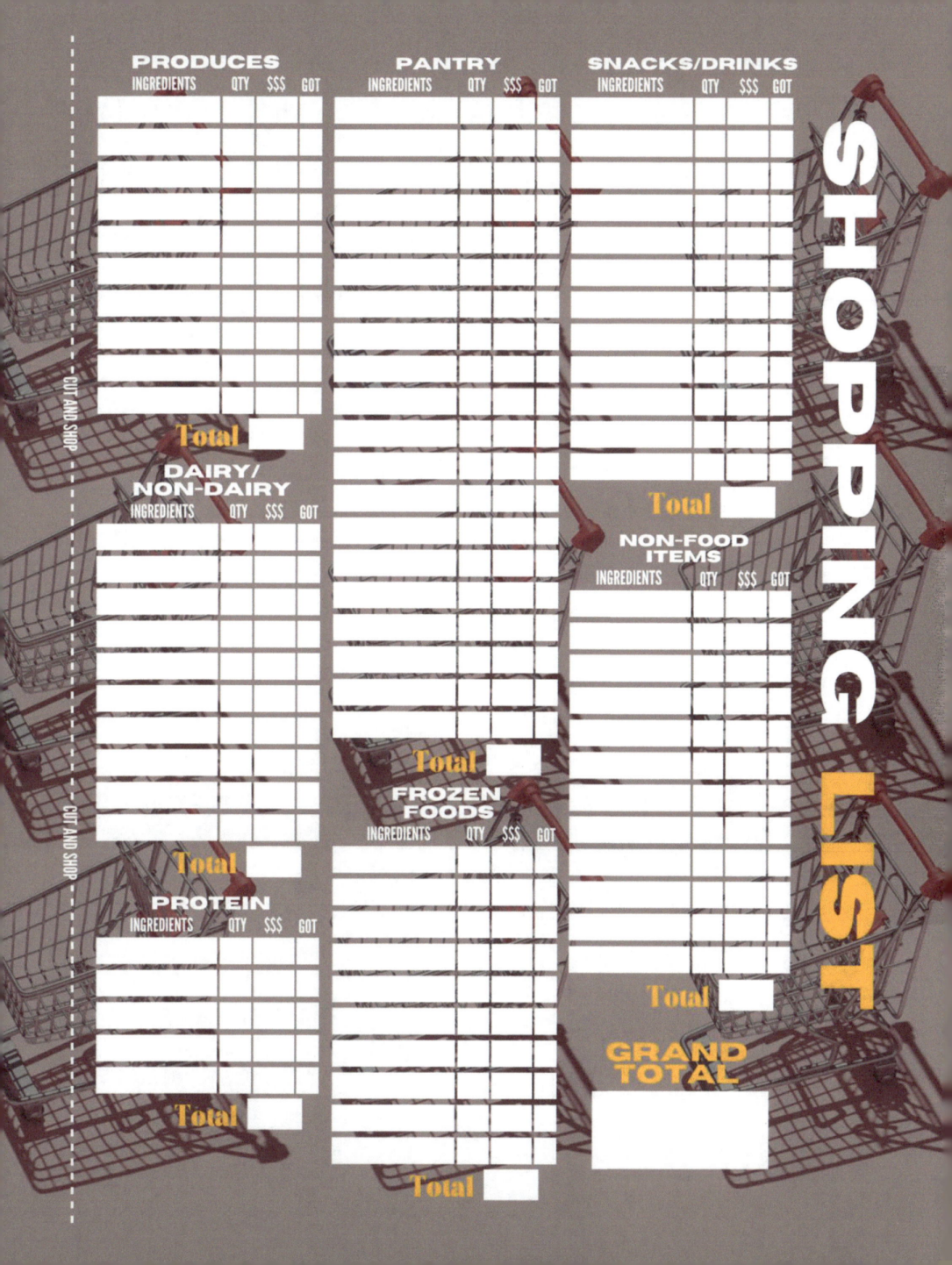

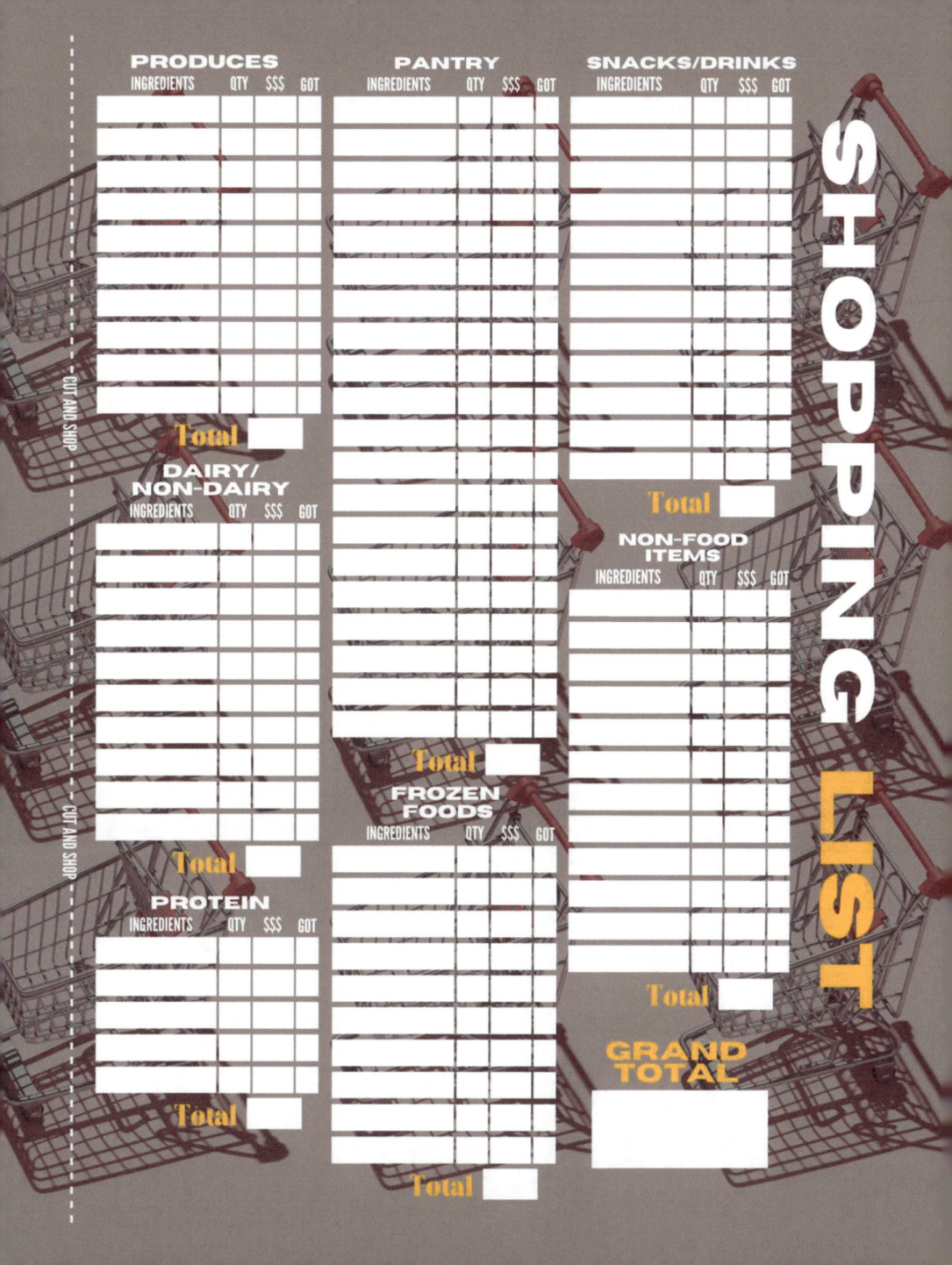

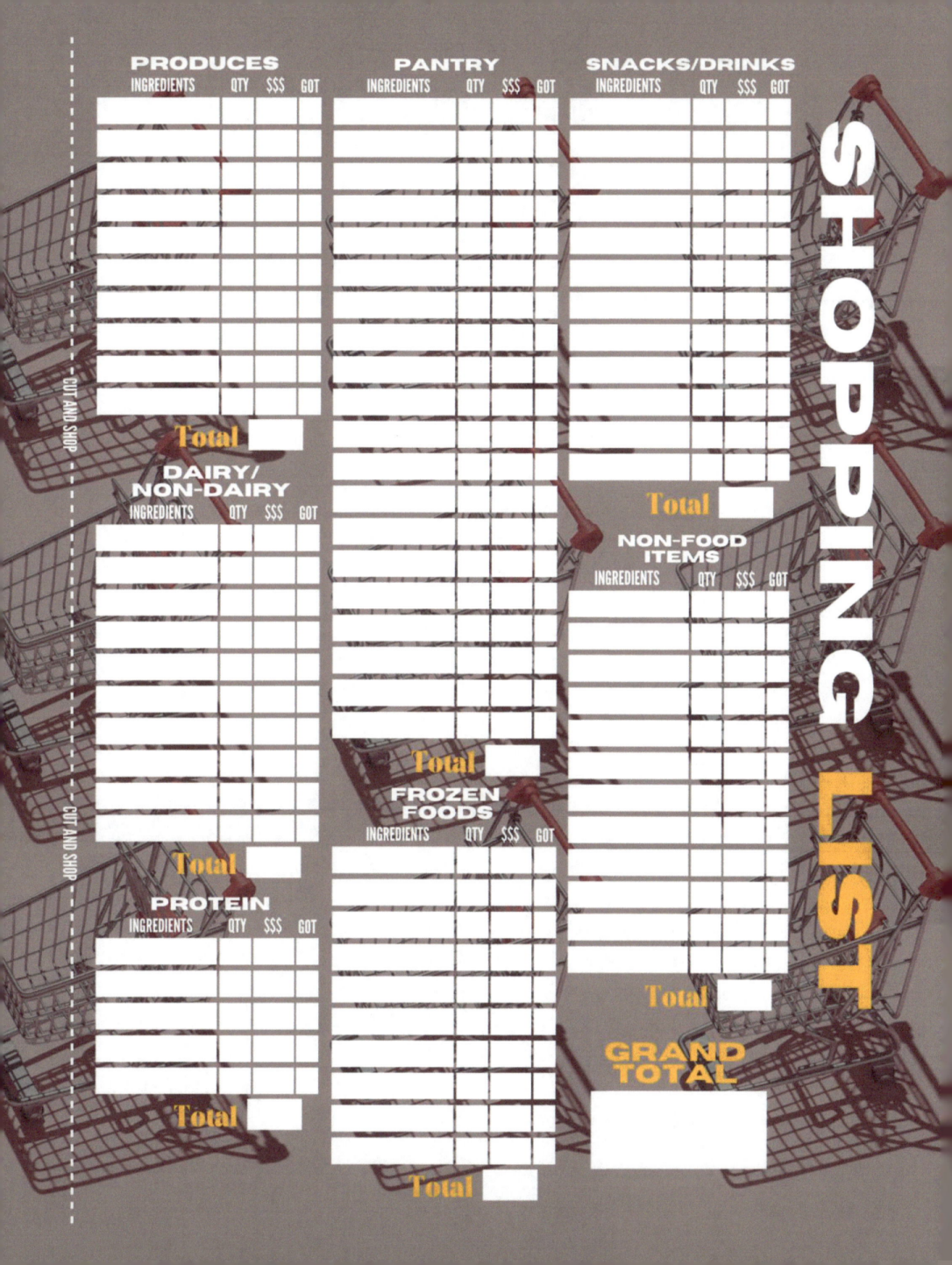

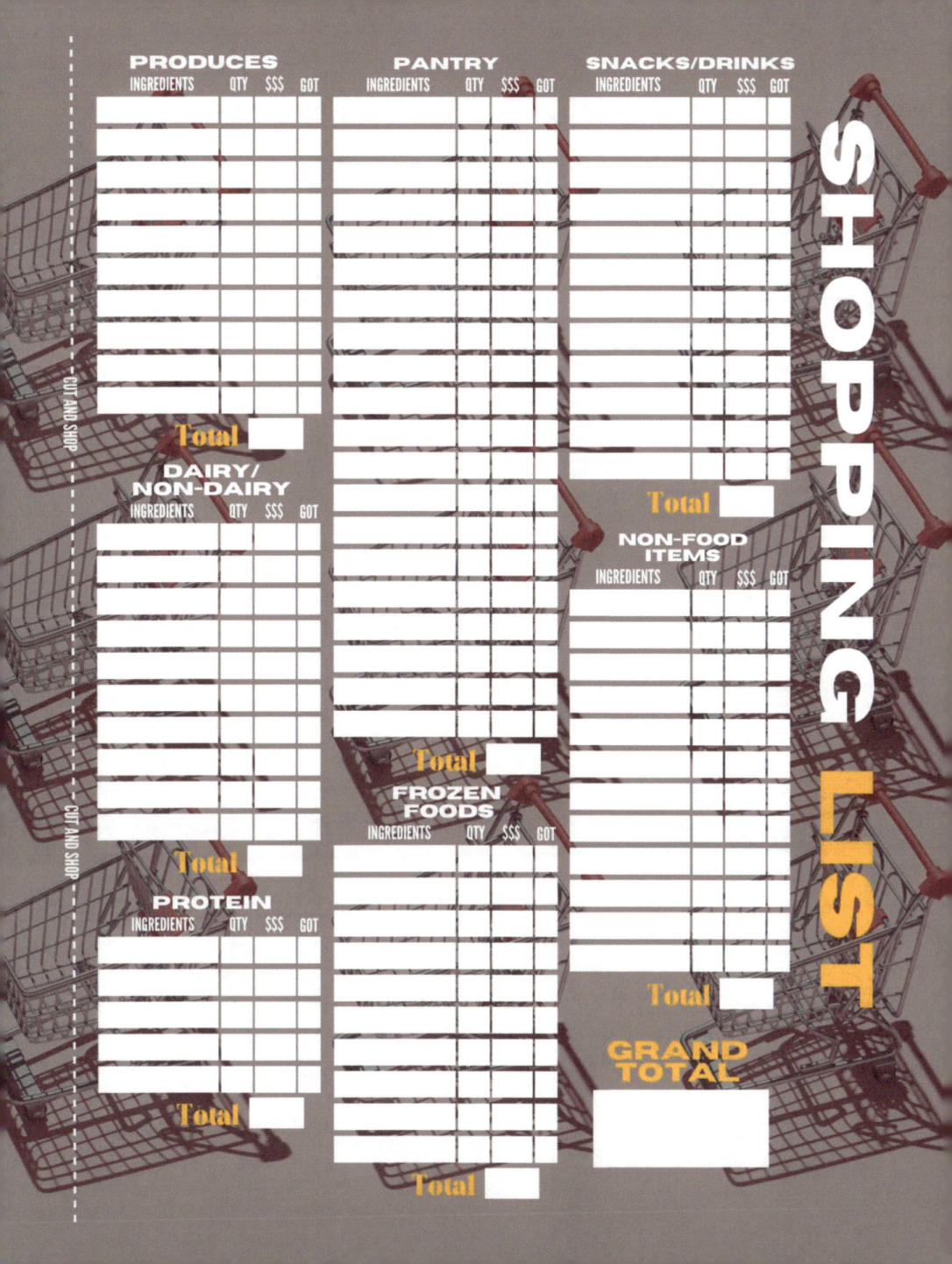

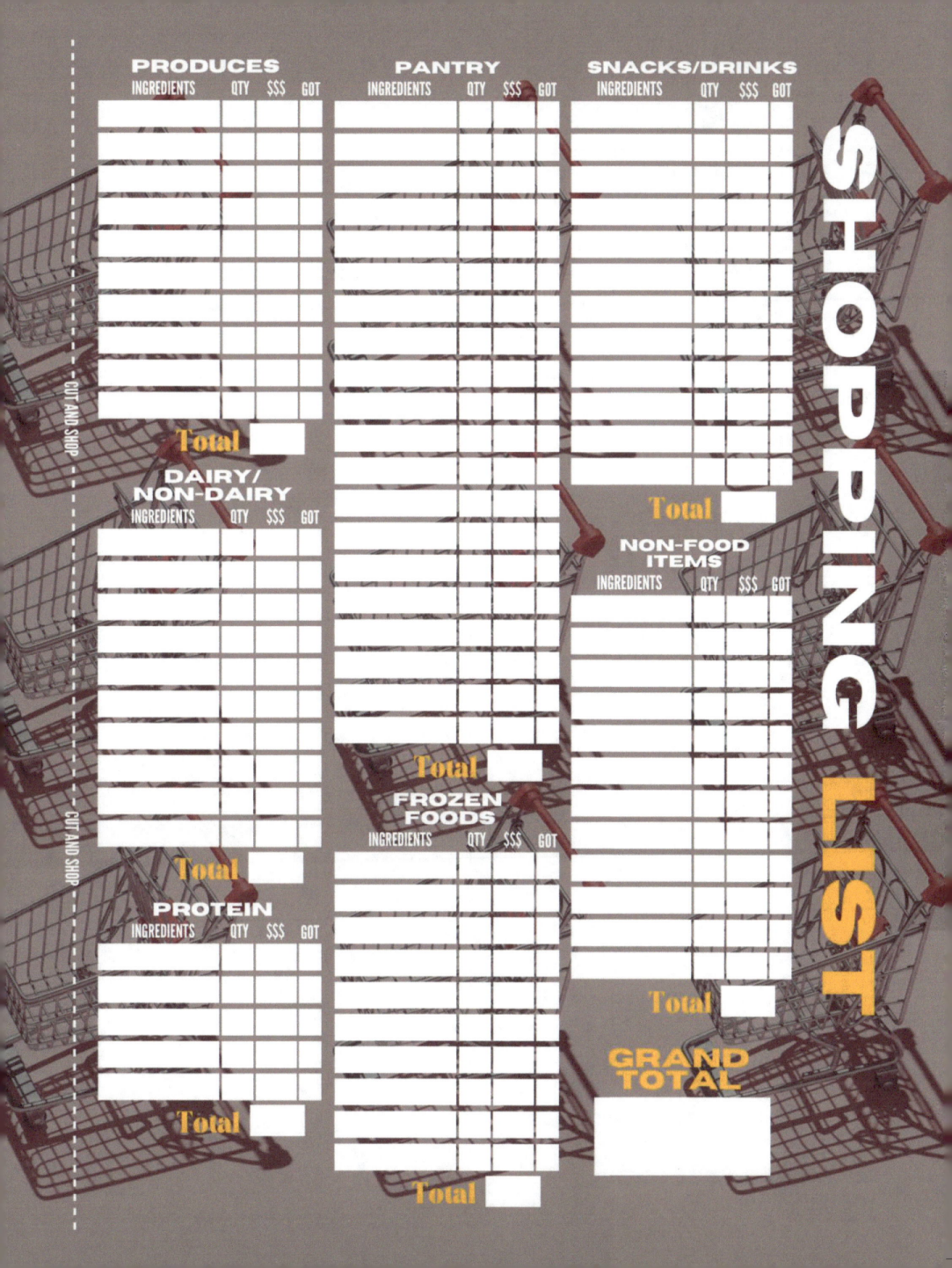

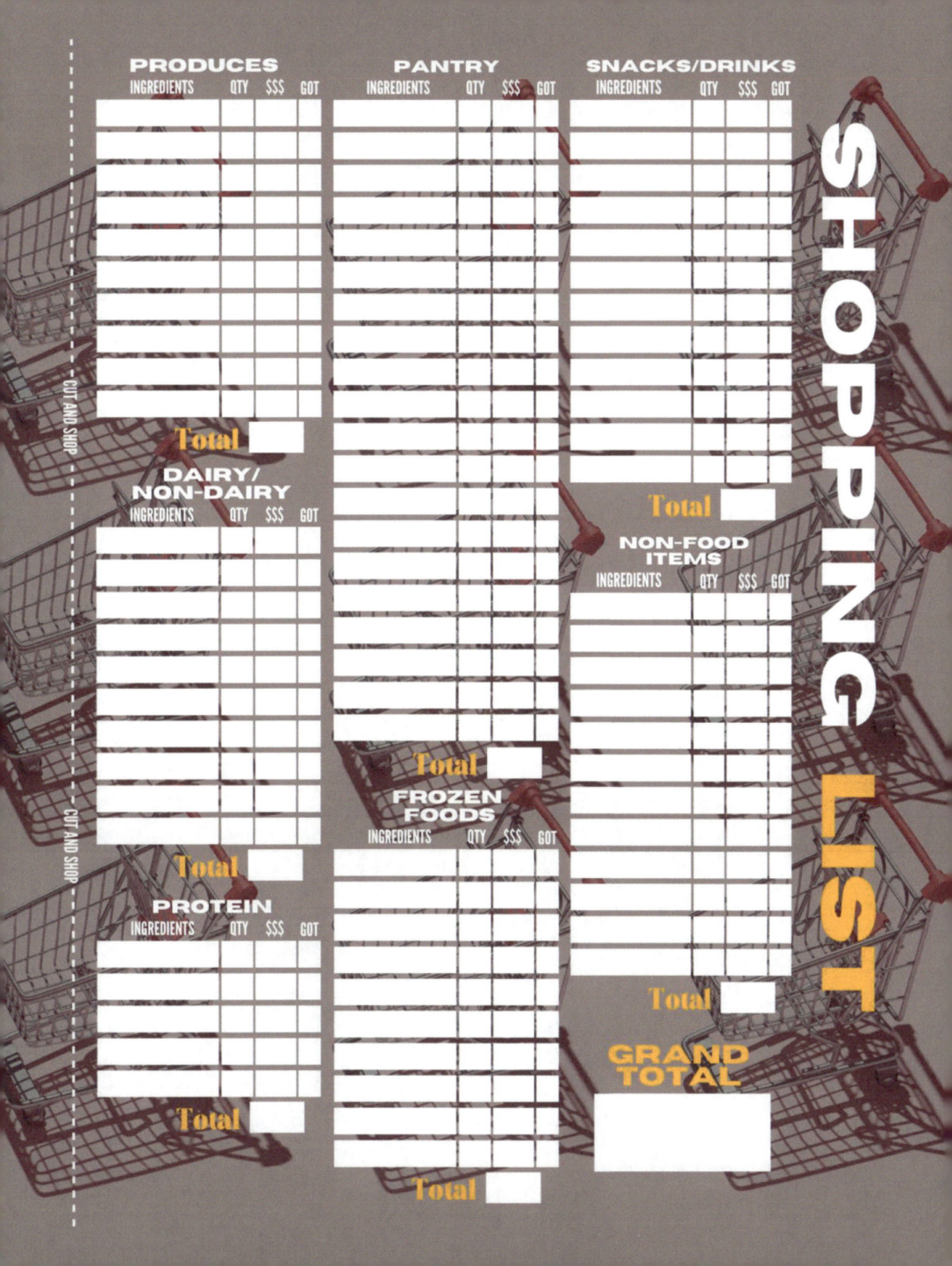

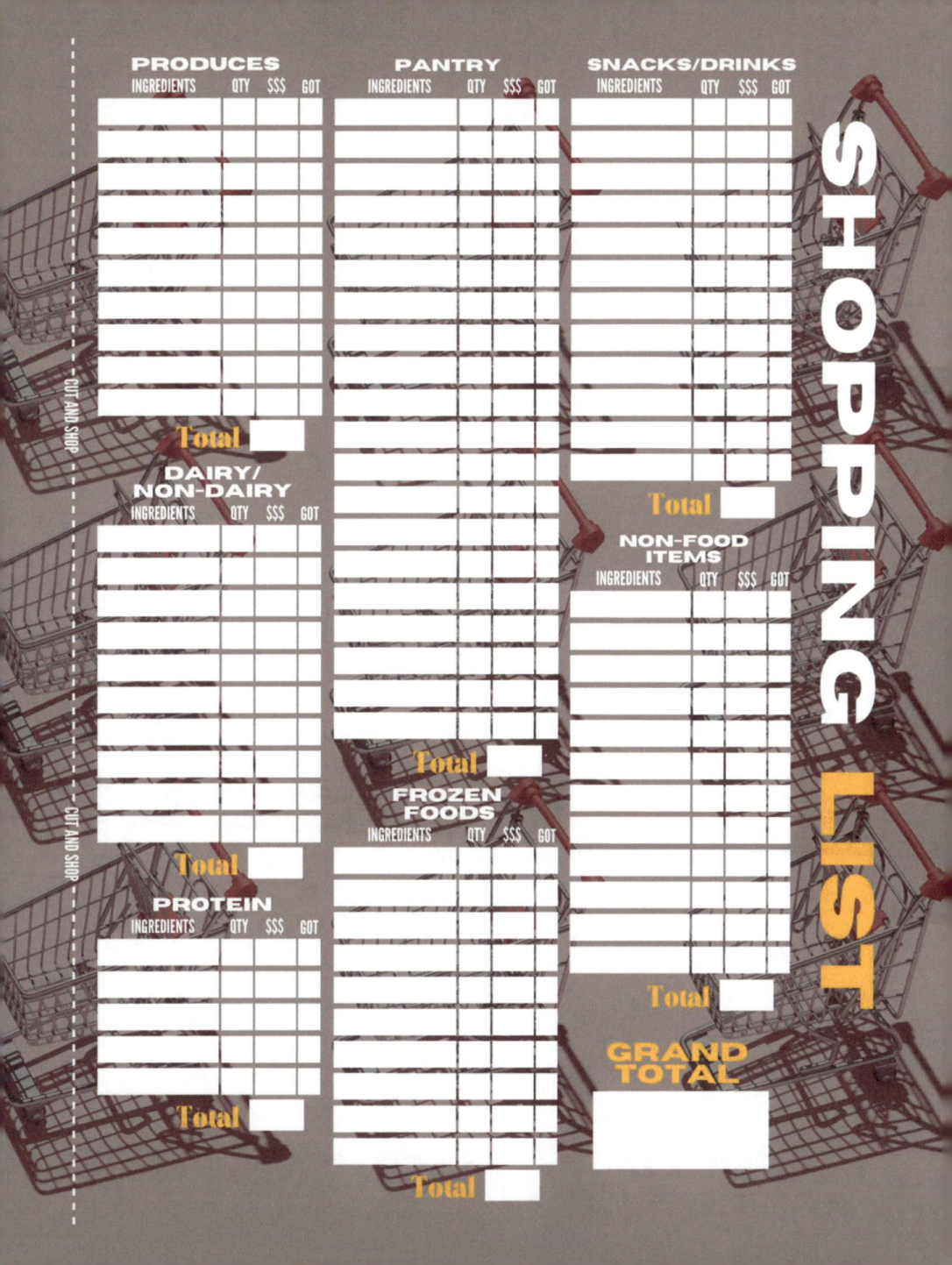

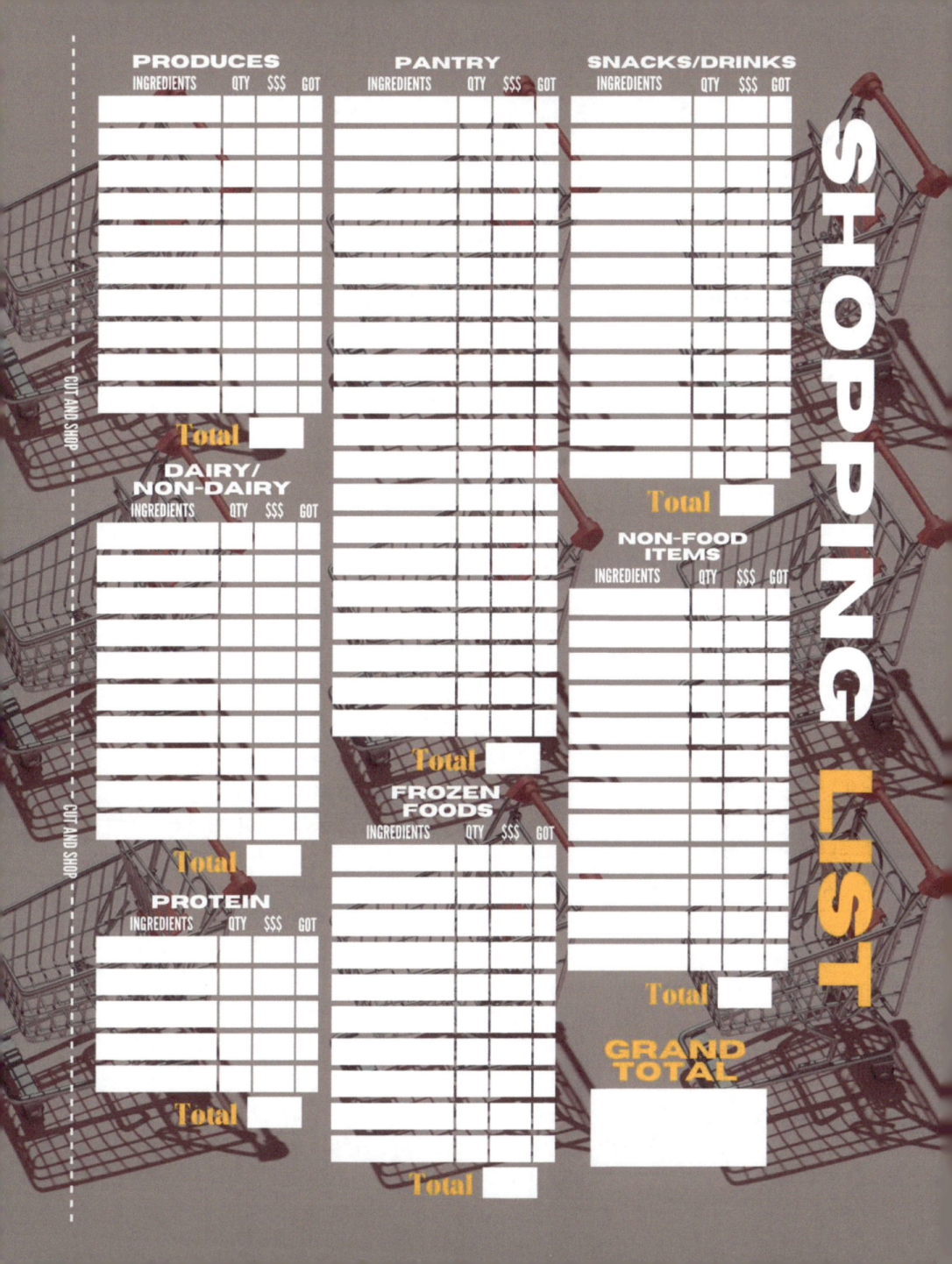

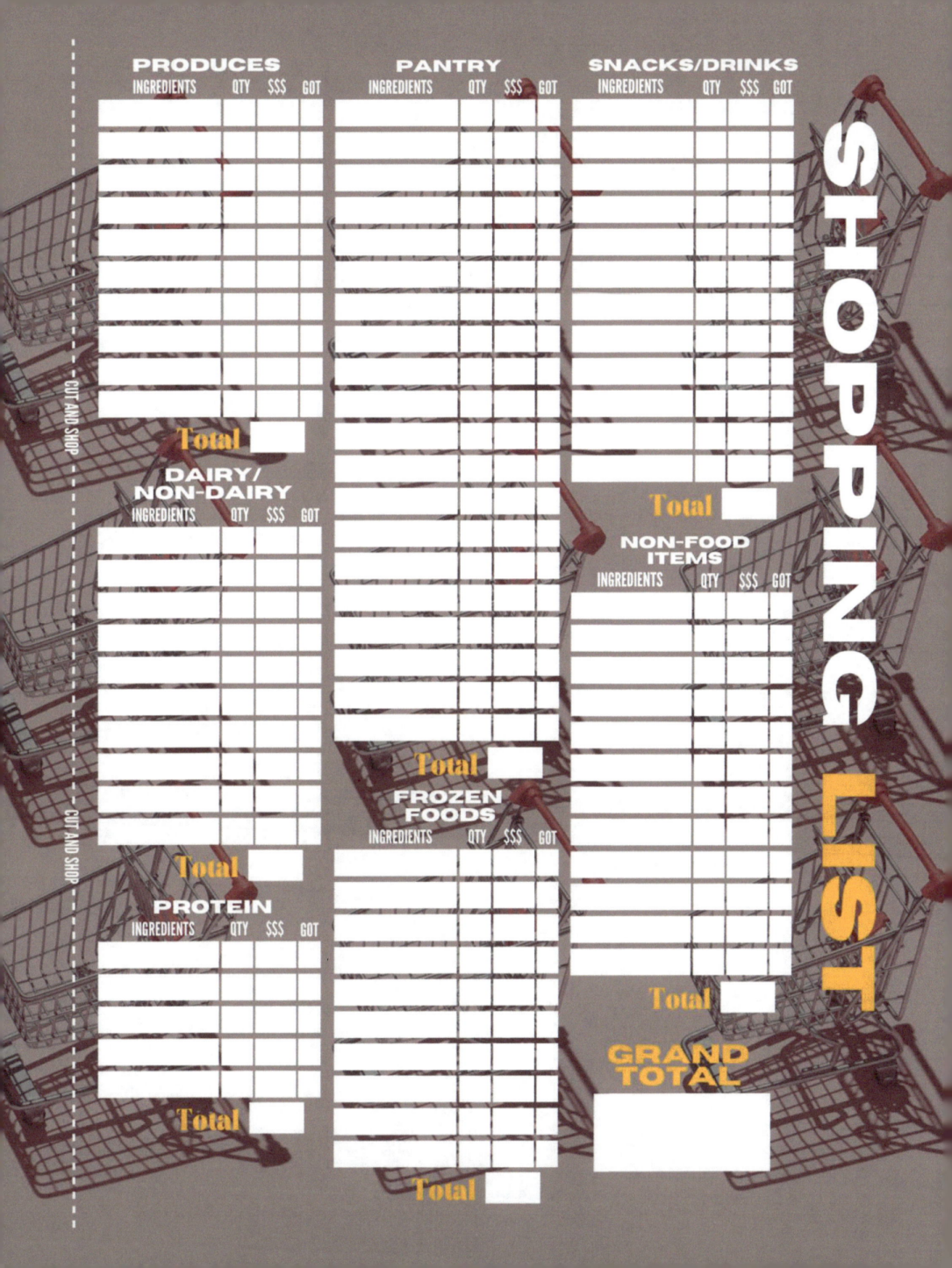

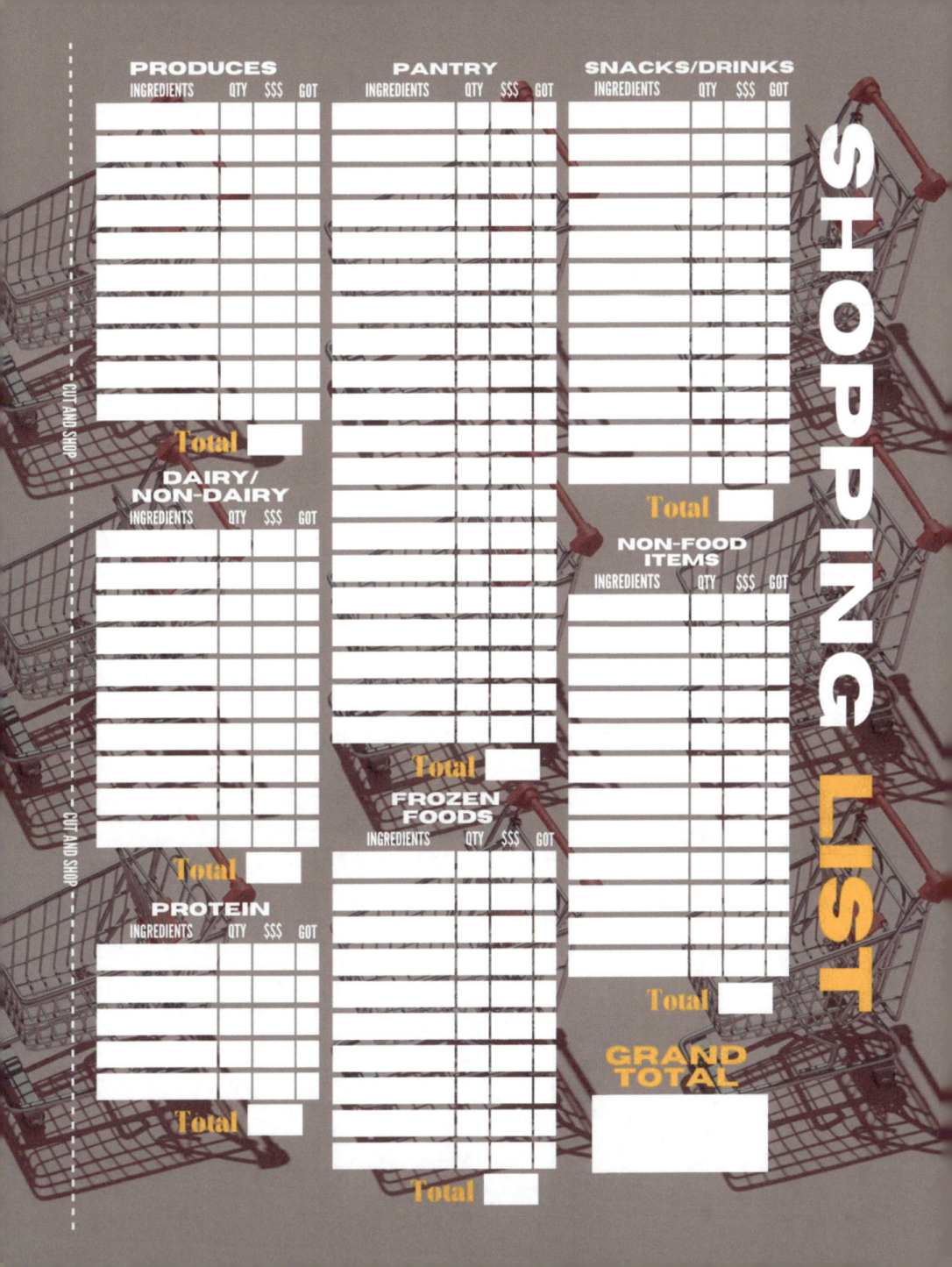

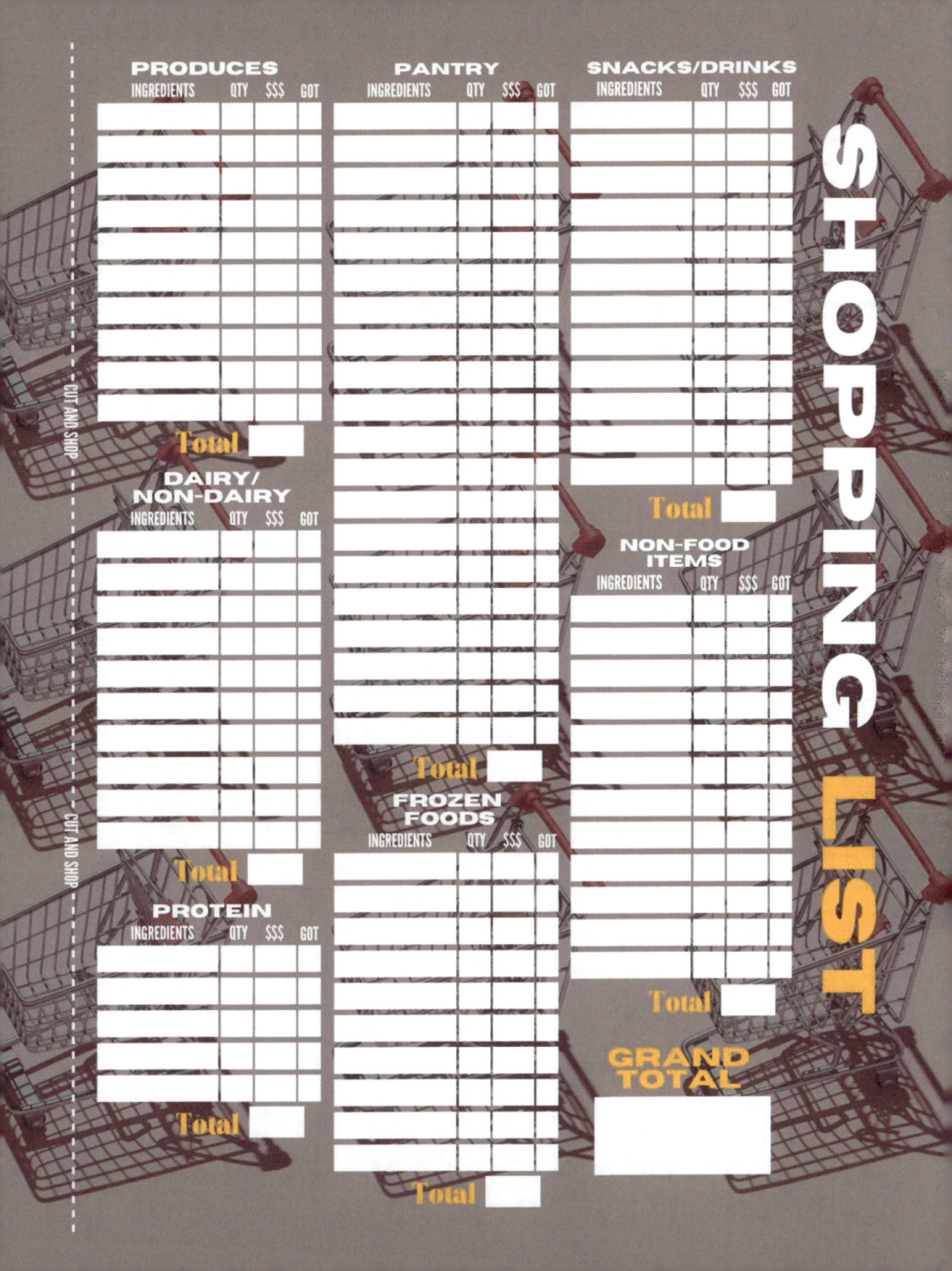

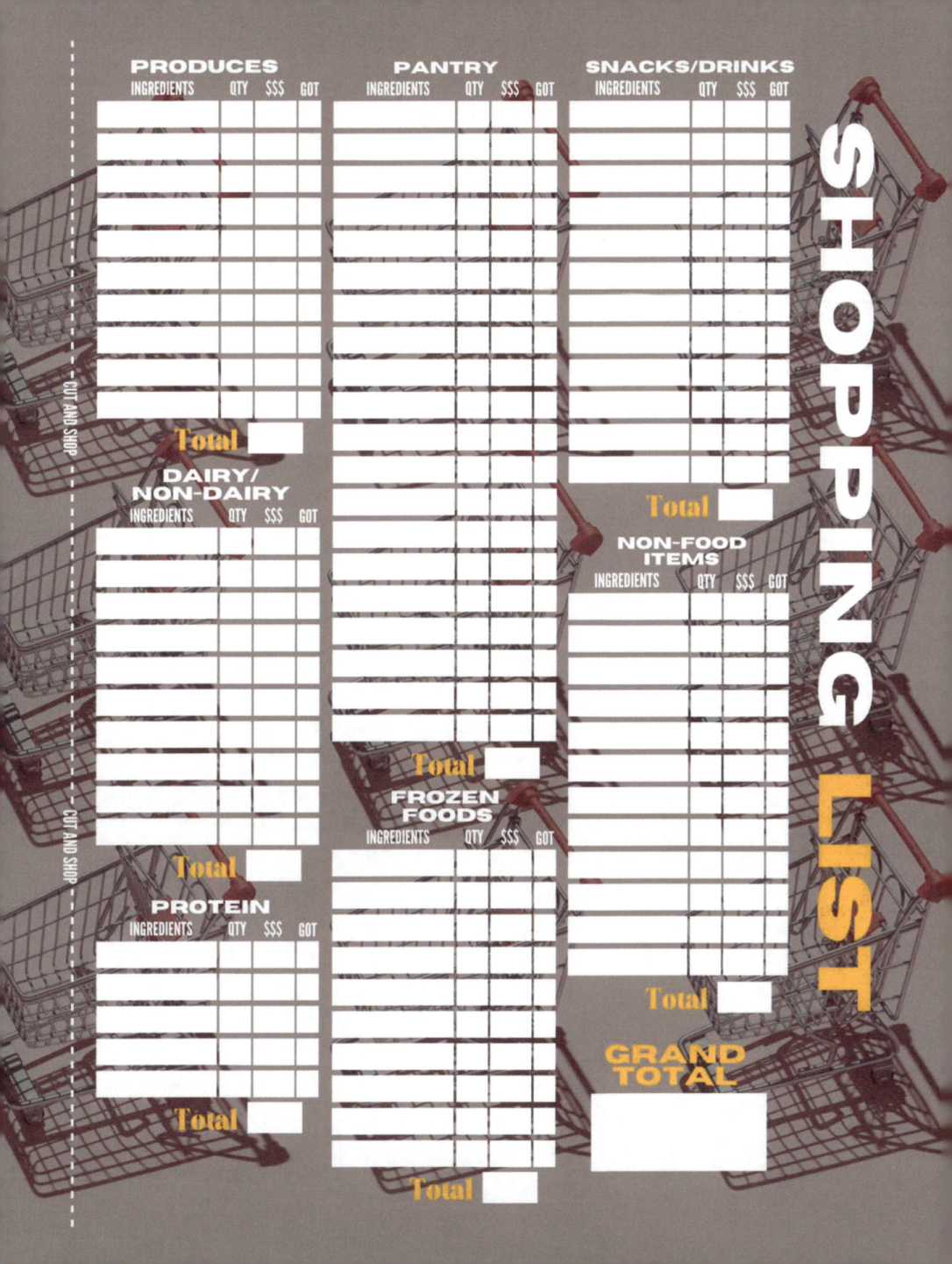

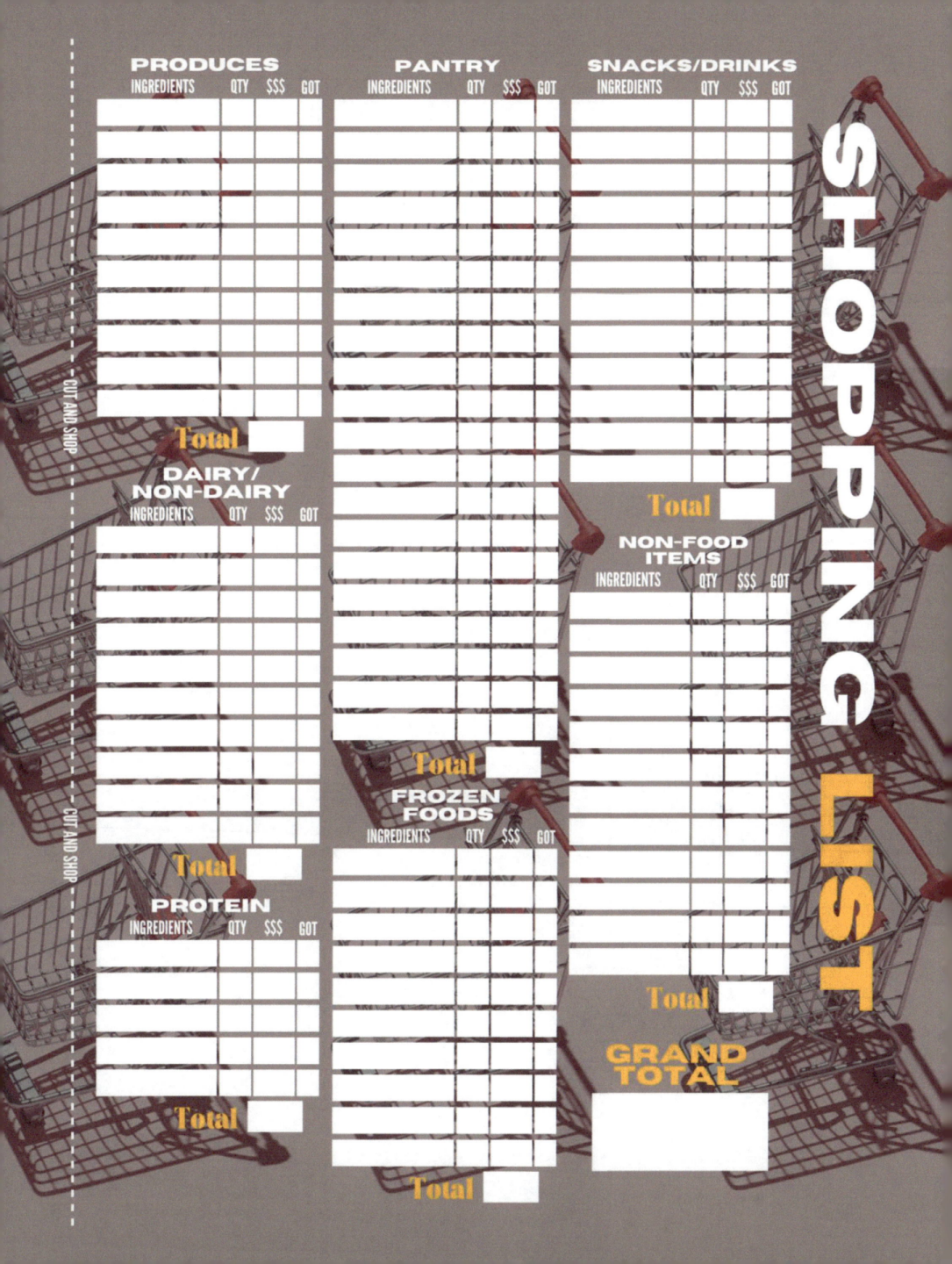

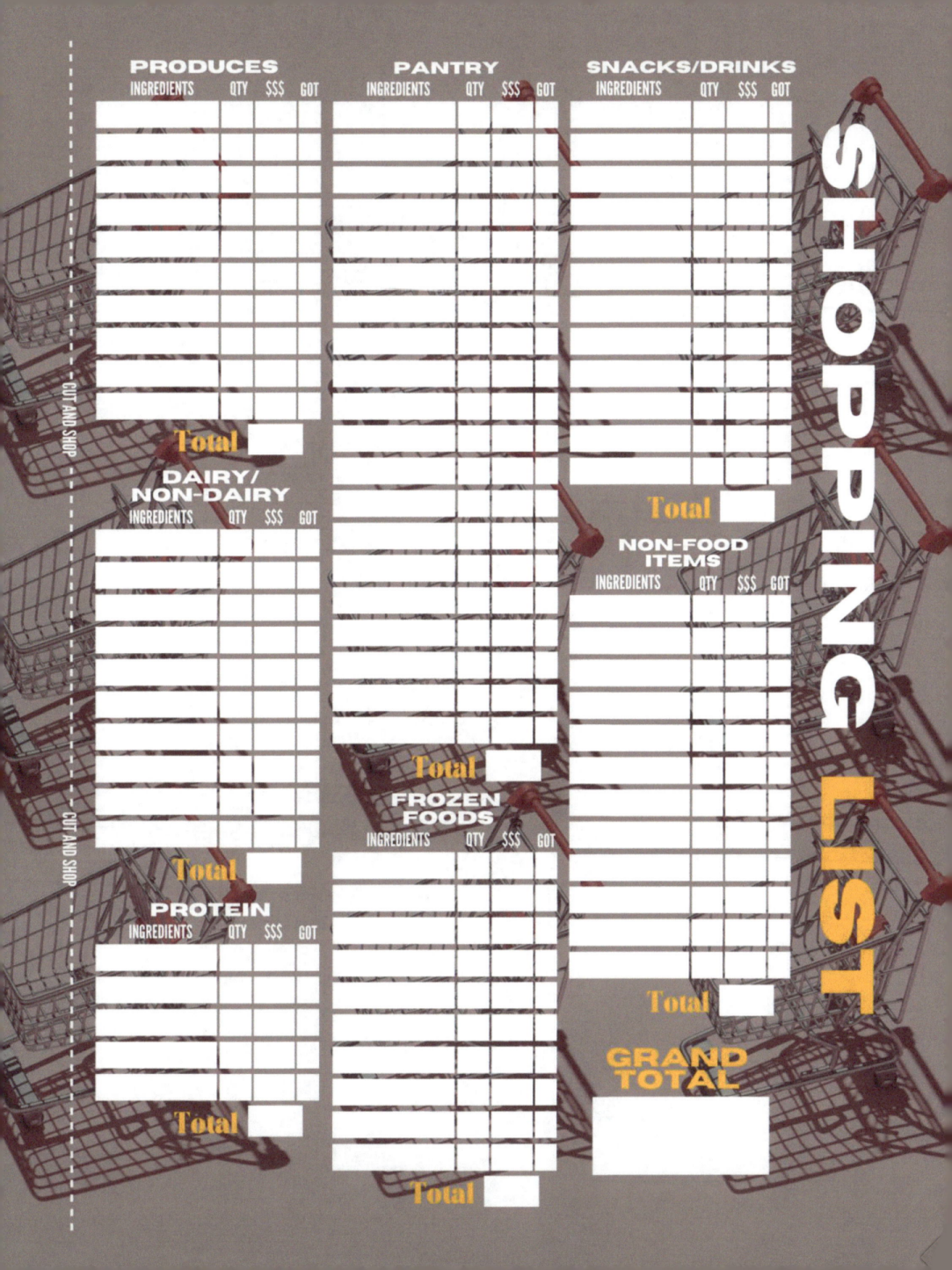

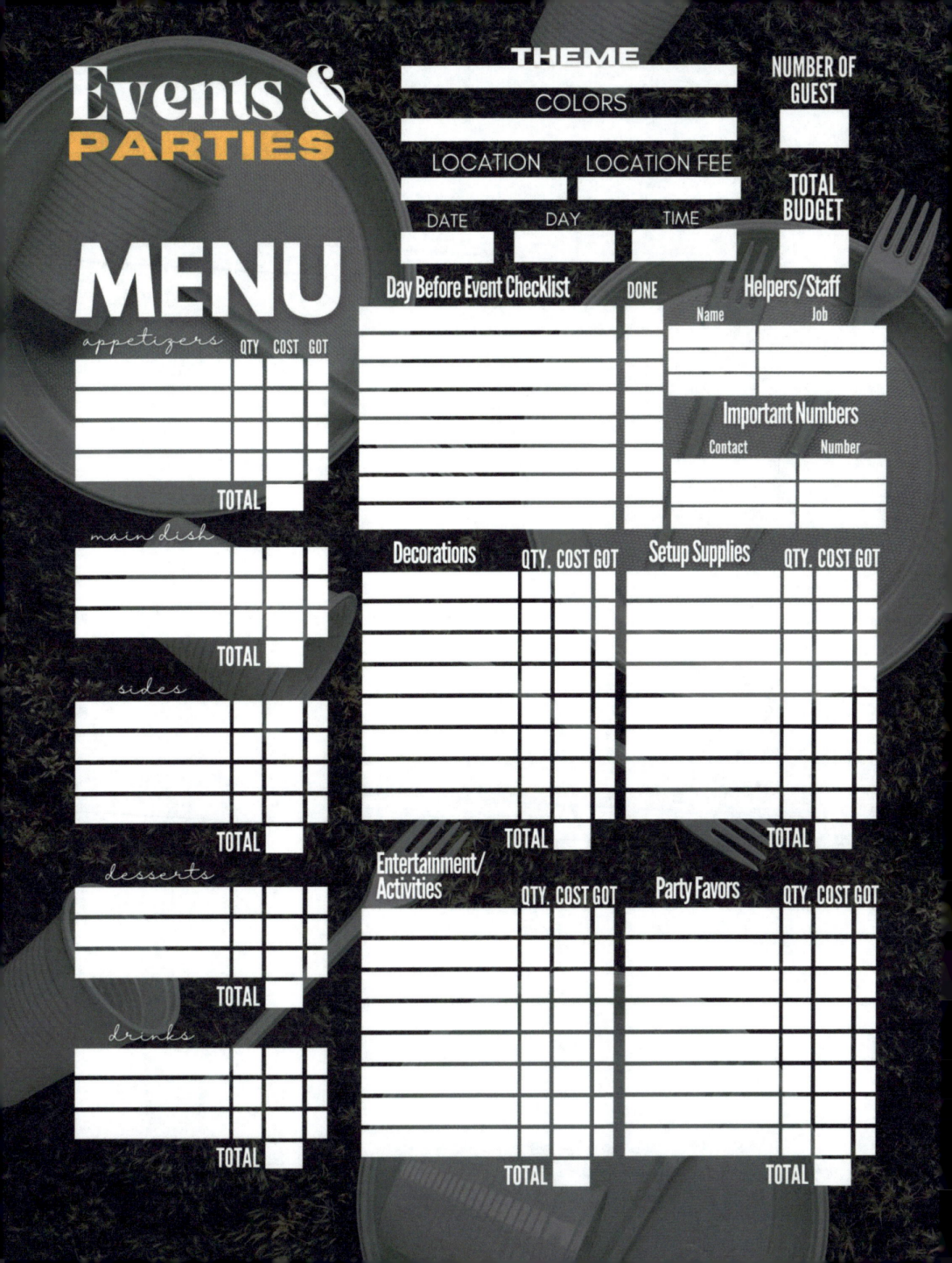

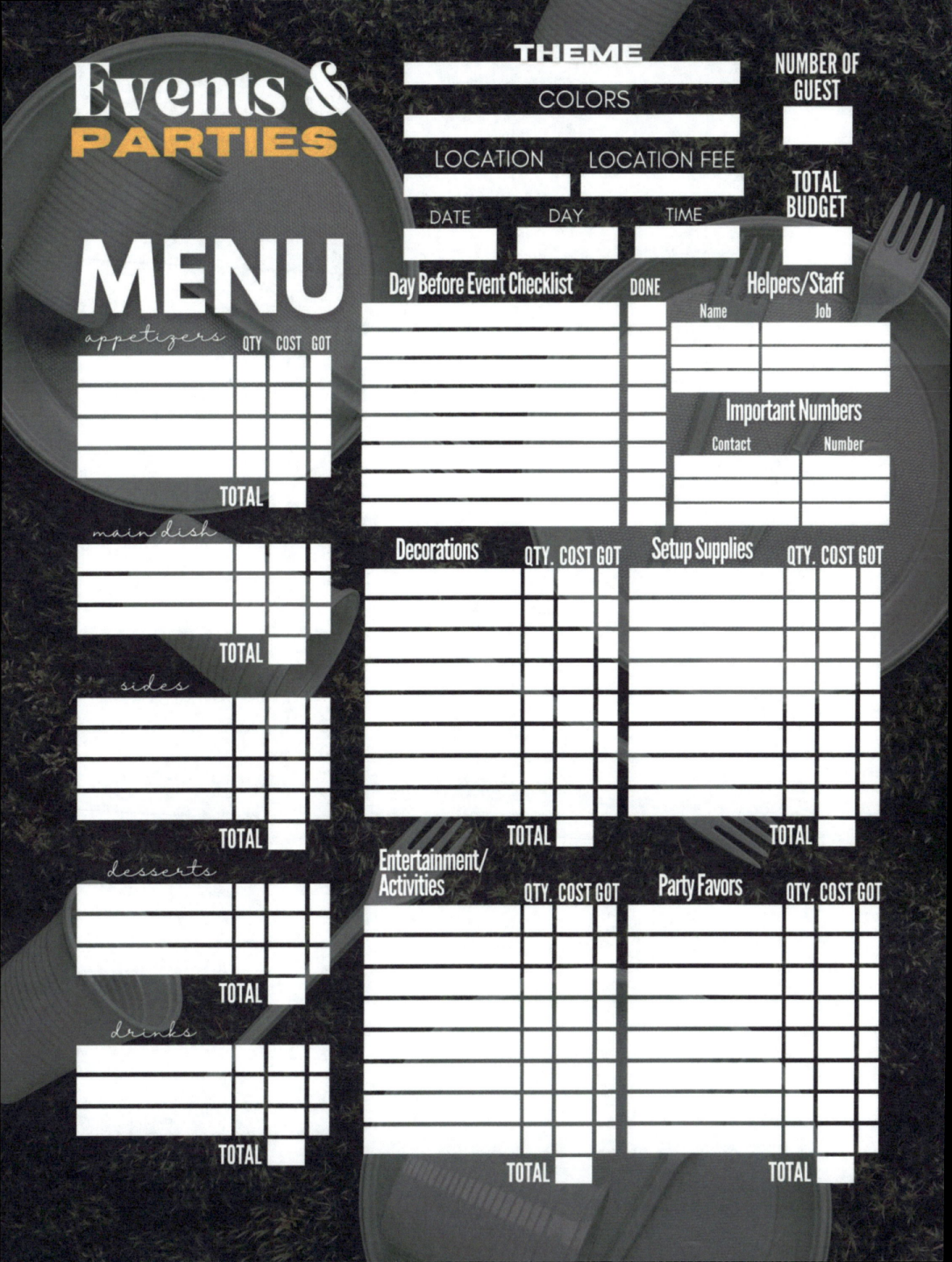

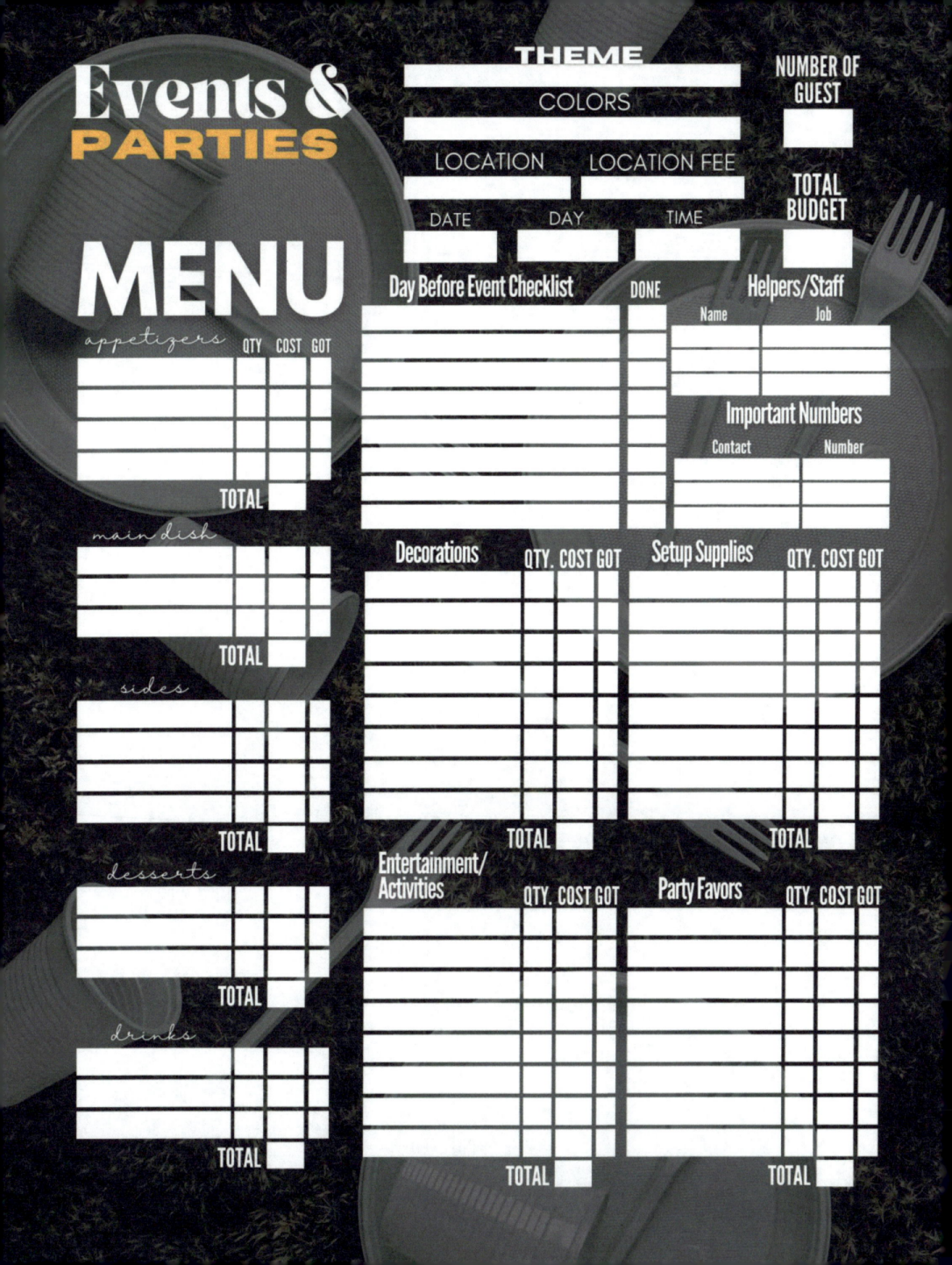

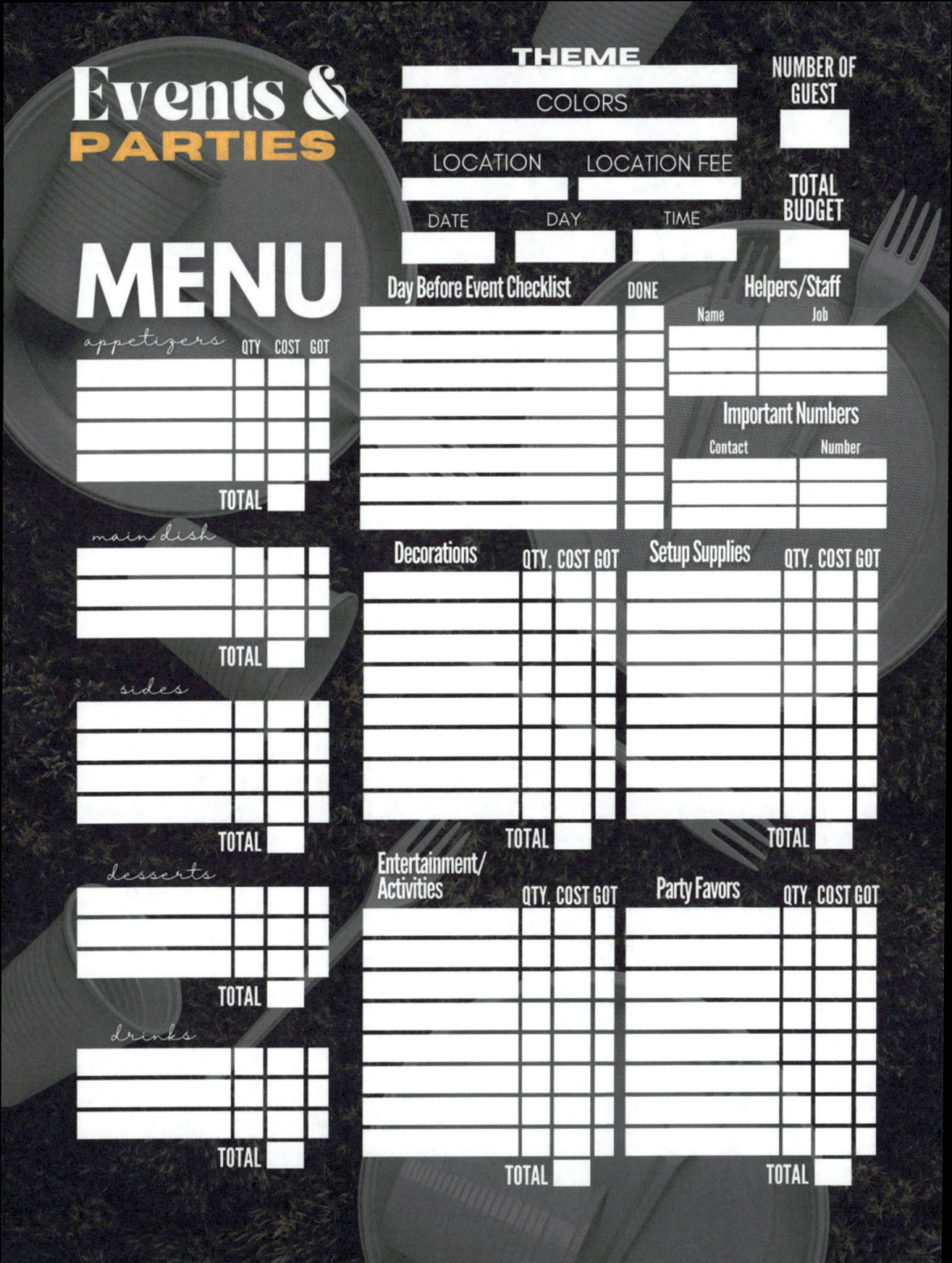

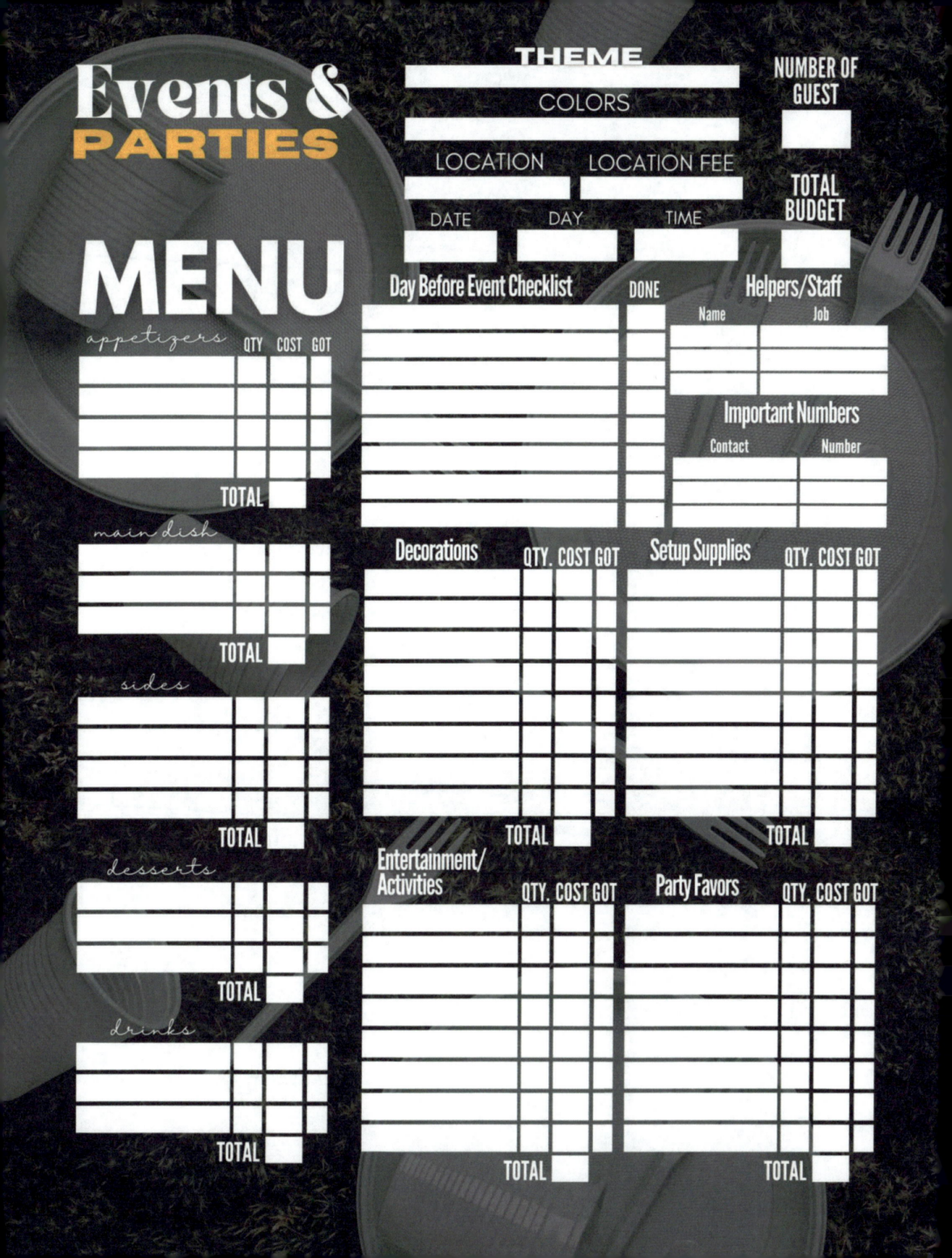

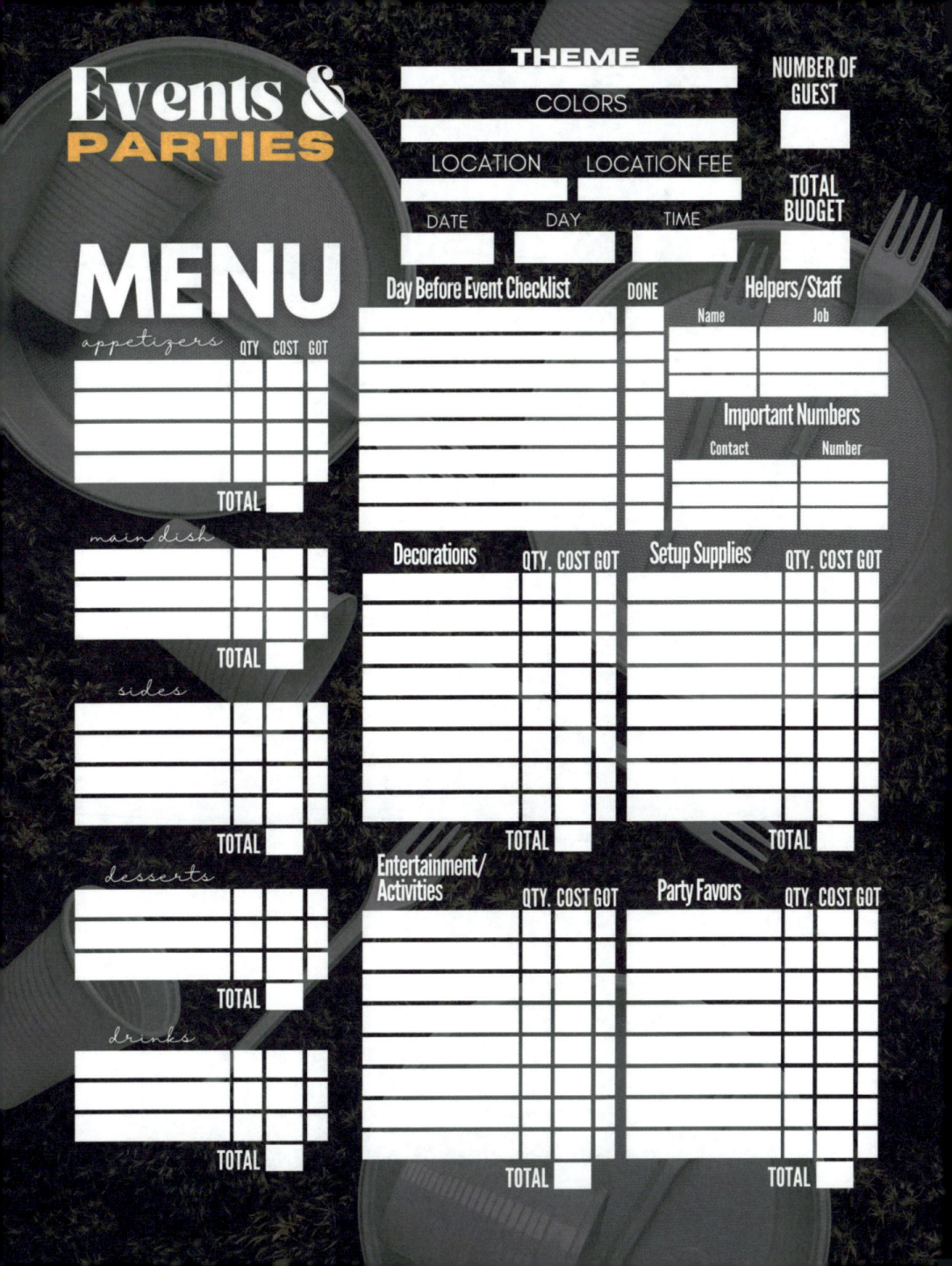

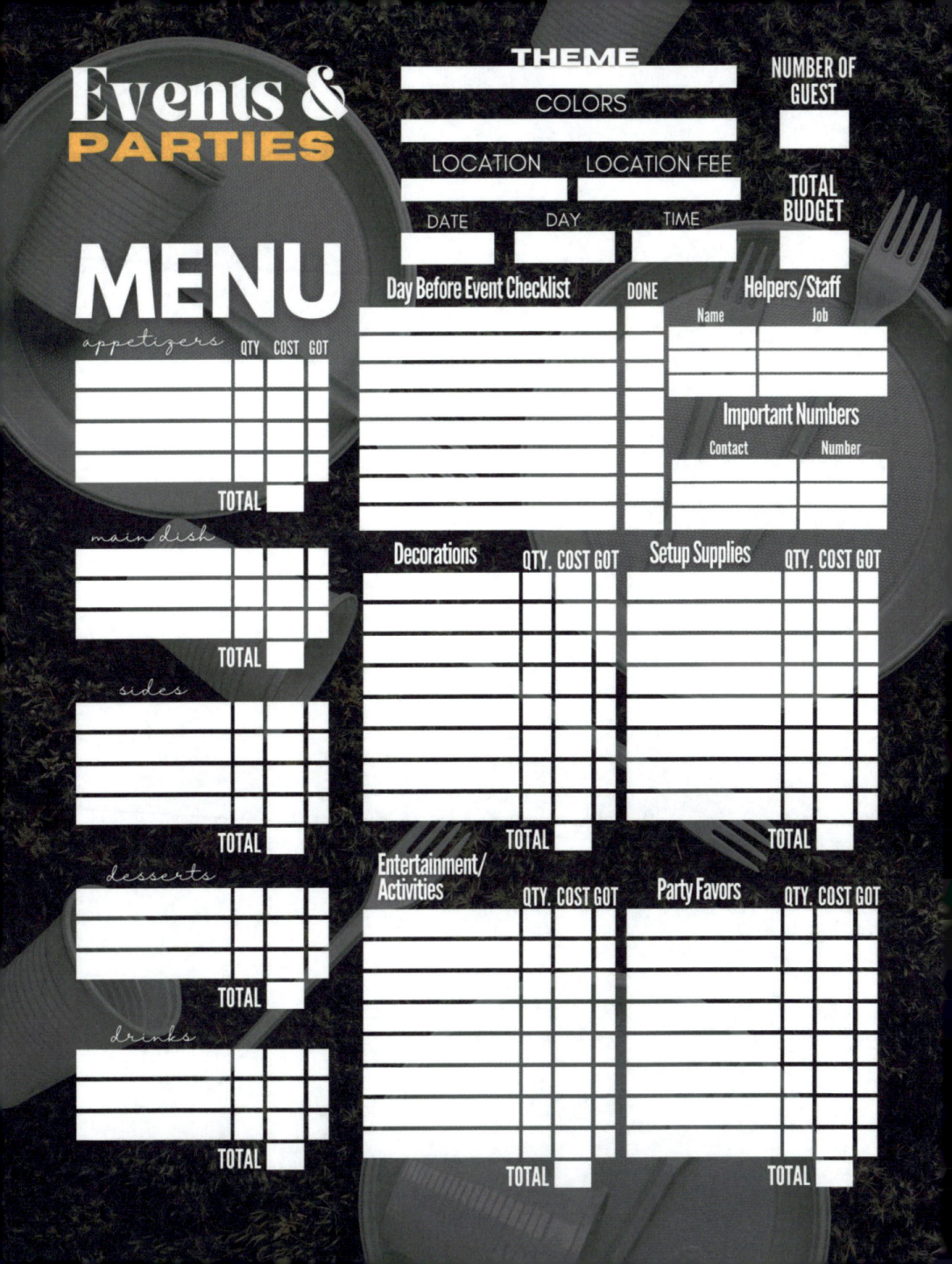

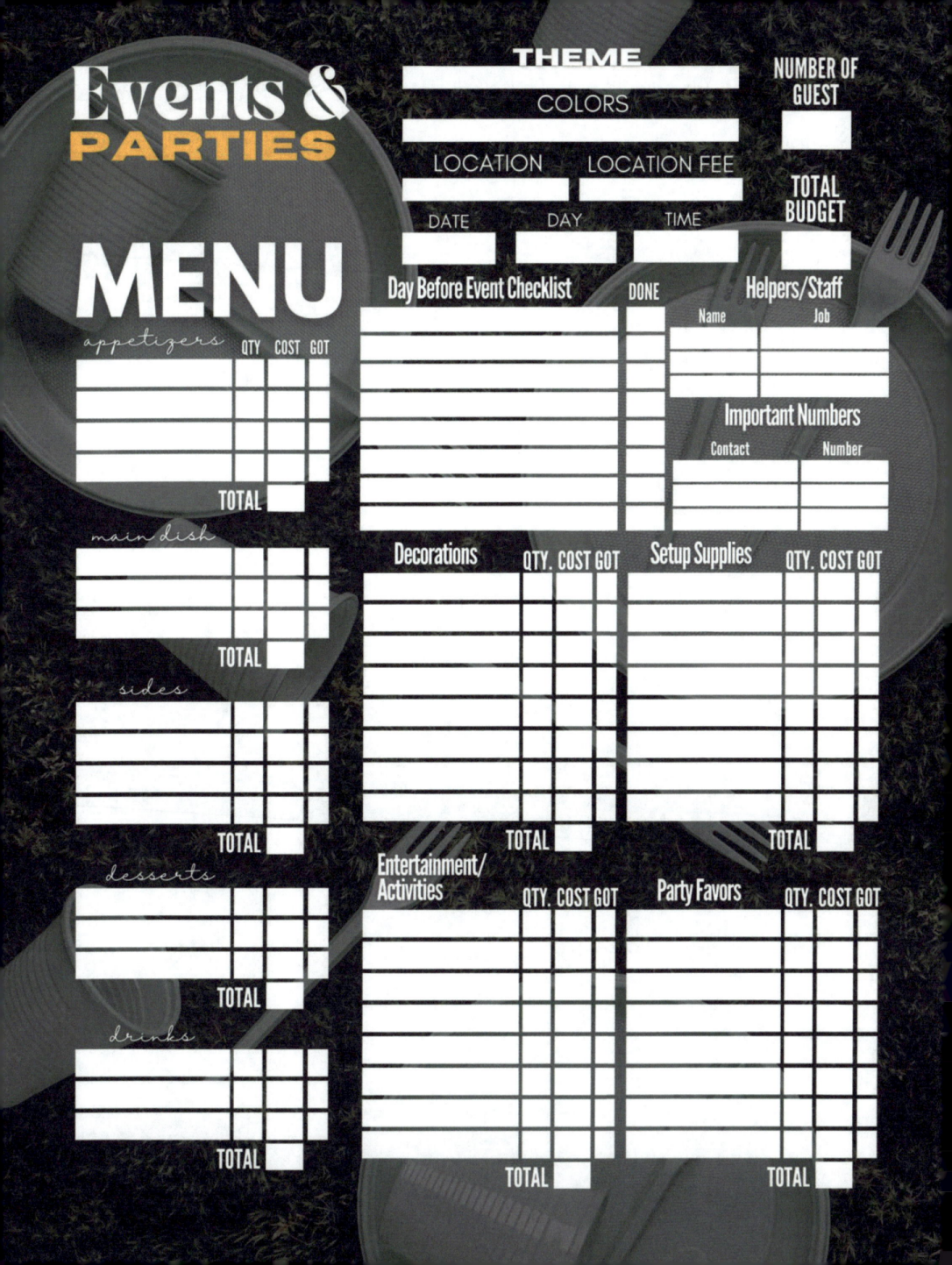

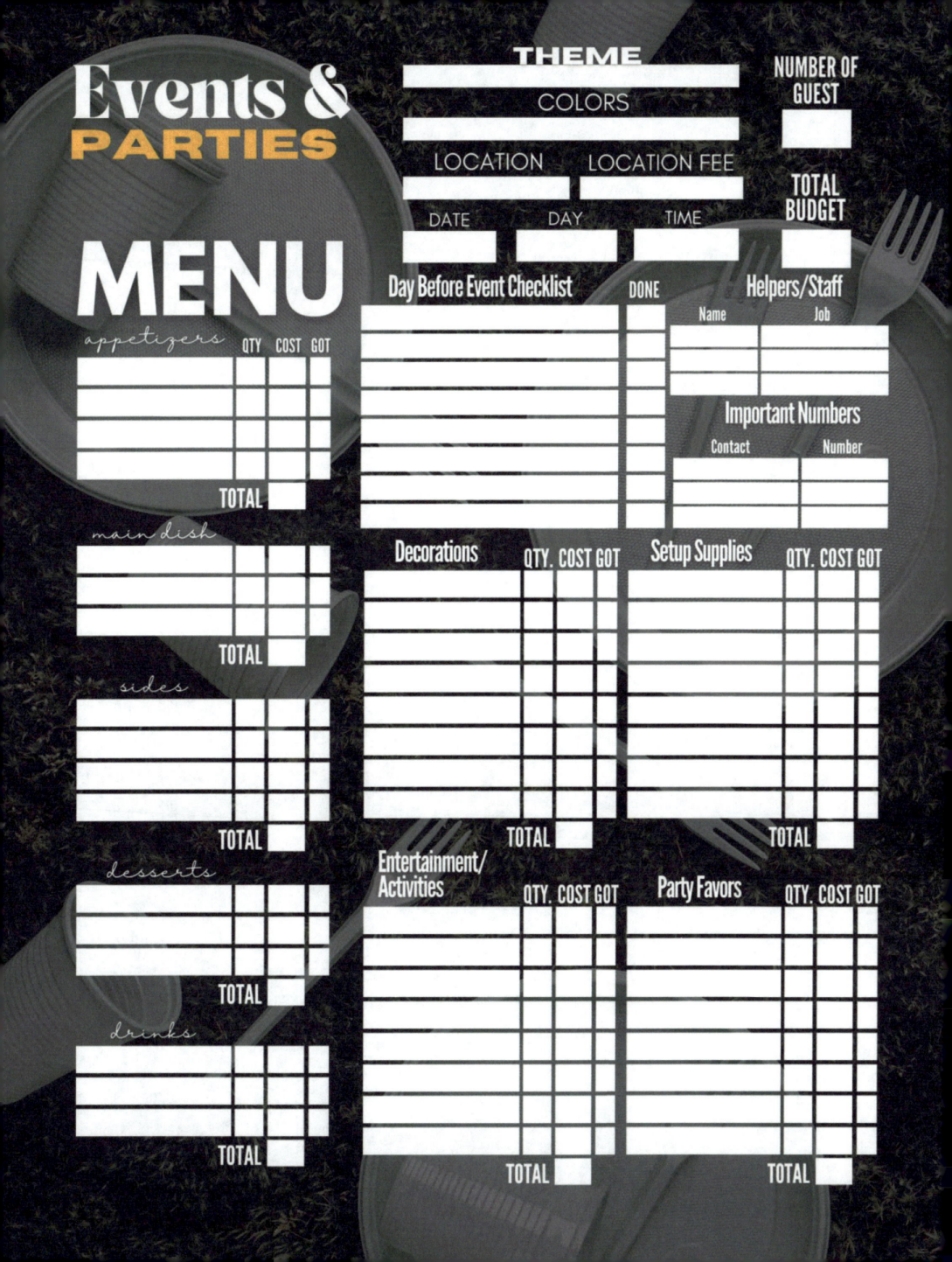

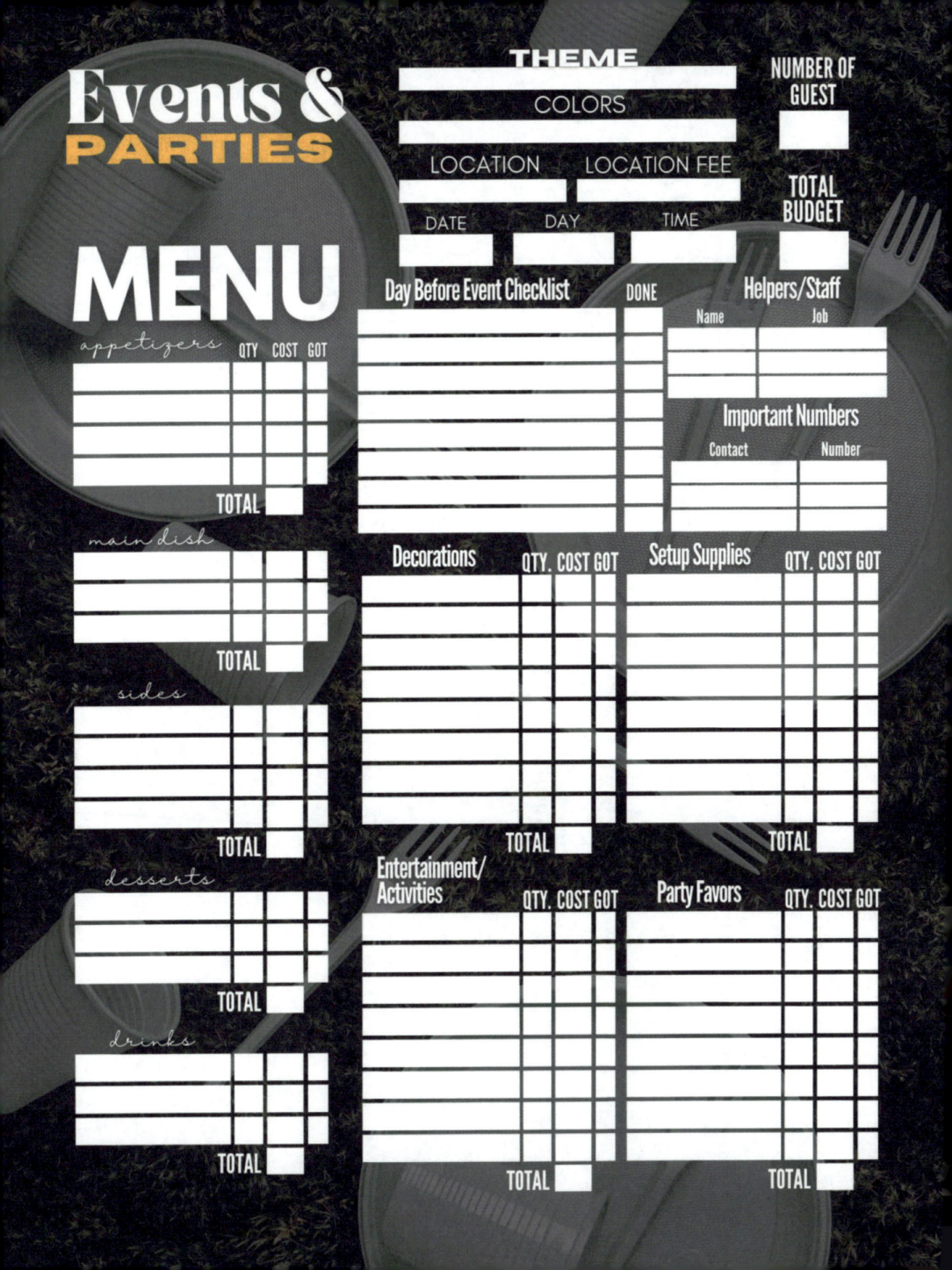

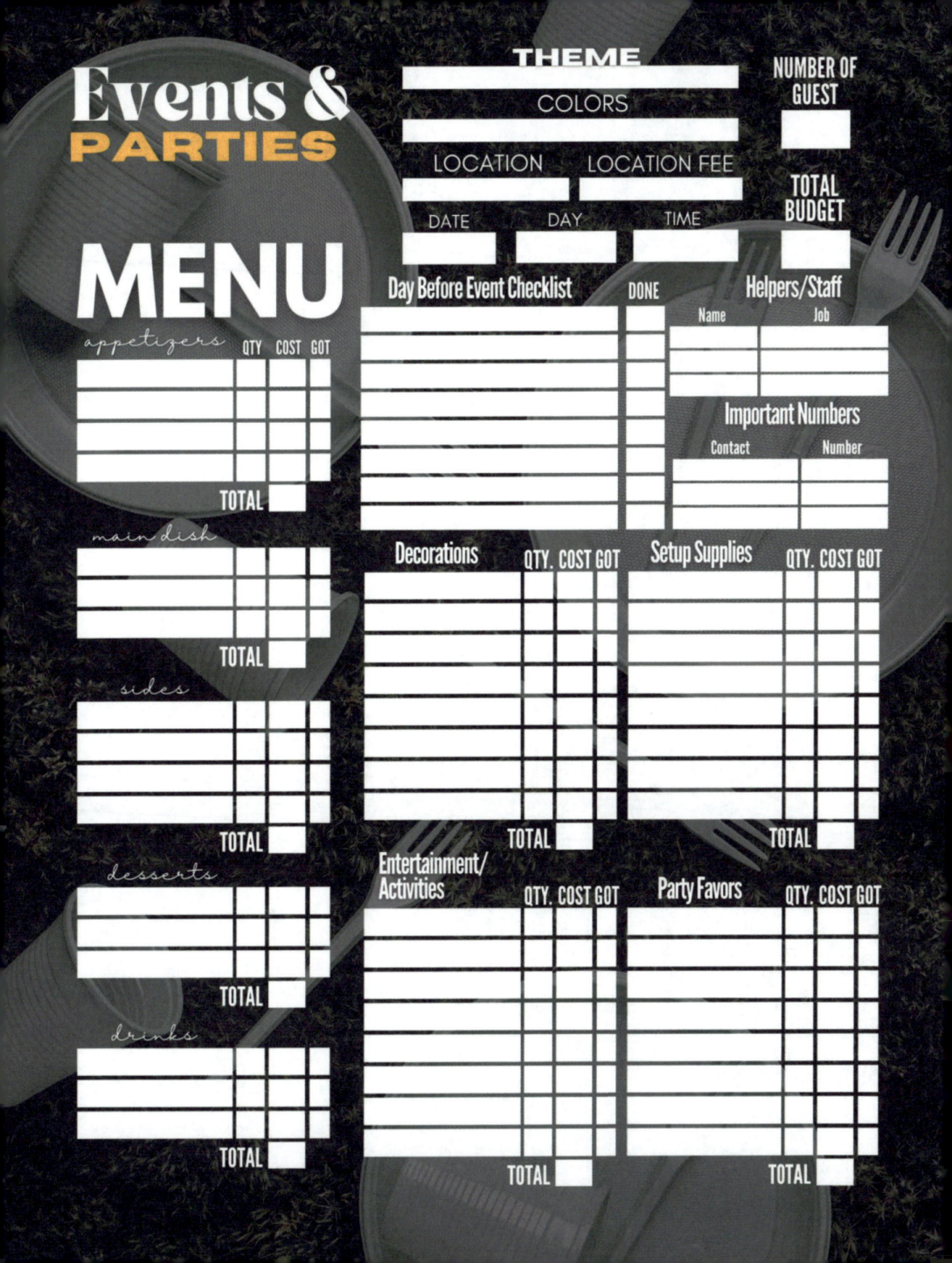

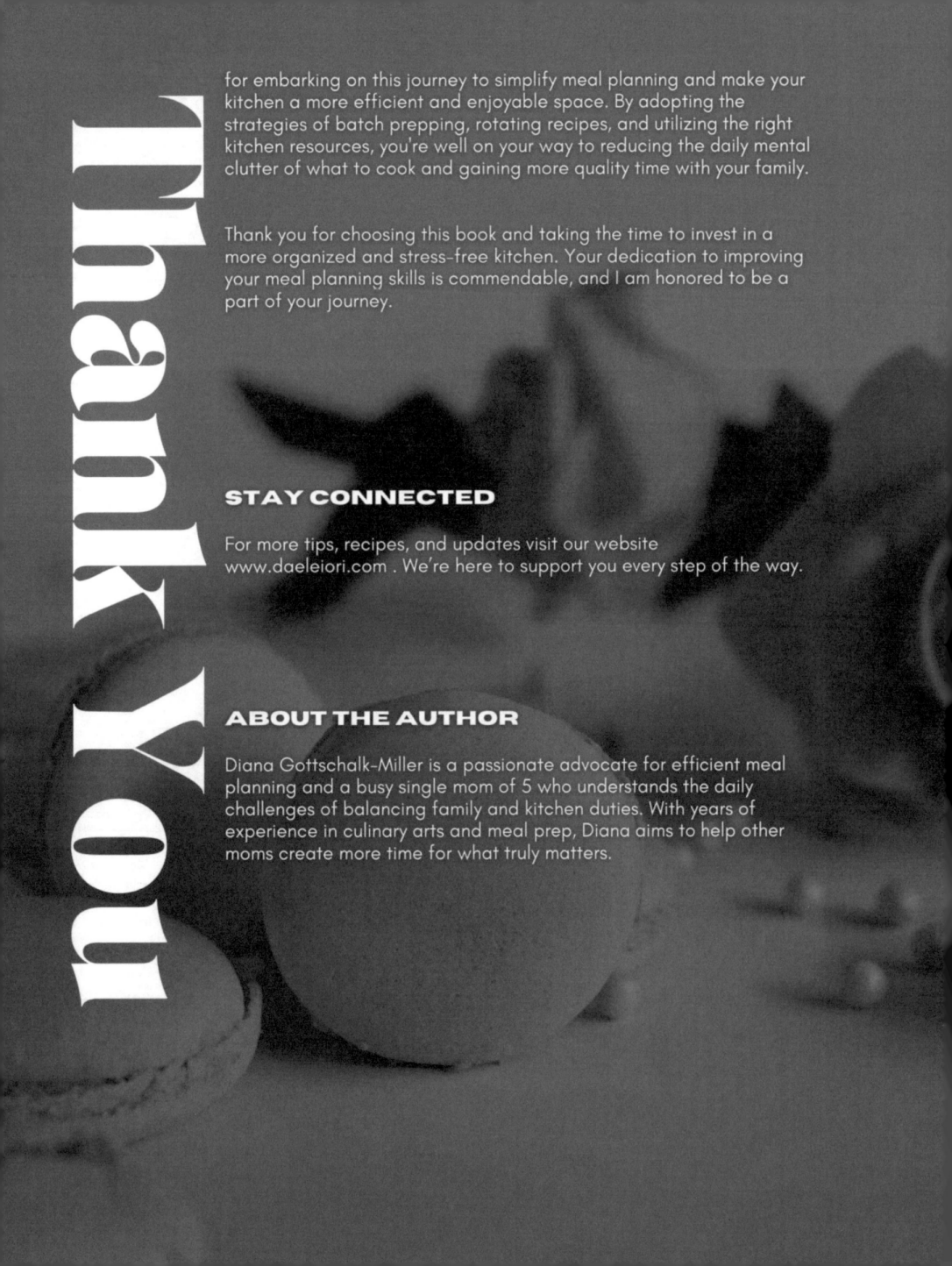

Thank You

for embarking on this journey to simplify meal planning and make your kitchen a more efficient and enjoyable space. By adopting the strategies of batch prepping, rotating recipes, and utilizing the right kitchen resources, you're well on your way to reducing the daily mental clutter of what to cook and gaining more quality time with your family.

Thank you for choosing this book and taking the time to invest in a more organized and stress-free kitchen. Your dedication to improving your meal planning skills is commendable, and I am honored to be a part of your journey.

STAY CONNECTED

For more tips, recipes, and updates visit our website www.daeleiori.com . We're here to support you every step of the way.

ABOUT THE AUTHOR

Diana Gottschalk-Miller is a passionate advocate for efficient meal planning and a busy single mom of 5 who understands the daily challenges of balancing family and kitchen duties. With years of experience in culinary arts and meal prep, Diana aims to help other moms create more time for what truly matters.

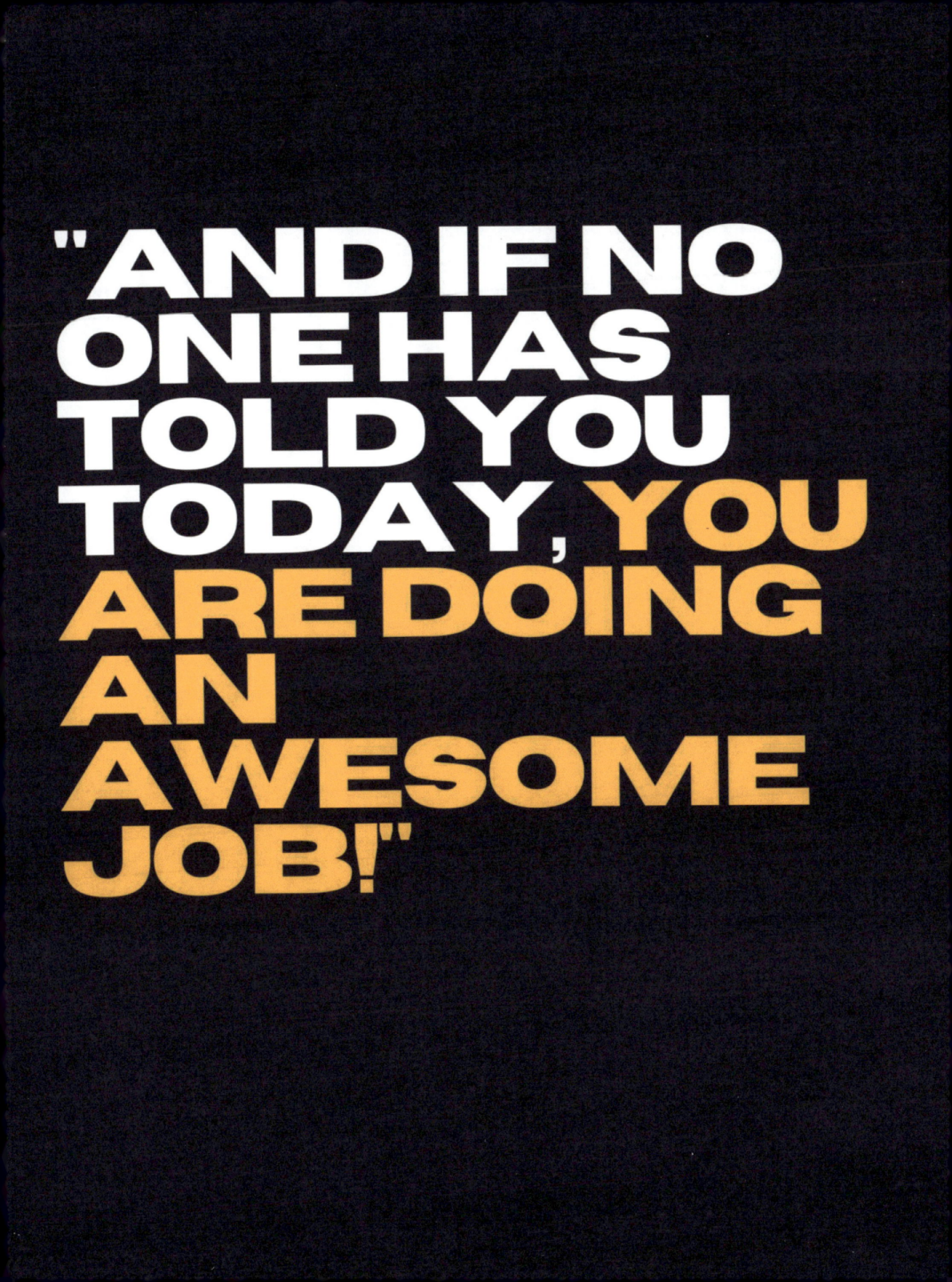

Made in the USA
Columbia, SC
25 July 2024

38868277R00154